CHAMPIONS
DAY

Shanghai Race Club

Autumn Race Meeting, 1941

1st Day—Saturday   8th November
2nd Day—Monday   10th November
3rd Day—Tuesday   11th November
4th Day—Wednesday   12th November

LIST OF ENTRIES

All Weights and Qualifications are as at 26th October, 1941

**FIRST BELL AT 1.15 P.M. ON 1st, 2nd & 3rd DAYS
AND AT 11.00 A.M. ON 4th DAY.**

Separate Lists of Entries will be published
for the 5th and 6th Days, Saturdays, 15th
and 22nd Nov., 1941, giving Handicap and
Corrected Weights.

CHAMPIONS DAY

DAY

The
End of Old
Shanghai

JAMES CARTER

W. W. NORTON & COMPANY
Independent Publishers Since 1923

For information about permission to reproduce selections from this book, write to
Permissions, W. W. Norton & Company, Inc., 500 Fifth Avenue, New York, NY 10110

For information about special discounts for bulk purchases, please contact
W. W. Norton Special Sales at specialsales@wwnorton.com or 800-233-4830

Manufacturing by LSC Communications, Harrisonburg
Book design by Barbara Bachman
Production manager: Lauren Abbate

ISBN 978-0-393-63594-2

W. W. Norton & Company, Inc., 500 Fifth Avenue, New York, N.Y. 10110
www.wwnorton.com

W. W. Norton & Company Ltd., 15 Carlisle Street, London W1D 3BS

1 2 3 4 5 6 7 8 9 0

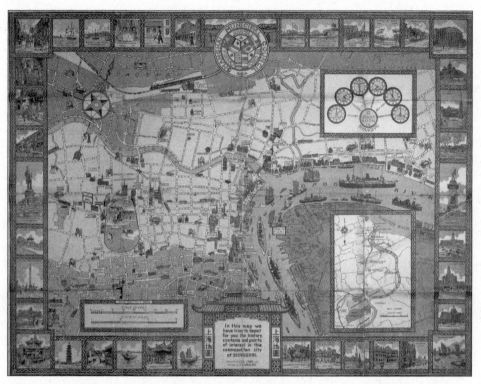

This map of central Shanghai, focusing on the International
Settlement, was designed by American journalist Carl Crow and drawn
by V. V. Kowalsky in 1935. The racecourse is prominent at center left (with
the outline of its former location visible in the roads just east of it). Arthur
Henchman's office is on the waterfront at Foochow Road ("H.&S. Bank").

CONTENTS

NOTE ON NAMES
AND ROMANIZATION

THERE IS NO SINGLE "RIGHT" WAY TO SPELL MANY OF THE names, especially place names, described in this book. Chasing twin goals of accessibility and consistency, for Chinese names, I have generally followed the pinyin romanization system that is standard in the People's Republic of China and for most international style and usage. However, for street names in Shanghai that would have been written in English at the time, I have tried to follow agreed-upon contemporary standard spellings. The three other exceptions to this are Canton (rather than Guangzhou), Hong Kong (rather than Xianggang), and Yangtszepoo. In a very few instances, I spell the same place differently depending on context (I write about Nanjing Road when describing the street in Shanghai today, but call it Nanking Road when writing about pre-1949 Shanghai).

This approach has led to some inconsistencies. Most Chinese personal names appear in pinyin, with the family name first (Fu Xiaoan and Mao Zedong, for instance). The major exceptions are individuals who have a common, nonstandard preference in English. Dayu Doon is one example. In this case the family name is second (English style), and the romanization is nonstandard (in pinyin he would be Dong Dayou). Unlike place names such as Nanking/Nanjing Road, personal names do not change over time.

CHAMPIONS
DAY

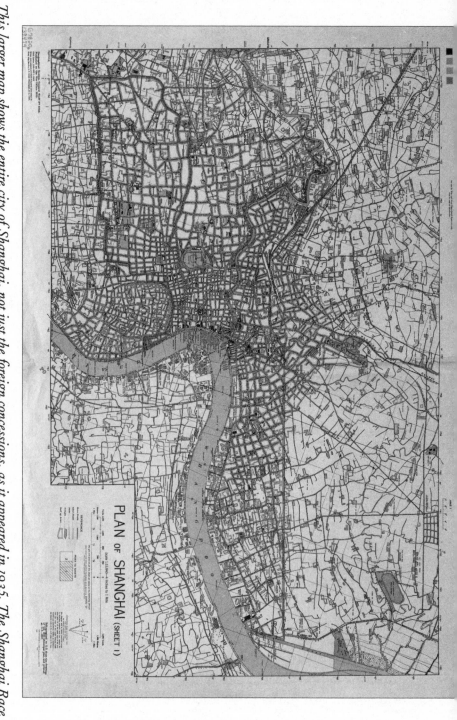

This larger map shows the entire city of Shanghai, not just the foreign concessions, as it appeared in 1935. The Shanghai Race Club is the gray oval left of center. The Jiangwan Civic Center and its racecourse are just off the top of the map. The Chinese Jockey Club course, at Yangtszepoo, can be seen at upper right, labeled "Far Eastern Racecourse." Hardoon Gardens (not indicated on the map) is at the corner of Bubbling Well and Hardoon Roads, near the Burlington Hotel west of the racecourse.

PLAN OF SHANGHAI (SHEET I)

PROLOGUE

...

The Center of a World

IF YOU WANT TO FIND HORSE RACING IN SHANGHAI, YOU NEED
to walk into its past.

Start at the waterfront, where all visitors to the city find themselves
eventually. Leave the Huangpu River and the skyscrapers of Pudong at your back and follow Nanjing Road west. For nearly a mile,
crowds, neon, touts, and video boards will remind you that commerce
built Shanghai and it remains a global marketplace. It may take a while,
depending on how successfully you resist the street's many distractions,
but eventually, the tall buildings that have been close all around give
way to open space ahead and to your left.

This is People's Park, and the adjacent People's Square, a transpor-
tation hub, civic center, and gathering place. There are a few buildings
inside its borders—the municipal government, as well as prominent
theaters and museums—but the park is mostly welcome green space
at the heart of a frenetic and often polluted city. Standing at the corner
where Nanjing Road encounters the park, you may notice that the road
continues not quite straight, but in an arc, bowing out to your right
before curving back.

People's Square isn't square.

That curve in Nanjing Road, out of place among the right angles of an
urban grid, is a clue to what came before. You won't see signs of anything
to do with horses, but this bend connects with other roads to make a rough
oval, the outline of what used to be a racecourse, built at this spot in 1862.

An immense shopping mall overlooks what was the backstretch, while Nanjing Road follows the contours along which horses carried their supporters' hopes for fortune and fame. Immediately to the east, Beihai Road curves in the same way, echoing the track's previous location in the 1850s.

Cross Tibet Road near the People's Square metro station and climb the stairs next to the Starbucks into the park. The horses that once raced here have been gone for seventy-five years, and where grooms and trainers once walked horses to the starting line, parents now push strollers, and couples hold hands or iPhones. Early in the morning you may encounter group *taiqi* sessions on the plaza, and in the evening, perhaps "dancing grandmas" and their line dances.

Continue on a little farther and look up. Through breaks in the foliage you can glimpse a brick clock tower, nearly 300 feet of neo-classicism and art deco that was the emblem of the Shanghai Race Club. It is no small feat that the tower has survived the political upheaval of China's recent past, for when it was completed as part of the Race Club's new clubhouse, in 1934, it symbolized European colonial power in China. The clubhouse was one of the world's largest and finest, an ornate refuge for a ruling class—where every morning, members surrounded by dark wood paneling checked the newspapers for the latest racing odds and news of the world and their city, and where Shanghai held its grandest parties and balls. The grandstands on race days could be filled with 30,000 people of dozens of nationalities.

This was the informal—but never casual—center of foreign power in China. Starting in the 1840s, when Shanghai began its rise to become one of the world's great cities, the Race Club represented the cosmopolitanism and excitement, as well as the racism and oppression, of a unique place. It was the center of a world.

This is the story of that world and its last day.

ON NOVEMBER 12, 1941, three crowds gathered in Shanghai. Each one, in different locations and with very different motivations, represented tremendous change amid the crises engulfing China. The smallest group celebrated the birthday of both an old revolutionary and a new nation at the insistence of Japanese military occupiers and their Chinese

*At the Shanghai
Race Club, 1928.
Introduced by the
British, racing
in Shanghai was
attended by people
of all nationalities
and social classes.*

collaborators. Another bid farewell to China's wealthiest woman: Liza Hardoon, the half-Chinese, half-French Buddhist widow of a Baghdadi Jewish merchant, whose death symbolized the passing of a generation that had seen Shanghai rise to global prominence. The third, and by far largest, crowd gathered at the racecourse to renew a semiannual ritual that had defined Shanghai for decades: Champions Day.

The locations of these three crowds help illustrate the geography of the city in 1941. Shanghai sits on a bend in the Huangpu River, a minor tributary of the Yangtze, which enters the East China Sea a few miles northeast of the city center. Travelers arriving by ship would steam up the Huangpu and land at the Bund (rhymes with "shunned"), the row of mainly European-financed office buildings that evoked London or New York more than China. Today, the mandatory view of Shanghai—almost the logo of twenty-first-century China—is the opposite side of the Huangpu: the skyscrapers of the east bank, Pudong, where dozens of towers, including some of the world's tallest, soar into the air. In 1941, though, little stood there besides warehouses on the waterfront. Behind those, a countryside of rice paddies and small villages extended toward the sea. Everything in 1941, and for most of Shanghai's history until the 1990s, was focused on the Huangpu's west bank. That's where November 12's three crowds were found.

Both the Hardoon funeral and the Race Club were in Shanghai's International Settlement, which, together with the adjacent French Concession, had functioned virtually, although not technically, as colonies since the 1860s. The Settlement, formed by a merger of the American and British Concessions, was administered not by foreign governments or governors but by professionals and merchants: a municipal council elected locally and composed of foreign and (after the 1920s) some Chinese representatives who managed the Settlement's affairs.

Originally larger, by 1941 the Settlement was effectively bounded by meandering Suzhou Creek on the north and the Huangpu River on the west—an irregular shape covering just 3 square miles. Close to the river, the Settlement was a densely populated city of concrete and masonry, but west of the Race Club, Shanghai became suburban. In earlier eras, the western reaches of the Settlement had been rural, almost bucolic, and some of Shanghai's most stately homes were built there. This is where Silas and Liza Hardoon had built their gardens, where Silas was already buried and where Liza would be laid to rest on November 12. This part of the city also included, to the north of the more residential regions and lining Suzhou Creek, cotton and other textile mills that employed the tens of thousands of workers—mostly Chinese—who made Shanghai China's industrial center. Farther west, ever since the Japanese invasion of 1937, the Settlement blended into the "Badlands," where Japanese, Chinese, and European jurisdictions overlapped—a place of little order and less law.

To the south of the International Settlement, separated by broad Avenue Edward VII, was the French Concession, smaller than the International Settlement and under the jurisdiction of the French consul. Originally combined with the other foreign-controlled territory, the French Concession had separated itself before the twentieth century. By 1941, "Frenchtown" residents enjoyed broad, leafy boulevards that were a comfortable alternative to the busy cityscape of the International Settlement a few blocks away. None of our November 12 crowds were gathered in the French Concession, though plenty of people from there made their way to the races.

Farther south, back along the Huangpu, the "Chinese city" had been Shanghai long before Europeans arrived in the 1840s. Before the Opium Wars, this walled, circular city had been an important regional port, well positioned to control trade into and out of the Yangtze River. Since the Opium Wars, though, the Chinese city had become marginal to the foreign-controlled areas of Shanghai—a situation that both Chinese and foreigners saw as representing China's decline.

To shake off that association, when the Chinese government in the 1920s sought to renew its authority in the region, it chose not the centuries-old walled city along the Huangpu, but instead a new urban center that would rise from farmland to the north. This new Shanghai was called Jiangwan, and that was where, on November 12, 1941, ceremonies celebrated the birthday of a Chinese revolutionary, the late Dr. Sun Yat-sen. Jiangwan was several miles from the Bund, and most foreigners in Shanghai considered it a suburb, though this dismissal had much to do with their belief that Shanghai was a foreign creation. In addition to the model city center that had been built in the 1920s and 1930s, Jiangwan consisted of farms and small villages. Other parts of greater Shanghai were similar, including pockets of development like Yangtszepoo, with a beach and its own racetrack, or Siccawei, where European Jesuits had built a library, orphanage, and weather station. Jiangwan—like all of Shanghai outside the International Settlement—was politically part of China, and foreigners played no role in its governance. At least, that had been the case before the Japanese invasion of 1937.

By 1941, the empire of Japan occupied all of Shanghai *except* the concessions. The tiny International Settlement remained technically neutral; the French Concession was officially a colony of Vichy France, and thus allied with the Japanese and the Germans, but it remained unoccupied. Chinese collaborating with the Japanese governed Jiangwan, supported by Japanese soldiers and armor. Shanghai in 1941 was a city divided. All of it was controlled by foreigners—parts by Americans and Europeans, other parts by Japanese—even though it was all formally Chinese sovereign territory. The crowds that gathered at the racetrack, at Hardoon Gardens, and in Jiangwan were in the same city but in different worlds, all of them Shanghai.

The heyday of Old Shanghai was art deco opulence, gambling and jazz, war and crime, and poverty and high fashion. Rickshaws jostled Packards in the city streets, the pullers' calls competing with clanging streetcar bells for customers. Gangsters elbowed taipans—bosses who may have operated no more scrupulously but on the right side of the law—on the sidewalks. American jazz played late into the night, as did Chinese opera, perhaps from live venues but just as likely from radios or phonographs. The smells of the city's cooking were international too. Street vendors sold steamed buns and pickled vegetables. Indian spices, sauerkraut, Worcestershire sauce, and locally brewed beer— these were the flavors of a city of migrants, from all over the world and all across China in search of new lives. The mostly British, mostly male, and mostly wealthy "Shanghailanders" dominated the city, living beyond the reach of Chinese law and often, it seemed, beyond any law at all. There were more foreigners in Shanghai than in any other Chinese city—but most of Shanghai was Chinese, including 97 percent of the people in the International Settlement.

Chinese were seldom thought of as Shanghailanders, and were often second-class citizens in their own country, but many Chinese in the city, like their European and American counterparts, lived urban lives separate from the typical experience of twentieth-century China. Shanghainese (understood as Shanghai Chinese) were a broad cross section of society: "multimillionaires who came to pursue an extravagant yet secluded lifestyle that could hardly be found in other Chinese cities . . . destitute who roamed the city's streets in search of bare survival . . . political dissidents who fled to the 'safety zone' of the foreign concessions . . . criminals who came to join China's largest underworld . . . flappers who found in this city the freedom they sought . . . innocent rural girls who were inveigled by labor contractors to come work in the city but who ended up being sold to brothels."[1] They were essential parts of this world too, and it was a world many came to love. "The happy lot of Shanghainese is indeed great," wrote one Shanghai Chinese entrepreneur. "To compare Shanghai with the hinterland is to compare paradise and hell."[2]

No institution better exemplified Old Shanghai than the Shanghai Race Club, and the pinnacle of the Shanghai Race Club's season was Champions Day. Twice a year—each fall and spring—Shanghai gathered for the city's biggest race, a contest among all the season's winners. The Shanghai races had started in the wake of British gunboats, on land taken from Chinese farmers seeking shelter from warfare, but they had become popular among Chinese in the city as well. Racing became such an institution in Shanghai that Chinese owners and riders built their own racecourses, emulating—in some ways exceeding—what the foreigners had created, but Champions Day at the Race Club remained the centerpiece of the spectacle.

Champions Day had persevered through the tumult of China's nineteenth and twentieth centuries: war against France in the 1880s and against Japan in the 1890s, the Boxer Uprising of 1900, and the fall of the Qing dynasty in 1911. A second revolution, warlordism, depression, Japanese invasion, and a battle in Shanghai itself—none of it stopped the running of the Champions' Stakes. But in 1941 time was running out. For four years, Japanese troops had surrounded the tiny International Settlement, and rumors of a wider war, one that would sweep away the European perch on China's coast, grew stronger every day.

The racecourse was the center of Shanghai and all it stood for. It was even shaped like the eye of a hurricane. For a hundred years it had been just that, but after this Champions Day, never again.

Morning in Shanghai

*Postcard of the Shanghai Race Club, looking west along
Bubbling Well (today Nanjing) Road, as it would have
appeared in November 1941.*

"WHAT OF YOUR FORTUNE, YOUR FAMILY, YOUR VERY LIFE?"
asked the fortune-teller. "If ever Humanity needed a glimpse into the
future, it is now."[1]

It was November 12, 1941. "Famous Clairvoyant Astrologer"
Madame Helen Piper offered her predictions to a city that wanted to
know what was coming next. Shanghai had bet on uncertainty for
decades, persisting through crisis after crisis and emerging each time,

somehow, both more prosperous and more precarious. Now, with the war between China and Japan entering its fourth year, Madame Piper peddled her "strange gifts"[2] to a place of contradiction that at once defied expectations and confirmed them, a world of make-believe made real.

Shanghai prided itself on blending East and West, but it was no haven of tolerance. It was a place of hard work and easy living, but usually Chinese worked hard while Westerners lived easy. White men held too much of the power to call the city truly cosmopolitan, but Shanghai was not a colony. British and Americans ran the center of the city— the International Settlement—and at this moment it was surrounded by Japanese armies on every side, but all of Shanghai was supposedly sovereign Chinese territory. It was hard to know what was real. Even "Madame Piper" was fiction, but who would begrudge Vera Hutchinson an alias in a place where so little was as it appeared?[3]

Arthur Henchman, the "dynamic, jittery manager"[4] of the Hongkong and Shanghai Banking Corporation (HSBC), would have seen Madame Piper's ad in the morning papers on his way to the Shanghai Race Club. What might the psychic be able to tell him? Hench— everyone called him Hench—had made a career and a reputation navigating China's financial system through trouble. He knew something was certain to happen soon, but just what, and just when, he couldn't tell. Maybe it would even be on this chilly Wednesday? But he could barely make out the street in front of him in this feeble dawn; a glimpse of the future was too much to hope for.

Before most of the city was awake, Hench made his way down Bubbling Well Road from his home as he had done hundreds of times before, but this was not the typical trip. More police than usual patrolled the road, some armed with machine guns. A temporary archway overhead and Buddhist fixtures along the road reminded Hench that Liza Hardoon's funeral would soon begin. Mourners had begun gathering around the gates to Hardoon Gardens all week, anticipating the rituals to come. Hench hadn't known Mrs. Hardoon well, though he certainly knew of her. Everyone in Shanghai knew about Liza Hardoon, born to a Chinese mother and French father, and the widow of Silas Aaron Hardoon, one of the richest of Shanghai's many rich merchants.

Liza had prospered along with Shanghai—some said she was

the wealthiest woman in all of Asia—and both had seen their challenges, but she no longer had any use for Madame Piper's predictions. Liza's mortal remains now lay in a silver casket that was soon to be entombed next to her husband, less than a mile from the race club that Silas had joined in 1897, on the estate that they had built in an eclectic and unlikely mix of English, Chinese, Buddhist, and Jewish styles. Widowed, deaf, and almost completely blind, Liza Hardoon had been increasingly reclusive in recent years—so much so that the *Shanghai Times* had called her "Shanghai's No. 1 Mystery Woman"⁵—but she was still a celebrity as China's richest woman. Ten thousand people would attend her funeral.

Henchman wouldn't be at the funeral. He and Silas Hardoon had been Race Club members together, but since Silas's death a decade earlier, the Hardoons had had little to do with the races. Holding a funeral on Champions Day proved that! As it happened, though, the weather suited a funeral more than a day at the races. Autumn had been mild up to now, but a cold front had pushed through overnight and was now blowing trash, bits of funeral decorations, and incense haphazardly down the streets. Flyers scurried by, pushed by the breeze, some calling on the people of China to join the government in exile and resist Japan, and others urging just the opposite: to support the peace movement and help the Japanese-sponsored government impose order.

These notices would remind Hench that November 12 was also the birthday of Sun Yat-sen, the Republic of China's founding father. For the first time since the Japanese invasion four years earlier, Shanghai's Chinese city government was commemorating the occasion, but was the celebration treason or patriotism? There were strong opinions—and armed partisans—on both sides. Shanghai was accustomed to propaganda skirmishes and the violence that often attended them. These fights over China's future would shape Hench's fate in ways that no one—perhaps Madame Piper?—yet knew, but Hench was not worried about Chinese politics this morning. It was Champions Day. He had a race to win.

At four o'clock that afternoon, Shanghai would renew a tradition that for two and a half minutes could distract a city in desperate need of it: the Champions' Stakes. Champions Day *was* Shanghai: stylish and obscene, bigoted and cosmopolitan, refined and ragtag. Banks and businesses closed so that the city—Chinese and foreigners alike— could crowd into the racecourse to watch. Henchman managed the most important branch of the most important bank in Asia, but on this day he was focused on getting a brown pony named Hindhead to run a mile and a quarter faster than its nine rivals. If he could, he would have won three Champions' Stakes in a row—something done just five times in 150 runnings. If the prestige and the tradition weren't incentive enough, maybe a purse worth as much as US$80,000 in today's money was.

Many would watch Henchman's run at history in style. Club members and their guests looked forward to elaborate meals and freely flowing champagne. In the owners' boxes, the latest fashions were on display. Furs too warm for the weather could nonetheless be worn by socialites impatient to show off their new coats. Thirty thousand people might turn up. Bettors would place wagers worth close to US$5 million.[6]

Britain had dominated Shanghai for a century, starting with the gunboats and diplomats that had forced the city open to trade with Europe on British terms in the 1840s. Hench's main rival at the track was British too: a Scot, Robert Aitkenhead. While Henchman had been raised wealthy in London, Aitkenhead was a middle-class Glaswegian who had turned an education in engineering into a job with a steamship company, eventually landing in Shanghai, where he had married and raised a family. His family wasn't with him now, though.

Aitkenhead had tried returning to Scotland when his oldest daughter was ready for university, traveling with the family back to the tiny Lowland village of Clunie, but he couldn't stay away and returned to Shanghai by himself after just a few months. He kept Scotland close through the names of his horses; it was a chestnut named Cluniehouse that Aitkenhead hoped to celebrate this November 12. Cluniehouse had been Champion once before, and had been favored twice more since, only to lose both times to Henchman's underdog horse Hindhead. Favorites once again, Aitkenhead and Henchman consulted their trainers and jockeys, wondering how to gain the upper hand in a racing rivalry that was the talk of the city.

While Hench and Aitkenhead puzzled over race tactics, grander strategy hung as a backdrop to Champions Day. For most of Shanghai,

Madame Piper's questions about "your very life" were literal. China was at war. Four years earlier, Japanese armies had overrun Beiping (the new name for Beijing, now that it was no longer the capital but still North China's most important city). They took the port of Tianjin, as well as Qingdao, colonized by Germans and made famous by their brewery. Farther south, Hangzhou and Suzhou, celebrated in poetry as China's most beautiful cities, fell. So did Ningbo and Canton, vital links between China and the West, with more than a thousand years of seafaring tradition. Japanese soldiers made Nanjing, the Chinese capital, a synonym for atrocity, raping and killing hundreds of thousands. The Chinese government fled up the Yangtze River and made its wartime capital at Chongqing, a thousand miles away but not far enough to escape Japanese bombers.

The war reached Shanghai in the summer of 1937. It had taken months, but when the city finally fell (exactly four years before this Champions Day), Japan stopped its armies at the International Settlement's boundaries just a half mile from the racetrack, close enough that residents of the Settlement began "crowding the roofs of buildings to watch the results of military bombardments"—a "very foolish practice" that the Shanghai Municipal Police warned against.[7] None of the European powers or the United States were at war with Japan, so the surrounded Settlement became a "lone island" of neutrality. The Japanese lines along Suzhou Creek seemed permanent fixtures, yet everyone knew that the present state of affairs couldn't last. Shanghai was a powder keg . . . a time bomb . . . on a razor's edge—the metaphors were endless and overused, but they weren't wrong. It had to end, probably soon, and few thought it would end well.

Shanghai's British consulate had been urging all British subjects, including Hench and his wife, Mary, and their two daughters, to leave the city since the withdrawal of British troops from Shanghai a year earlier had ended four decades of continuous British military presence in China. But Hench wasn't leaving. "[We have] been smoking on a powder magazine for about ten years on and off," he wrote to colleagues in Hong Kong, "but I suppose are becoming hardened for, after giving the matter a lot of thought, we struck a match and carried on."[8]

While the dozens of foreign consulates advised their nationals to leave Shanghai, millions of Chinese refugees streamed in, doubling the

Settlement's population and straining resources and facilities. Hoarding and speculation led to inflation and shortages. Food riots were not uncommon. Commerce, the city's lifeblood and raison d'être, was possible only at Japan's pleasure. Western governments restricted imports, for fear that goods shipped to Shanghai would, sooner or later, fall into Japanese hands and be used against them when the war expanded.

The International Settlement was completely vulnerable as it clung to fragile isolation. Hench had written his superiors in 1937 that he sensed Shanghai's time was running out. It seemed absurd to worry about racing while Chinese and Japanese armies and aircraft fought all across the Yangtze delta, but in the end the foreign community decided it needed its amusements. The 1937 fall Champions' Stakes had been delayed by a few weeks, but it had still been run. Since then, the city had carried on, but for how much longer?

The British weren't the only Westerners in jeopardy.

Cornell Franklin was an American who, like Henchman and Aitkenhead, hoped to become Champion this November 12. The *North-China Herald*'s front-page editorial cartoon that morning showed worried foreign residents contemplating their future, prompted not by a fortune-teller's pitch but by rumors that FDR was about to order the US Marines out of Shanghai. Cornell Franklin, who had himself served briefly in the army, might have paid the cartoon particular attention. He was used to risk and had made a fortune on the China coast, but fortunes had been lost there too, and even the most seasoned and savvy Shanghailanders were nervous. That August, the US secretary of state had authorized a $10,000 loan—perhaps $150,000 today—to help the Shanghai consulate find American citizens passage home, and just two weeks earlier the consulate had issued permission to travel on non-US-flagged ships because no American vessels were making the journey.[9] But Franklin was staying—at least for Champions Day.

Franklin's trip to the Race Club that morning was longer than Henchman's—a drive from his mansion in the suburbs that had once been appealing for their quiet remove from Shanghai's hectic center, but were now at the very edge of the Settlement's protection. Franklin had come to Shanghai in the 1920s to build a law practice and make a fortune representing American companies in the seemingly boundless China market. He succeeded in both and made Shanghai his adopted

"Judge C. S. Franklin,"
in Men of Shanghai
and North China.

home, even serving as chairman of the Shanghai Municipal Council, the closest thing to a mayor that the Settlement had. Americans had always been fewer than Brits in China, but as the United States' global role had grown, so had the influence of Americans in Shanghai.

Judge Franklin—the title recalled his time as a US circuit court judge in Hawai'i, though he had long ago left the bench—became unofficial head of Shanghai's American community. The marines may have boosted Franklin's patriotic pride, but their presence was mostly symbolic. Their departure boded ill for Shanghai's prospects, but a thousand men at arms could hardly protect the Settlement if Japan chose to invade. Never mind, though. Franklin wasn't focused on his country's global security commitments this morning. He had the speediest pony in Shanghai and his heart set on the winner's circle.

Like Hench and Aitkenhead, Franklin began his day at the crowded Mohawk Road stables. Seven hundred fifty horses could fit there when it was full, and it had been overfull for years. Invading armies had closed or ruined Shanghai's two Chinese-run tracks—the International Recreation Club at Jiangwan and the Chinese Jockey Club at Yangtszepoo—in the 1930s, and the Shanghai Race Club had welcomed those horses and their owners into the protection of the International Settlement. But most of the thousands who would soon pack the grandstands weren't concerned with how many horses filled the stables.

Their focus was on just ten ponies: the ones entered in that afternoon's featured race. The Champions' Stakes wouldn't ensure Shanghai's safety or make the Japanese armies any less ominous, but it would provide a welcome diversion.

The club's members were European and American elites, but most people at the track for Champions Day were not wealthy foreigners, or even foreigners at all. Most of the crowd that afternoon would be Chinese. Excluded from membership in the Race Club, Chinese were the great majority of Shanghai's population, and their fates were even more uncertain than those of Henchman, Aitkenhead, or Franklin.

Ing Tang, educated in Chinese and English, could have read Madame Piper's promises to foretell the future of her family and fortune. She had been born and raised in a suburban section of Shanghai's International Settlement, and riding had been a favorite pastime since childhood; she wouldn't have missed Champions Day. Chinese of means occupied an important spot in the city, moving between foreign and Chinese circles centered on the turf ring at the heart of the International Settlement.

The daughter of a doctor who had tended to both Shanghai's Chinese and Western communities, Ing Tang was among those people. She was a staple of society functions, educated in the city's best schools and once called "the most popular society beauty in Shanghai," although because she was a woman, she could not get the Ivy League degree that her brother earned.[10] She had opened an haute couture clothing store near the racetrack and had even been recruited to star on Broadway, though that opportunity had evaporated alongside her first marriage. In the fall of 1941, she lived just a few blocks from the racecourse, and the Champions' offered her a chance to forget the uncertainty of the present and the lost opportunities of the recent past.

Also focused on forgetting lost opportunities was Wang Naizhi. His foreign friends knew him as Nates Wong, and he had lots of foreign friends. An interpreter, translator, lawyer, editor, and amateur actor, Wong moved regularly among Shanghai's many worlds. The relationship had not always been cordial. British police had hauled him into their stations more than once, demanding explanations for his magazine's transgressions. He had worked at the racetrack, and he was a founding member of an association of Chinese professionals who used the Race Club's facilities to promote their cross-cultural vision for the city, even though Chinese couldn't be members there. Champions Day was just a short walk from his home on Yates Road, where he lived in a neighborhood of traditional *lilong* ("alleyway houses")—distinctive Shanghai residences, with numerous rooms opening onto a central courtyard. Built largely in the late nineteenth century to accommodate Shanghai's burgeoning population, they combined Western and Chinese features (they were built in rows, as in many European or American cities, but their interiors followed the traditional Chinese courtyard design).[11] In blending Chinese and Western influences, the alleyway houses exemplified Shanghai, and they have come to be seen as a valuable and vanishing contribution to world architecture, but for Shanghai Chinese they were, as historian Lu Hanchao described, "merely the place most people called home."[12]

Although the Shanghai Race Club never accepted Chinese members, attendance at the races became part of the social fabric for many Chinese denizens of the International Settlement. In neighborhoods like Jiufuli, just a few blocks from the racetrack, race days were important social occasions. Certainly on Champions Day, residents like newspaper publisher Y. S. Fong, Peking Opera star Cheng Qiuqiu,[13] and their neighbors made their way to the races. The Shanghai Race Club made lots of money from the public grandstand filled mostly with Chinese. And although some Race Club members objected to Chinese racegoers as low-class, many Chinese who attended the races were foreign-educated and wealthy. Some had, literally, helped to make Shanghai what it was.

Dayu Doon was one of these men, cutting a stylish figure with a pencil mustache and wire-rimmed glasses. Doon had graduated from Tsinghua University in Beijing and had studied architecture in Minnesota and New York City before returning to China to design what was meant to be Shanghai's future in the suburb of Jiangwan, north of the International Settlement. Doon's modernist utopia had been bombed and burned twice during construction and then, as it neared completion, occupied by invading soldiers.

On this morning, Doon's new Shanghai was under Japanese control and preparing to host the awkward celebration of Sun Yat-sen that Hench had seen praised and condemned in the posters strewn across Bubbling Well Road. Three thousand people would crowd into the square that Doon had designed a decade earlier, but Dayu Doon wouldn't be there. He was safe only in the foreign concessions, where one kind of foreign power could protect him against the incursions of another.

Ma Xiangsheng had also fled to the protection of the International Settlement, where he was commonly known by his English name, C. S. Mao. He wasn't the kind of man who was used to needing protection. Rising through the ranks of the Green Gang—Shanghai's most notorious organized crime syndicate—to acquire wealth and power, he had invested in casinos, theaters, and racehorses.[14] The horses had become his passion, and he stayed in Shanghai to race even after the Japanese invasion and after his patron, "Big Ears" Du Yuesheng, had fled the city. Mao's was the largest Chinese-owned stable in Shanghai, and even though the tracks he had helped found were now shut down by war, he was still able to run his ponies in undercard races at the Race Club downtown. His horses had already won several races that fall, including one of Shanghai's important classics, but he arrived at the track this November morning as a spectator: none of his horses were entered on the season's biggest day.

Whether a spectator or a competitor, it was still Champions Day. Mao would join Doon, Franklin, Nates Wong, Ing Tang, Henchman, Aitkenhead, and tens of thousands of others making their way to the Shanghai Race Club. Such an international scene would have been unimaginable just a few generations before. To make sense of the city in 1941, and the changes it was undergoing, we must go back a hundred years to see where it came from.

PART ONE

CITIZENS OF SHANGHAI

(1843–1937)

Europeans who by fate have been exiled in the far
East are probably not so much to be pitied as their friends
in Europe are inclined to believe.

—*NORTH-CHINA HERALD*,
NOVEMBER 24, 1860

. . .

"The Pleasures of Exile"

LONG BEFORE EUROPEANS IN SHANGHAI WOULD ENJOY WHAT
the *China Press* called "the pleasures of exile,"[1] Shanghai was very different from the place where Madame Piper prophesied. Its streets even
then heard many tongues, but mostly various Chinese languages spoken by migrants from throughout China. Often mutually unintelligi-
ble, belying the label "dialects" that they are sometimes given, they
showed that the city's diversity was never simply a matter of Chinese
versus foreign, or entirely a product of the arrival of Europeans. A few
miles away from the walled city along the Huangpu River, what would
become the racetrack and everything that surrounded it—stables,
offices, apartment buildings, hotels, theaters, shops—was farmland or
marsh. Nothing was more than a few stories tall. No European faces
were to be seen.

China's rulers had carefully managed their interactions with foreigners since the 1500s, when a handful of merchants and Jesuit priests
began to expand European interest and presence in China. For a century or more, these Europeans were managed ad hoc or fitted into existing categories devised to regulate border trade with central Asia or
maritime commerce in the South China Sea. Their first lasting outpost
was the Portuguese enclave at Macau, in the far south.

Although focused on trade and religion, the Europeans also brought
horses, and raced them. Racing at Macau began as early as 1637, with

horses brought from Europe or raised by the Spanish in the Philippines. The English raced East India Company cavalry horses on Macau's black-sand Areia Preta beach in the 1790s. But racing there was small in scale, a hobby for people stationed far from home to pass the time. There was no possibility of racing local horses. Not only did the treaties regulating the European presence forbid interaction between Chinese and foreigners outside of official government-authorized trade, but few horses could be found in southern China; the caravans that brought ponies from the steppes down to Chinese cities stopped a thousand miles north of Macau.[2]

The European presence in China concerned the new Qing dynasty, which came to power in 1644 and confined European overseas trade to Canton, the southern city that had long been one of China's most important maritime entrepôts. This restriction clashed with the desires of traders who, driven by their expanding seaborne empires and China's immense potential market, continued to illegally develop trading opportunities in other ports. Tensions grew between Qing officials and merchants from Britain, France, Sweden, the Netherlands, and other European states, who complained that they could not resolve or even express disputes adequately. The Europeans wanted their delegations to meet with the representatives of the Chinese government, ideally at the capital, but the Qing preferred to handle trade disputes locally, and in any case, no office at court quite matched European notions of diplomacy.

In response to the increasing demands, Qing authorities tightened their control. They reaffirmed the maritime-trade restrictions stipulating that Europeans could trade only with Canton, adding regulations to formalize what would come to be known as the "Canton System" in 1757. Trade could be conducted only with officially licensed government monopolies, which would assess duties and tariffs on their transactions. The trading season was limited, and permanent settlement was not allowed. Women were not permitted. The men who came could bring neither families nor firearms. They could not study the Chinese language. No foreigner could own property. Attempts to spread Christianity, which China's emperors had once formally tolerated, were forbidden.

The British, especially, complained that this Canton System was oppressively restrictive. The system *was* intended to manage trade and keep Westerners both closely supervised and at arm's length, but Canton was as free and open as most international ports at the time. (Though in the minority to be sure, some, even in Britain, recognized that trading at Canton was in many ways freer than at London.)[3]

Whatever its strengths and weaknesses, the Canton System facilitated China's trade with Europe (and after the 1780s, with the new United States), but it did not satisfy the ideals of Britain's expanding commercial empire. A British mission to Beijing in the 1790s asked to establish formal diplomatic relations and open more Chinese ports to commerce, but the Qianlong Emperor replied that China "possesses all things in prolific abundance and lacks no product within its own borders."[4]

Qianlong's letter has long been put forward as an example of the emperor's narrow-mindedness; recent scholarship suggests that its importance has been overstated to justify British imperial policies and priorities.[5] Nevertheless, the emperor rejected both the idea for an exchange of ambassadors and British requests to expand trade. The emperor might be forgiven his attitude. British demand for Chinese goods, especially tea, was strong, but the Chinese bought little from the Europeans in return. Silver paid for Chinese tea and porcelain; China enjoyed a substantial trade surplus as the eighteenth century drew to a close.

Chinese dominance did not last. Global recession, spurred in part by declining silver flows out of Latin America as countries there fought for and won independence from European colonizers, slowed foreign demand for Chinese exports. And around the same time, Britain finally found a product it could reliably sell to help balance its accounts: opium, grown in British-controlled India.

Opium has come to dominate impressions of nineteenth-century China. This image is misleading, not because opium was unimportant but because overemphasizing the opium trade diminishes larger internal and external trends. The Chinese economy had been slowing for decades, starting in the late eighteenth century, and the conflict between the British and Qing empires was less about opium specifically than about competing approaches to trade. But while the conventional wisdom that state-sponsored drug pushers from England undermined China's prosperity is at least overstated, British merchants did seize their opportunity to sell Indian varieties of opium that were more addictive than what had been in China previously. The market surged despite the Qing government's ban on the narcotic. A triangular trade emerged: British merchants sold their cargoes of tea in Europe, using the proceeds in India to acquire opium, which they then traded for tea and other goods in China. Declining Chinese exports and growing imports of opium combined to reverse the balance of trade.

Chinese officials responded as they had in the past, redoubling efforts to regulate and control commerce. Meanwhile, British traders skirted the Canton System and the ban on opium by working with Chinese smugglers and their boats, called "fast crabs," that could avoid officials, not only enabling the illegal opium trade but also evading the tariffs and duties owed to the government monopolies. In 1839, Qing officials confiscated supplies of opium (mainly British, but also American and Dutch) in a grand display at the waterfront that included the recitation of a classical Chinese poem apologizing to the creatures of the sea for fouling their habitat as opium stores flushed into Canton's harbor. As part of the crackdown, Western traders were confined until they agreed to surrender all their goods to Qing officials and cease the illegal trade in opium.

British traders demanded war, both as retribution for their losses and to reopen and expand their trade. After heated debate, Parliament voted by a narrow margin—9 votes, out of 533 cast—in favor of war.[6] Prescient members of the Qing government had wanted to avoid conflict, suspecting they could no longer dismiss Britain as Qianlong had forty-five years earlier, and their fears were realized. *Nemesis*, the world's first oceangoing iron steam-powered warship, arrived on the Chinese coast in 1840. Her six large guns and rocket launcher, in addition to steam power and an iron-plated hull, overwhelmed Chinese defenses and decimated the Qing navy.

Within two years of *Nemesis*'s arrival, the Treaty of Nanjing ended the war and dismantled the Canton System by ceding to Britain the colony of Hong Kong and opening the ports of Canton, Xiamen, Fuzhou, Ningbo, and Shanghai to trade. In these "treaty ports," there were few limits on what foreigners could do. Subsequent treaties extended rights won by the British to other "most favored nations," principally France and the United States, and permitted the construction of churches and

The 1842 Treaty of Nanjing ended the First Opium War and established five treaty ports in China, including Shanghai. This print from 1847 depicts Shanghai before its opening as one of these "treaty ports," though it takes liberties (there are, for instance, no mountains on Shanghai's marshy plain).

residences. Foreigners could now come in unlimited numbers, learn the language, and work directly with local businesses. They could not technically own land—it had to be leased, except in the crown colony of Hong Kong—but foreigners were able to acquire Chinese land to do with as they pleased. Commerce thrived; Chinese sovereignty foundered.

By no measure was Shanghai considered the most promising of the newly opened ports. Canton had a greater volume of trade, and Ningbo had a richer maritime history. But Shanghai—in part because it was a less prominent port, in part because of its strategic location near the mouth of the Yangtze, and for a dozen other reasons that historians debate—quickly became the most successful and important of the treaty ports. The world's largest empire now encountered its most populous country, and both were transformed.

The foundation of these treaty ports, and the basis of the special status that Arthur Henchman and other Shanghailanders would enjoy a century later, was extraterritoriality. Negotiated in the treaties ending the Opium Wars and extended to nationals of Britain, France, the United States, and eventually twenty-five other nations, extraterritoriality made foreigners in China subject not to Chinese law but to the laws of their own countries. Paralleling extraterritoriality was the creation of tiny colonial entities, called "concessions," in those parts of treaty ports made available for foreigners to settle.

Officials in London and Washington asserted that "non-Christian" governments in Asia and Africa were not civilized enough to be trusted. Instead, European and American citizens abroad would remain subject to their own laws, enforced by consular, not Chinese, officials. Caleb Cushing, the American diplomat who negotiated treaties establishing extraterritoriality, put it bluntly: American citizens in China would not be left vulnerable the "sanguinary barbarism of their inhabitants" or the "narrow-minded policy of their governments." "To none of the governments of this character," he wrote, "was it safe to commit the lives and liberties of citizens of the United States."[7]

Extraterritoriality applied throughout China, but the concentration of wealth and opportunity in Shanghai meant that foreign autonomy there went even further. Lured by newly opened ports and protected by extraterritoriality, European (mostly British) merchants and money began arriving in Shanghai in 1843. The Qing authorities granted them the right to rent land not in the existing walled city of Shanghai—both the Chinese and the British wanted more separation than that—but a short distance upriver along the Huangpu. This was the beginning of the British Concession, which would evolve into the International Settlement.

This settlement would become the focus of Western power in China, but in 1843 it was simply the start of a community that foreigners could inhabit, though not quite possess. Not all were English and not all were men, but from the start these foreigners aspired to reproduce English sporting life in China, and that included racing. Less than a decade removed from the First Opium War, Englishmen in Shanghai met to race horses near the confluence of Suzhou Creek and the Huangpu River.

Just a few years earlier, the emperor had rejected Britain as irrelevant and trivial, prohibiting foreigners from Shanghai (and virtually everywhere else in China). Now, these first British riders—just like Henchman, Aitkenhead, and Franklin in 1941—lived beyond the reach of Chinese law and with little regard for local authority. As in Macau two centuries earlier, sea captains and cavalry officers started looking for flat land on which to race their horses, and flat land was one resource that Shanghai held in abundance.

The first informal races in Shanghai ran on the muddy banks of the Huangpu near the Bund sometime between 1845 and 1847. Austin Coates—a British civil servant and author of the first history of racing in China—asserts that in the 1840s, "virtually every Briton in Shanghai owned a horse and rode every day."[8] (This may not have been an exaggeration, since only a few dozen British subjects lived in the city prior to 1850.) The early races were social events for people of means; owners usually rode their own horses, and the races were mainly for their own entertainment and recreation. Official race meetings began in 1848, and the Shanghai Race Club itself was established in 1850 "to encourage and promote horse and pony racing amongst its Members."[9] The Race Club constructed its first permanent course, the "Old Park," near the corner of Nanking Road and Honan Road (today the site of an Apple store). When the "Shanghae [sic] Park Stakes," went off on April 22, 1851, only 200 foreigners lived in the city, and the foreign community was not even a decade old. A second race meeting took place that October.

The club sold the Old Park's land and used the profit to buy a new course farther west, near the corner of Nanking and Chekiang Roads, which opened in 1854. There was little coordination among the various foreign jurisdictions and stakeholders in Shanghai, and the land was purchased piecemeal, with predictable problems. Some of the property enclosed by the racecourse—a patchwork of houses, shops, and even cemeteries—was never acquired at all. New buildings began to rise up in the middle of the track on land beyond the club's control.[10]

Who controlled what in Shanghai during these years was a muddle. The regulation that foreigners could not own but only lease land was unevenly understood and enforced, and after 1845 both British and American citizens could rent land "in perpetuity," begging the question.[11] Chinese sovereignty constrained foreign actions in Shanghai but didn't dictate them. American (1848) and French (1849) concessions were established. The confusing situation was easily, sometimes willfully, misinterpreted; competition among jurisdictions became an essential aspect of living and working in Shanghai. Extraterritoriality ensured that Chinese law did not apply to most of the Europeans living in Shanghai, but foreign countries' activities there were typically limited to trade and protection of their own citizens.

The vast and bloody Taiping civil war changed that in the 1850s. The Taiping movement tapped into social and economic unrest: familiar motives for rebellion. But this insurgency combined Christianity, utopian socialism, and nepotistic monarchy in a unique ideology backed by formidable armies that threatened to topple the Qing dynasty altogether. Hong Xiuquan, the self-identified younger brother of Jesus Christ, led his Taiping soldiers to victory after victory in the first years of the war. In 1853, Hong captured Nanjing—just 200 miles from Shanghai—and made it the capital of his "Heavenly Kingdom." Many foreign observers not only expected Taiping victory to soon follow but welcomed it, believing that their long-cherished ideal of a Christian China was at hand. This optimism, though, diminished after missionaries met with the Taiping leaders and found in Hong's Christianity more heresy than hope.

The impact of the Taiping war on China is hard to overstate. Killing more than 20 million people, the war laid waste much of southern and eastern China.[12] Taiping forces never reached Shanghai, but by threatening the city, the Taiping war transformed the role of foreigners there and expanded their autonomy. The main danger to Shanghai was not the Taiping kingdom itself, but a bandit group, called the Small Swords, that took advantage of the chaos created by the war, even capturing Shanghai's Chinese city from the Qing for a short time in 1851.

Whether the Taiping would overthrow the dynasty itself or merely undermine law and order, foreigners in Shanghai feared losing the land and livelihood that they had extracted from the Qing government. They banded together to protect their interests and take advantage of the Qing dynasty's weakened position to expand foreign power, creating a Shanghai Municipal Council in 1854 to administer their part of the city.[13] The American and British Concessions formally united in 1855 to establish the International Settlement, encompassing about 9 square miles of land. The French, after some uncertainty, formally declined this arrangement in 1862, incorporating their concession as a department of the French government administered, technically, directly from Paris.

The International Settlement was not a colony, because it remained sovereign Chinese territory. This distinction was a technical one, and had little impact on the extent of colonialism in the settlement, which many foreigners treated as a colony, technicalities notwithstanding. Trying to make sense of a place that embodied colonialism yet was not a colony, historian Isabella Jackson rejects labels like "semicolonial" or "quasi-colonial," instead applying the term "transnational colonialism" to Shanghai's International Settlement. What distinguished colonialism in Shanghai, Jackson argues, was not a lighter touch, but that the variety of imperial actors prevented any one imperial power from having its way.[14]

Colony or not, to defend its new territory the Municipal Council created its own army, the Shanghai Volunteer Corps. The SVC was said to be the first army in which British and American soldiers fought as allies, but whether or not that is the case, they fought their only engagement at the racecourse: the "Battle of Muddy Flat." Appropriately, given the confusion of sovereignties in Shanghai, the SVC fought not against the Taiping, or even against the Small Swords, but against the Qing army, encamped so close to the foreign areas that fire from its battle against the Small Swords threatened the International Settlement. When Qing generals refused to move away from the foreign-administered territory, British and American marines from vessels anchored in the Huangpu joined the volunteers and fired on the Qing camp. For this one day, the racecourse became a scene of literal and not just metaphorical combat, as foreign and Qing troops exchanged fire across the homestretch. Some fifty Qing troops and four foreigners were killed.[15]

The battle was no epic, but it helped to affirm the independence of the International Settlement and demonstrated that foreigners would protect their private state with force of arms. Merchants and professionals residing in the Settlement elected and operated its Municipal Council, which, in addition to protecting extraterritorial rights through its own police force and court system, acted as a local government, collecting taxes, fighting fires, and paving roads. Amid war and government weakness, the strength and stability of the International Settlement attracted Chinese, from the surrounding region and also from the Chinese city of Shanghai, seeking the protection of foreign governments. Shanghai became both more Chinese—as many as 500,000 Chinese refugees entered the foreign concessions during this time, and from then on the great majority of the International Settlement's population was Chinese—and more foreign, as foreign autonomy expanded and intensified.[16]

The Race Club could now acquire land more systematically and ambitiously than before. Operating freely now within this virtual colony, the club bought land—at less than market value and backed by implicit threats of force—from Chinese farmers desperate for protection and money after years of fighting.[17] The racecourse resumed its westward migration and established its third and final location at the end of Nanking Road, where it met Bubbling Well Road. There, the Race Club built a ⅝-mile turf track, grandstand, and clubhouse that defined Shanghai's International Settlement around two centers of power: the Bund and the Race Club, about a mile apart with Nanking Road linking the two. This was the track that would remain in operation into the 1940s. After fits and starts, the Shanghai Race Club was settled.[18]

The first races finally went off in April 1862, following days of thunderstorms that left the new track "more fitted for a sampan regatta than a horse-race." Foreshadowing the 1930s and 1940s, Shanghai's new foreign playground opened against the backdrop of a war, but "the recent warlike demonstrations against the rebels, or the prospect of hot work against them close at hand," did not diminish the crowd's enthusiasm for sports, the *North-China Herald* assured its readers.[19]

Shanghai was perched on the edge of the deadliest civil war in history, but racegoers preferred to imagine their racetrack as a haven "where the rival stables of Shanghai struggled for the peaceful palm of victory, beneath the smiles of the fair, and amidst the plaudits of our sporting friends." And although most of the crowd was Chinese, the *North-China Daily News* saw the races as a slice of England. "The touching confidence with which the sporting Briton pins his faith upon the stable of his friend, or the sayings of the learned in stable lore, forms one of the brightest traits in our national character. We may say that to be an Englishman is to be a judge of a horse and horseracing." Knickerbocker, the first winner on the new course (in the appropriately, if not creatively, named "New Course Stakes") launched an institution in the Settlement for the next eight decades.[20] And the spectacle of thousands of people gathered to cheer on the races with their backs to the smoke rising from encroaching war—kept barely at bay by imperialism—established a theme that would recur throughout the racetrack's history and right to its end.

If "to be an Englishman" was to judge horses, one has to wonder what sense those first race fans made of what they had come to see. As impressive as the Shanghai races were—"a Course and a Grand Stand which many a more important city would be proud to possess"[21]—the animals competing there were not. Strictly speaking, they weren't horses at all, but ponies, and not any pony was a China pony (China ponies themselves, ironically, were not bred in China at all, but in the Mongolian grasslands).

These "China ponies" that starred in Shanghai were puny beasts, very different from the Thoroughbred racehorses running in Europe, America, and Australia. Whereas Triple Crown winners like Secretariat or Justify stood more than 16 hands (about 5 feet 6 inches) at the shoulder, China ponies were only a bit over 13 hands (4 feet 8 inches). Owners and trainers in Shanghai routinely stood taller than their horses! (Australian Thoroughbreds raced at Shanghai too, but they were never as popular as their shorter cousins.) And the ponies were distinctive not just for being short. Broader, shaggier, and more durable than their Thoroughbred cousins, they had a heavy mane, a low-set tail, and an unusually large head on a short neck.

Some maintained that these ponies were closely related to the Przewalski horses, small horses native to Mongolia that were named for explorer Nikolay Przhevalsky (Przewalski) after he brought some back to Europe during his nineteenth-century expeditions. The short and shaggy China ponies impressed everyone with their spirit, "speed, sturdiness, soundness, and stamina." Enthusiasts in Shanghai praised the breed as "a wonderful weight carrier" able to "bear equally well torrid heat and Arctic cold," and above all, having "the determination to get from start to finish first, which is the mark of a true racehorse."[22]

Purchased at horse bazaars in the spring and the fall, the China ponies remained the focus of the Shanghai races, not always without controversy. With no hard-and-fast rules to define what a China pony was, and without the strict attention to breeding that characterized Thoroughbred racing, it could be hard to prove that a racehorse was a genuine China pony (despite later assertions by one expert that "every-

Chinese grooms, known as "mafoos," pose with China ponies
for a group photo. Shanghai, ca. 1880.

body who has taken any interest in racing in China would immediately recognize a 'China pony' if he saw one in the street in London, or Timbuctoo, or the North Pole"[23]).

Anytime a pony began to dominate, or seemed a little too fast or a little too tall, rumors would begin to circulate that the horse was a hybrid, crossbred with Australian horses descended from European and Arabian stock. But these disputes did nothing to dampen Shanghai's enthusiasm for its unique horses. How they first came to the attention of British racing enthusiasts in treaty ports isn't clear, but from the very beginning the races on the China coast were contested mainly among China ponies—whatever those were.

CHAPTER

3

· · · ·

Shanghailanders

Esmé "Dolly" Hutton Potts leading a winner at the Shanghai
Race Club, ca. 1910.

THE FIRST BRITISH RESIDENTS ARRIVED IN SHANGHAI IN
November 1843—just a year after the Treaty of Nanjing ended the
First Opium War—and a census taken that year listed just 25 Europeans in the city.[1] A decade later, the foreign community had expanded
tenfold, but still only 250 foreigners lived in a city of more than a
million. Some of those were temporary residents who moved among
the treaty ports—by the end of the nineteenth century there were

dozens—up and down the coast. By 1865, about 2,800[2] foreigners lived in Shanghai. Some, although not all, would come to see themselves as Shanghailanders.

A "Shanghailander"—the term was used as early as 1886—was understood to be a foreign resident of the city, usually western European and most commonly British.[3] Most definitions excluded Russians, though that stigma became more prominent with the Russian diaspora of the early twentieth century. In a city of temporary and permanent migrants from across China and around the world, Shanghailanders ran the show.

The idealized Shanghailander was a Briton abroad, but the category could be flexible. One of the first examples was Norwegian. Nils Moller came to the city via Hong Kong in the summer of 1863; soon his red-and-white anchor flag was flying at the Race Club. He sponsored a trophy and may have owned horses, but whatever his specific role at the racecourse, Moller was a polarizing figure. Part progressive entrepreneur and part conniving cheat, he insisted on being called "Captain Nils"—a demand that grated on his business partners because it was not clear that he had ever held a naval rank or commanded a ship.

Moller's charismatic personality attracted many, but his charms seldom lasted. Lawsuits against him alleging damages to ships or goods, breaches of contracts, and other commercial disputes were constant. These cases were brought to Her Britannic Majesty's Supreme Court for China, the court established in the 1860s (as the Supreme Court for China and Japan) to hear cases involving British citizens, but Moller rarely even appeared in court. Although he worked on and with British-flagged vessels, he was not a British citizen, and judges consistently affirmed that their jurisdiction did not extend to Swedish citizens, as Moller had been and, presumably, was[4] (Norway and Sweden were united under one crown from 1814 to 1905). But when subpoenaed to appear before the Swedish and Norwegian consular court, Moller rejected that too.

Responding to allegations that he used "flags of convenience" to avoid tariffs and other consequences, Nils Moller wrote in 1891 that he had "expatriated [himself] from all jurisdiction of the Swedish and Norwegian consulate" more than twenty years earlier. "Since which time," he went on, "I have practiced business as a Citizen of Shanghai."[5] He went on to protest that he claimed no European citizenship at all, and rejected extraterritorial protections.

Nils Moller was an unusual case. His disdain for nationality and professed affection for the Chinese set him apart from most Europeans in Shanghai, including the Swedish consul, who was shocked by "the strange spectacle of a European voluntarily giving up his rights as such to be subject to the laws of a nation like China."[6] Moller, in turn, was indignant at the consul's "vulgar" denigration of the Chinese people. It was not Moller's last time in court; he tried to hold the Shanghai Municipal Council responsible for damages to his property resulting from faulty drainage on city roads.[7] His own children sued him more than once over business dealings gone wrong, and it was these children who would carry on the family name, making it eventually one of the most important in Shanghai, especially at the races.

If Nils Moller was too eccentric and not English enough to be the ideal Shanghailander, Augustus White, another Race Club member whose family would become a fixture in Shanghai, better fit the bill. Like Moller, White came to Hong Kong in the 1860s, part of the migration of Europeans to China after the Opium Wars. The combined energies of China and Britain would make Hong Kong a center of international commerce in the twentieth century, but this version of the city did not emerge until after World War II.

At first, the British regarded Hong Kong as so remote that they sanctioned their negotiator who obtained it after the Opium Wars for acquiring such a meager prize. When Augustus White arrived there, just twenty years after Britain took possession, he was one of only 2,000 Europeans out of a total population of 125,000, and this outpost on the edge of empires was, above all, a Chinese place. White seemed to exemplify the English colonist: born in Middlesex, traveling to Asia in the wake of a war that provided Britain with colonies and trade on its own terms, growing rich as the empire expanded.

In Hong Kong, White met Sewey Hong, a Chinese woman; their daughter, Fanny, was born in 1864. Relationships between Europeans and Chinese—usually European men and Chinese women—were commonplace, though they rarely resulted in marriage, even when they produced children. The relationship between Augustus and Sewey was not casual. They left Hong Kong together for Shanghai soon after

Fanny was born. There's no indication that they left because of their relationship, though it is possible that social stigma drove the couple out of Hong Kong. For whatever reason, Augustus, Sewey, and Fanny, not yet a toddler, arrived in Shanghai around the same time as Nils Moller. Augustus began working in the first Shanghai office of Chartered Bank, one of the several banks that financed the growth of British commerce in China.

Augustus and Sewey never married, but they were a family. Together they had seven more children over the next ten years. After that, we don't know what became of Sewey Hong (she may have died in 1877—at what age is unknown). In 1878, Augustus married an Englishwoman, Maude Pratt, who bore two children with him before she died at the age of just twenty-five, in 1883. The ten White children grew up together and shed important light on the nature of Shanghai society. That eight of the children were half-Chinese and two were not was unusual, but not beyond the capacity of the International Settlement's bureaucracy. All of the half-Chinese children were registered at the British consulate, with the notation that Sewey Hong was their mother, and that she and Augustus were not married.[8]

Augustus White left Chartered Bank to establish his own brokerage in about 1870, and the new firm, White and Co., grew along with Shanghai. Neither White nor Moller arrived in China wealthy, but they amassed fortunes there and spent their leisure time accordingly, running with the same crowd. They shot clay pigeons at the Shanghai Gun Club (Moller was the better shot) and played cricket on the International Recreation Ground, which was the racecourse's infield.

The extended White family became one of the most powerful in Shanghai finance and regulars on the society pages, throwing and attending extravagant parties. Augustus Harold—each generation named the eldest son Augustus, so the middle name was important to distinguish among them—built an estate, which he named "Clatterhouse," in the countryside west of the French Concession along Siccawei Road (later renamed Avenue Haig). It was quintessentially British and colonial: a leopard-skin rug in the foyer welcomed visitors. Nearly every room featured animal-skin rugs and antlers on the walls; scenes of English military escapades or hunting scenes of foxes, pheasants, horses, and hounds hung alongside Japanese objets d'art, Chinese vases, and family photographs. And of course, there was a bar outfitted for Shanghailand: French and Italian vermouth; Dawson's scotch; Asahi lager; Guinness stout.[9]

Moller and White were names that would become Shanghailander aristocracy, prominent at the Race Club to its very end. It is revealing that neither of these families at the heart of Shanghai society neatly fit the stereotype of the Shanghailander. Nils Moller wasn't English and refused to be assigned nationality. He railed against racism and imperialism, though he benefited from both. The Whites exemplified British colonial society, yet the family was thoroughly Eurasian. A close look at the Shanghailanders who made the Race Club, and other Shanghai clubs, their personal playgrounds, reveals that backgrounds like these were, if not quite the rule, not very exceptional. Another family fitting this description was the Cumines.

The first generation of Cumines in Shanghai—Winifred Greaves and Henry Monsel Cumine—were both Scots who were born and raised in China. Their fathers had come, like Nils Moller and Augustus White, as part of the China trade—one trading in tea, the other a ship's captain. Winifred's mother, Josephine Ng, was from southern Guangdong province. The identity of Henry's mother is uncertain, but she likely was Chinese as well, probably from Shanghai. This mixed parentage put Winifred and Henry under intense scrutiny. As early as the 1860s, the *North-China Herald* editorialized about the peril facing Shanghai if it failed to recognize the growing problem of "the intermediate race that is arising," and called on the city to establish an English-style boarding school for "Eurasian" children, so that they might become a "civilized link between Foreigners and Chinese." The Shanghai School for Eurasians, established in about 1870, was deemed a great success for "replicating as near as possible the European standard" while remaining segregated from "pure blood" Europeans.[10]

Nowhere was the racism of Shanghailand more evident than in its clubs. A dozen or more sprang up in the nineteenth century, led by the Shanghai Club, "pre-eminent among the social clubs of the place, not only for the priority of establishment, but for the important place it occupies in this community."[11] Founded in 1864 on the Bund, it boasted a "Long Bar," reputed to be the longest in Asia, and the place where business was transacted "at the witching hour of noon, under the beguiling influence, as some cynics have it, of the soothing cocktail or insinuating sherry and bitters."[12] The Shanghai Club was decidedly British in membership. Though the Shanghai Club was foremost, Shanghailanders also had at their disposal the Club Concordia (predominantly German in membership), the Country Club, the Masonic Club, the Customs Club, and numerous others, not to mention the sporting clubs, of which the Race Club was most important.

One description of the Shanghai Club extolled it as "thoroughly cosmopolitan, and its members are of every nationality."[13] Its membership was restricted to white males, illustrating clearly the sort of "cosmopolitanism" Shanghailanders envisioned, especially in the first decades of the International Settlement. Cosmopolitan implies an equality that was absent in Shanghai. The infamous sign declaring "No dogs or Chinese allowed" in the city's public garden is apocryphal, but the sentiment behind it was not (dogs and most Chinese *were* excluded from the park, but not in the same sentence).[14]

At the Race Club, Chinese were permitted, encouraged even, to attend race days—their bets made up the bulk of the club's revenue—but Chinese could not join the club as members. Physically, financially, socially, and culturally, the Race Club was at the center of the Shanghailanders' world, and though it was in China, it was not meant to be *of* China. The Shanghailanders celebrated their new course as an imperialist achievement, an example (using rhetoric that would earn the condemnation of Communist Chinese authorities in the 1950s) of "the changes taking place in this corner of the old decayed, misnamed Celestial Empire, and the material progress of THE FOREIGNER IN SHANGHAI."[15]

As the nineteenth century drew to a close, Shanghailanders were proud of the little piece of Britain they had constructed. "Europeans who by fate have been exiled in the far East," wrote A. L. Robertson in the *North-China Herald*, "are probably not so much to be pitied as their friends in Europe are inclined to believe. . . . [S]eeing that probably no place in the world could be more favored in the facilities offered for each individual enjoying to the fullest extent the special sport in which he is interested. . . . The course is perfect, level, and smooth, a billiard table."[16]

Their facilities may have been the finest in China, but the early race meets were amateur affairs. Professional jockeys were few, and most owners rode their own horses. Royal Navy musicians provided music, but only if a ship carrying a band happened to be in port. Decorations and entertainments were arranged by the club stewards. These modest beginnings laid the foundation for what was to come.

The Race Club named most of its races after (seemingly random) locations in China. Others were named for a sponsoring individual or group: the senior Chinese official in Shanghai presented the Taotai's Cup, Shanghai's German community put up the purse for a German Challenge Cup, and so forth. Still other races described the participants, such as the Griffins' Cup for new horses or the Consolation Cup for non-winners. The most important race of those early meetings was the Tsatlee Stakes, named after a commonly exported form of raw silk that formed the foundation of some members' fortunes. The 1850 Tsatlee Stakes offered a purse of $100 (about US$3,000 in today's currency).

In their quest to replicate English sporting life as best they could, club members named the most important Shanghai races after English races and, also in keeping with English practice, designated the most important races as "classics." Named after the oldest of the English classics, which had begun in 1776, the first Shanghai St. Leger was run (as the North China St. Leger) at the fall meeting of 1851 and became a staple of the second day of each race meeting. The Criterion Stakes (its English namesake first run at Newmarket in 1868), became the featured event of each meeting's first day. A "Shanghai Derby" was first contested in the 1850s, but it didn't become a regular part of the racing program until 1867. (Hong Kong, which began racing around the same time as Shanghai, followed a similar practice, running a Hong Kong St. Leger, for instance, and a Hong Kong Derby as well.)

As the number of races grew, so did the crowds and the number of wagers, but what would become the most important race in Asia began modestly, in 1869. The *North-China Herald* announced the first Champions' Stakes subtly amid the details of the upcoming race meet: "There is also to be the Champion Sweepstakes, a forced entry for all winners, on the third day."[17] Although there were "champions" races during the 1850s, the November 1869 Champions Sweepstakes was the first to require all the winning horses from the meeting to compete. The requirement came not just from a sporting desire to see whose horse was fastest.

In the early days of the races, the small community of owners could easily manipulate the results through gentlemen's agreements, deciding among themselves how to distribute the best horses so that everyone would be guaranteed a win. Top stakes races might get only two or three entrants, and in some cases the jockeys visibly held back their mounts to ensure the desired outcome. The integrity of the races did not greatly concern the owners, who were, in effect, dividing the purses among themselves, but betting required confidence in fair play, and from the very start, gambling drove the races in Shanghai (as elsewhere). Newspapers—both English and Chinese—printed odds and payouts, and crowds packed the grandstands looking for chances to cash in. If races were thought to be fixed, interest—and betting—would dry up.

The very first Champions' Stakes went off on November 5, 1869. Mors aux Dents ("bit between the teeth"), the first winner, belonged to French customs official Baron Eugene de Meriten (one aspect of the treaty port system was that Europeans and Americans took over the collection of Chinese customs and staffed the agency). The distance was a mile and a quarter, and it never changed.[18]

For decades to come, the four classics would define the race meetings, predictable parts of each spring and fall in Shanghai: the Criterion Stakes on day one, the Shanghai Derby and the Shanghai St. Leger on day two, and—most important of all—the Champions' Stakes on day three. Dozens of other races were contested, but attention focused on the classics, and especially on the Champions' Stakes, the standard against which all horses were measured. Champions Day became a holiday in the foreign concessions. Repeat winners of the Champions' became celebrities: Ravenshoe in 1873 and 1874; Teen Kwang back-to-back in 1875; Strathavon in 1878 and 1879. Black Satin and Prejudice each won three Champions' in the 1870s and 1880s. When Henchman, Aitkenhead, Franklin, and all the others set their sights on the Champions', they were joining in a tradition that dated back to Mors aux Dents in 1869.

The races and Shanghai grew together. More races were added—so-called "extra" race meetings that complemented the spring and fall meetings. Crowds and wagers continued to grow, but even as the races attracted more fans, more horses, and more money, most owners rode their own horses, and jockeys were, for the most part, amateurs. By the 1880s, racing was a spectacle for the entire city, but still a hobby for many of its participants.

David Sassoon, for one, was not interested in racing as a hobby.

The Sassoon family wrote one of the most important chapters in the growth of foreign business in Shanghai and also in the Race Club. Sassoon businesses, built on cotton and opium, emerged after the American Civil War and the Taiping war as some of Shanghai's most profitable enterprises. David Sassoon (David Elias Sassoon, 1865–1938, not to be confused with the founder of the Sassoon dynasty, his great-uncle David Sassoon, 1792–1864) never showed much interest in the family business, though he was pleased to spend the family money. As successful as his relatives were in boardrooms and stock exchanges, David Elias was just as expert at the Race Club. The Sassoon name transformed business in Shanghai, and he ensured that it had the same transformational effect at the Race Club.

The Sassoons exemplified Shanghai's status as a city of migrants. The Jewish family started its migration from Baghdad to Shanghai in the 1820s, driven by the pogroms of Dawud Pasha, the last Mamluk ruler of Iraq. One of these refugees, an elder David Sassoon, arrived in Bombay in 1831, where a Jewish community dated back to the sixth century. Sassoon's good fortune was that, at just the time he was arriving, Bombay was poised to explode commercially, thanks first to a cotton trade that would link Britain, India, and China. By 1831, English mills were the world's most productive—protectionist tariffs and laws that undermined the Indian textile industry saw to that—and as a global textile producer, Britain relied on its overseas colonies and former colonies for raw material. English mills preferred varieties grown in Alabama or the West Indies, but some balked at the high prices fetched by American cotton and sought cheaper alternatives from India.

Also at the same time that Sassoon arrived in Bombay, the British East India Company's monopoly on all trade in India was ending; Parliament completely abolished it in 1833. After the Opium Wars, Indian textile producers found themselves thousands of miles closer than their English competitors to newly opened Chinese markets.

Indian entrepreneurs began building their own mills to compete with the British factories, opening the first cotton mill in Bombay in 1854. Rather than shipping raw cotton to England and then importing finished textiles, Indian cotton mills were now competing directly with the Lancashire mills.

Their connections and knowledge of the Middle East and regional trading networks were important to their business success, but the Sassoons also benefited from an unlikely confluence of events spread across the globe. The increasing price of American cotton, the availability of new machinery for cleaning and refining cotton in India, and the end of the East India Company's monopolies all played a role, but politics on the other side of the world may have been the crucial piece. In the United States, a Union blockade reduced cotton exports from the southern states by 95 percent during the American Civil War. The decimation of its cotton trade helped doom the Confederacy, but its impact was almost as great on the British textile mills. The early 1860s became known as the Lancashire Cotton Famine, or Cotton Panic. Starved of raw cotton to turn into cloth, mills slowed and shuttered.

While Lancashire languished, Bombay surged. Indian cotton exports and prices increased because of the dearth of material from America. Meanwhile, new mills opened in Bombay—ten were operating by the time the American Civil War ended—as Indians refined the cotton rather than exporting it to be processed in Britain. Tens of millions of pounds sterling flowed into the Bombay economy. Land speculation fueled a bubble, with an entire financial industry devoted to inflating it. By January of 1865, Bombay had more than thirty banks and more than sixty joint-stock companies, as well as dozens of other companies selling insurance, shipping, and services for the cotton industry. But within a few months of Lee's surrender, American cotton exports resumed and Lancashire mills turned away from Indian cotton. The price of Bombay cotton dropped by more than a third, and interest rates rose. The Bank of Bombay failed; thousands of speculators went bankrupt. That same year, David Elias Sassoon, who would transform the Shanghai Race Club, was born.

Sassoon & Co. survived the boom-and-bust of the 1860s. The Sassoons had not stockpiled raw cotton, so the drop in prices affected them little. The immense profits they had made—in textiles, but also in opium, the second crucial commodity for British trade during this period—during the previous decade had given them lots of cash on hand, so rather than having to borrow money at high rates, Sassoon could buy the assets of his competitors at a discount. Although the Bombay bubble had burst, the boom of the 1860s had laid the foundation for industrial development. Sassoon & Co. was now positioned to become a vital pivot between the North Atlantic economy, dominated by Britain, and newly opened China.[19]

The opium trade burgeoned after the war of 1839–42 and was soon generating enormous profits. Almost all of the opium sold in China originated in British-controlled India, and new trading companies saw opportunities in new markets that lacked existing infrastructure. The Sassoon family, emboldened and enriched by its successes during the American Civil War, entered this competition and established itself in Shanghai by the 1850s. Two Sassoon firms—often bitter rivals—thrived off of this mix of cotton, opium, and real estate, trading between Bombay and Shanghai, but the younger David Sassoon—David Elias—showed little personal interest in business.

Born in Bombay, David Elias came to Shanghai when he was about eighteen years old, in the early 1880s. He was never active in managing the Sassoon firms, but his share of the family fortune made him nevertheless a very rich young man. Befitting an Englishman of leisure, he took his place among the local elite at the Race Club (he became a member in 1886), spending his time and money on philanthropy and, especially, horses. When he was just twenty years old he bought a stable of many of the best horses, including Councillor, the reigning Champion. His results proved that he judged horses better than anyone else in Shanghai. Sassoon went on to dominate the Champions' for the next decade. Councillor won three in a row. Zephyr won back-to-back and set a record for the distance. Sassoon's stable, appropriately labeled "Leviathan," was soon the largest in the city.

David Sassoon's Leviathan Stables dominated the Shanghai Race Club, but his success was not appreciated. Many club members viewed Sassoon as a bullying outsider who had bought his success rather than earning it. Criticisms were widespread. A letter to the *North-China Herald* complained that Sassoon's dominance had taken the joy out of the races, reducing attendance:

It is a general belief that [Sassoon's] stable is going to carry off more prizes than ever, and this throws a wet blanket over the meeting. No one has any objection to the owner of the stable personally, who is praised as a true sportsman and a plucky rider; but his apparently exhaustless purse crushes out the opposition which is the soul of racing. When one man can buy up all the best ponies, and command the services of the best grooms and the best jockey. . . . [N]obody cares to go out to the rails to see one foregone conclusion after another.[20]

Critics went out of their way not to insult Sassoon personally, but it is hard to avoid the implication of anti-Semitism from the clubby, Anglican members. One, calling himself "Fairplay," called out Sassoon's riding tactics, asking, "When will the genial 'David' learn even the rudiments of the ethics of racing?"[21]

The pinnacle of the Leviathan era was Hero, widely regarded as the best horse ever to run in Shanghai. Frank Dallas rode Hero to six Champions' wins in seven tries between 1890 and 1893. Stony silence greeted his wins more often than not: "Four successive Sassoon wins were received in absolute silence in the Grand Stand . . . silence for a Sassoon victory, tumultuous enthusiasm for a Sassoon defeat," wrote Austin Coates of an afternoon at the club.[22] The contempt was confined, it seems, to the foreign crowd: Sassoon's success attracted more Chinese fans to the track than ever, requiring the construction of an additional stand reserved just for Chinese women, all cheering enthusiastically as the winning horses passed the stand.

Hero surely would have added to his own record, but just hours after winning his sixth Shanghai Champions' he fell ill with colic. In enormous distress, he was put down at noon the next day, his death casting a pall over the Settlement.[23] Hero's *North-China Herald* obituary mourned him as "the pony of the century."[24] (Hero's jockey, Frank Dallas, died young and unexpectedly as well, passing away of liver disease in 1905 at just forty years of age.)[25]

After Hero's death, David Sassoon had had enough. Losing his champion may have taken the joy out of racing for him, or perhaps the relentless criticism and complaints of the club members wore Sassoon out. Or maybe he just grew bored, having mastered the Shanghai races.

From the time he first sent a horse to the line in Shanghai, David Sassoon won the Champions' eleven out of sixteen times and dominated the Criterion and Shanghai St. Leger too. But he left Shanghai abruptly in the fall of 1894. The *North-China Herald* could barely conceal its glee. "As one result of the withdrawal of the leviathan stable," the paper crowed, "it will be noticed that the nine races . . . were divided among eight owners, only two . . . carrying off two first prizes."[26] Hero's record of six Champions' was challenged, but never equaled.

Race and the Races

Racing was a foreign import, but the people of Shanghai, regardless of nationality, embraced it. Two statues that stood on Bubbling Well Road, a few yards from the entrance to the Shanghai Race Club's grandstands, bore witness to the races' popularity among Shanghai Chinese. On race days, thousands of people on their way to the track flowed past these sculpted deities. A chance for a good payday was worth a minute's pause, and many fans—though very few foreigners—made offerings to the golden statues, hoping for luck in the races to come.

Racing had begun as a social club for agents of imperialism, but its appeal went beyond European men of means. Chinese residents loved the races. Chinese-language newspapers reported regularly on the "Westerners' horse-racing" with colorful metaphors of "flying clouds" and "electric fire"[1] racing through the mud at the racecourse. In the 1870s, race meetings might attract 20,000 Chinese spectators, meaning that 10 percent of the city's Chinese population was at the races. A nineteenth-century Chinese observer showed his fascination with Shanghai's new spectacle:

> During fine weather in the spring and autumn, [the Westerners] hold horse races, once in each season, each time for three days, from noon until around six in the evening. Sometimes three or

The two statues of Chinese deities, near the entrance to the Shanghai Race Club, often visited by Chinese racegoers before attending races at the club. The statues remained in place until 1948, when they were torn down because the crowds gathered in front of them regularly disrupted traffic.

four wide, and at other times there are six or seven. They dress in different colours: yellow, red, purple and green. The horses vary, too: pure black, yellow, red with black mane and tail, white with black mane. Neck and neck, they run, swift like the wind and quick as lightning. . . . On the third day, wall jumping, ditch leaping, fence jumping and other such tricks are added. On this day, the spectators, everyone from high-ranking gentlemen to lowly peddlers, jostle together in the crowd, and late arrivals hardly have a place to stand.[2]

In the early days the Race Club prohibited Chinese from even entering the grandstand, so spectators lined the track, craning their necks for a better view.[3] Soon, though, the club permitted nonmembers of any nationality, including Chinese, to pay an admission fee to enter the Race Club grounds on race days, where they could sit in the grandstand and place wagers.

Even while most of the people on the club grounds were Chinese, membership was whites only. This racism was not written down. To become a member, a man—at first, only men—"of legal age" needed to be nominated by a member and voted on for membership. The rules allowed for members to be expelled if their "nationality or political status may in the opinion of the stewards render him unfit to continue as a member," but this provision was never specified or elaborated on.[4] Whether or not these rules were printed, club members understood that Chinese were not appropriate nominees, even though plenty of wealthy Chinese who would otherwise fit the bill for membership called Shanghai home.

Zhu Baosan was one of these men who, had he been white, would have been a Shanghailander in good standing, with a box at the Race Club and membership in the Shanghai Club on the Bund. He was Chinese, though, and therefore excluded from those establishments. Zhu's career in Shanghai mirrored those of men like Augustus White and, later, Arthur Henchman: bankers who made fortunes through the China trade and, along the way, fell in love with racing.

Zhu's family had based its businesses in the city of Ningbo, some 50 miles from Shanghai at the southern entrance to Hangzhou Bay. Ningbo, not Shanghai, had long been the most important port in the region, a center for fishing, shipping, and banking. These economic engines made Ningbo one of the richest cities in China (and, therefore, in the entire world). A European settlement at Ningbo had been the very first in China, established in 1522 by Portuguese merchants. Complete with hospitals, churches, inns, and a courthouse, the settlement lasted twenty-five years before Chinese troops violently dismantled it, killing some 800 Europeans in the process and relocating Portugal's Chinese presence to Macau.[5]

Ningbo remained a prominent, thriving port, and Zhu Baosan's family had prospered there. One British East India Company representative described the city as "[surpassing] anything Chinese which we have yet seen, in the regularity and magnificence of the buildings, and is behind none in mercantile fame."[6] Such accounts made Ningbo a target to be among the first five treaty ports opened in 1842, but by then the city was already in decline. Fuzhou and Canton, farther south, could more efficiently handle overseas trade; and Shanghai, at the mouth of the Yangtze, had better access to inland markets.

Much of Ningbo's own merchant and banking community was shifting its focus to Shanghai. Rather than the jewel in the treaty port crown that many expected, Ningbo became a backwater at the very edge of Western influence. One disappointed British observer described Ningbo as "the quietest place under the sun. A handful of merchants lived there, buried without the trouble of dying."[7] In Shanghai pidgin, the language of traders in the port, to go "Ningpo more far" (meaning "beyond Ningbo") was to disappear into China, beyond the reach of laws or creditors.

Although past its peak, Ningbo's influence remained important. By the 1790s, Ningbo merchants were the most powerful in Shanghai, and their native-place associations—usually translated as "guilds"— provided vital social and commercial networks, helping people with family ties to Ningbo find everything from food, jobs, and shelter to entertainment, security, loans, and burial plots. These native-place associations could also play political roles: in 1874 and again in 1898, the Ningbo native-place association in Shanghai (called, using one of Ningbo's classical names, the Siming Association) organized protests against French authorities during land disputes. Zhu Baosan, Zhou Jinzhen, and other leaders of Shanghai's Ningbo community were at the top of the city's Chinese hierarchy.[8]

Coming of age in the 1860s, Zhu Baosan played a critical role in financing this development, expanding the Commercial Bank and the Zhonghua Commercial and Savings Bank at a time when Shanghai needed capital for building. He was involved also in manufacturing and shipping, and became president of the Chinese Chamber of Commerce in the International Settlement, a position of outsized importance because businessmen rather than governments administered the Settlement.

In addition to serving as this sort of internal ambassador from China to the Settlement, Zhu helped reorganize the Ningbo native-place associations to serve a broader segment of society (always focused on men, though they did eventually serve some women). Much of their work was charitable. They did help those in need but were not radical institutions serving the poor. Leaders of the association created elaborate and often luxurious facilities, exemplified by a new headquarters for the Siming Association at Thibet Road in the International Settlement. The five-story Western-style building housed a library, banquet hall, theater, and exhibition hall for Ningbo goods. It was, just like the Race Club a few blocks away, a place for men to pass their leisure time, develop connections, and establish contacts.[9]

With institutions like the Siming Association at their disposal, Chinese of means in Shanghai had access to elaborate and often luxurious social amenities. But not to all of them; the Race Club was a sticking point between the Chinese and white communities.

Because the Shanghai races were a foreign import with a mostly Chinese audience, questions of race dogged them from their very start. Neither side was completely satisfied with the arrangement that allowed Chinese to attend the races but not join the club. As the races drew more and more spectators, the mostly Chinese crowds troubled members. No one was complaining about the money being spent at the track, but about the class of people that were coming. The Race Club members perceived not a gathering of gentlemen like Zhu Baosan, but an unruly crowd bent on gambling without attention to the social niceties of the races (a description that applied to many in attendance, without regard to nationality).

Zhu Baosan, the "merchant prince of Shanghai," was one of the founders of the International Recreation Club at Jiangwan, the first racetrack in Shanghai to admit Chinese members.

Repeatedly, club members—all men—framed their concern as the protection of public order, not segregation: the rowdy race days, they worried, made for a scene that discouraged women from attending (all the while refusing to admit women as members). At the Race Club's 1897 general meeting, members deplored the atmosphere on race days, blaming it on an insatiable Chinese thirst to gamble. "I do not think that a Chinese cares a rap about seeing a pony win or lose," a Mr. Midwood declared, "as long as he could gamble on the races."[10] One of the course stewards agreed that the club had become "nothing but a seething mob!" thanks to both Chinese gamblers and the new "totalisator" machines that automatically adjusted the odds and payout for each horse according to the money wagered (this principle remains the standard method for gambling on horse racing to this day).

Midwood proposed "to kill two birds with one stone—getting rid of the Chinese and the Totalisators."[11] Midwood directed his ire at the Chinese, even though many Chinese at the track were as fancy as any Western Shanghailander. Nonetheless, race, rather than racing, carried the day: the Shanghai Race Club enacted policies intended to maintain the revenue stream from gambling while excluding most Chinese from the racecourse altogether.[12]

The SRC removed the totalisator machines from their location under the grandstand, where they had created the "mob" that members found objectionable, and relocated them to a viewing stand on the far side of the track, where people—mostly but not entirely Chinese—could bet on and watch the races away from the members' grandstand. At the same time, the SRC ended the policy of accepting paid admission to the grandstands on race days. No longer could nonmembers gain access to the SRC facilities (unless they were invited guests). The new policy did not ban Chinese—or any other nationality—per se, but since Chinese could not be members and had to rely only on daily admission for entrance, the change effectively excluded them from the Race Club's grounds. The change, enacted for the fall 1897 meeting, touched off a firestorm. The Chinese press, led by the newspaper *Shenbao*, attacked the SRC as "Pleasure Palace for the Arrogance of the White Race."[13]

Denied entrance to the Race Club, Zhu Baosan and Tse-ung (T. U.) Yih, another prominent merchant with Ningbo roots, decided that if they couldn't join 'em, they would beat 'em, and they led a group of Chinese investors to plan a new race club that would admit Chinese members. The new club, to be known as the International Recreation Club (IRC) would be located in Jiangwan district, outside the International Settlement and thus avoiding the complicated politics of the all-but colony.

Just a few miles north of the Shanghai Race Club, Jiangwan was in some ways a world apart, but it was close enough that the SRC perceived it as a threat (for although the SRC was now prohibiting Chinese attendance, the new club would welcome paying spectators of any nationality).[14] Furthermore, the SRC's more restrictive admission policies were having unintended consequences: the new regulations "cannot be said to have been an entire success," reported the *North-China Herald* as it described "virtually deserted lawn and rails."

> The great merry crowd of non-members was absent; the bustle and jollity of former Meetings were unknown quantities, while dull decorum reigned supreme, and even if members and their families enjoyed the luxury of ample accommodation, they lacked the fun, liveliness, and hilarity which are considered inseparable from a Race Meeting.[15]

Faced with having less fun—never mind the economic losses and ethical considerations—the SRC found a solution that was quintessentially Shanghai: cosmopolitan, racist, pragmatic, cooperative, and cynical all at once. The policy excluding Chinese from the Race Club grounds was modified. Paying customers of any nationality were once again able to attend race days, and, starting in 1908, the Race Club would admit Chinese as honorary or social members—as guests, really. But rather than admit Chinese as full members, as Zhu Baosan and others sought, members of the Shanghai Race Club—led by John Johnstone, the head of the trading house Jardine Matheson—underwrote the new IRC. British Shanghailanders literally bought into the new club and helped promote it as a symbol of international, multicultural goodwill. But their Shanghai Race Club would remain white.

The International Recreation Club opened its new clubhouse in the spring of 1910, even before its racecourse was finished. Zhou Jinzhen, who had succeeded Zhu Baosan as Chamber of Commerce president, addressed the club's opening ceremony by tying the new club to the revival of the Chinese nation, foreshadowing the republican revolution that would overthrow China's imperial government just a year later. "Many, perhaps, may think that many other things are far more import- ant than horse and pony racing, sports and other kinds of recreation," Zhou told the gathered Chinese and foreign dignitaries. "But we must not forget the fact that in the regeneration of our country, we depend a great deal upon a body of men who possess a healthy and strong phy- sique, and in order to enable us to realize our object, I think there is no better way than to have such a club." Following Zhou, T. U. Yih emphasized the new club's international mission. It would be open to foreigners and Chinese: "If the Chinese and foreigners can be got to feel and believe that they can play together harmoniously and honor- ably, the more serious union of working together for their mutual social and commercial advancement will follow."[16]

Rain delayed the new track's opening, just as it had the Shanghai Race Club fifty years earlier. The first races finally went off on April 15, 1911, before 2,000 race fans, including Zhu Baosan; Yu Xiaqing; the chair, Zhou Jinzhen; and three members of the Yih family: T. U., T. C., and T. S. A handful of foreigners also played key roles at the track, including the starter and timekeeper. The English press praised the new facilities' spirit of international cooperation, even if there was a note of condescension in their report that "it was pleasing to note that Chinese riders competed against foreign riders, of perhaps more experience in racing, and held their own very well indeed."[17] A month later, the track had its official opening. Appropriately, a Chinese jockey won the first race: T. N. Yih rode Piston across the finish line three lengths ahead of Eric Moller on Australia.[18]

The new racetrack fed the love of racing among Shanghai residents of all nationalities. The *Shishi xinbao* (in English, *China Times*) adver- tised and reported on the new IRC races, boasting of the crowded trains arriving at Jiangwan station, carrying Chinese and Western spectators to the first formal meet on June 1 (the paper emphasized that Western women were among those on the train). The paper presented the meet as a competition between the Shanghai Race Club and the new IRC, describing the elaborate grandstands, well furnished bar, and expansive grounds, as well as a competition between Western and Chinese horse owners (Westerners held a narrow edge).[19]

The advent of Chinese racing in Shanghai had a big impact on a small world. That Chinese and Britons were sitting side by side, whether on horseback or in the grandstands, probably felt revolutionary to many in the city, but the impact of this newly integrated pastime paled next to the genuinely revolutionary change beginning some 600 miles up the Yangtze. In the city of Wuchang, on October 10, 1911, the discovery of a revolutionary cell led to a chain of events that brought down China's Qing dynasty, in power since 1644. On January 1, 1912, Sun Yat-sen proclaimed the founding of the Republic of China. The last Qing emperor abdicated a few months later.

And in Shanghai? "The unified Empire of China was founded in the year 221 BC. After 2,131 years, it had come to an end. This did not interfere with the Shanghai races."[20] Austin Coates's glib description overstates the continuity of China's imperial past but sums up many foreigners' perception of Shanghai's relationship to China: a cork floating in a Chinese sea. Waves rocked Shanghai as they passed but left the city unaffected once they had moved on.

This picture wasn't entirely wrong. After the Qing fell, the new Chinese Republic was beset by violence, internal division, and predatory imperialism, but the treaty ports, led by Shanghai, grew at record pace. These ports—even the International Settlement—were still nominally Chinese territory, yet foreign residents, protected by extraterritoriality and foreign police, soldiers, and ships, could justifiably feel invulnerable. Even without the formal protections of extraterritoriality, the many Chinese residents of the Settlement were able to live largely beyond the reach of the Chinese state too.

The IRC showed that even outside the Settlement, Shanghai remained a part of China, yet apart from China. While the nation struggled, the Jiangwan racetrack thrived. A new grandstand was completed in 1923, touted as the largest not just in Shanghai or even China, but in the entire world, and it became not just a stadium but a national symbol. At its opening, a military band played the Chinese national anthem as a stand full of military officials and business leaders looked on. General He Fengling, the military governor of Zhejiang province (including the Chinese-administered parts of Shanghai) spoke about the success of racing in Shanghai as an example not only of "a manly sport" but also of the cooperation between foreigners and Chinese.

The new English-designed and Chinese-built 6,000-seat grand-stand, bigger and better than the SRC's "City Course" a few miles away, illustrated He's ideas. Beneath a national flag, with the immense new grandstand as a backdrop, He presented T. U. Yih with a silver pagoda in appreciation of Yih's efforts in the club's success. John Johnstone, the Jardine Matheson trader who had helped manage the initial financing of the IRC, took part in the ceremonies as well, and then leapt into the saddle; he entered, and rode, three of his horses that day and won all three races, including the Grand National Steeplechase.[21]

The IRC's art deco facilities drew an even mix of Chinese and foreign riders and owners, as well as crowds, such that every Sunday (the SRC did not race on Sundays) a traffic jam extended from the International Settlement to Jiangwan. Membership at the two clubs remained technically separate, but the privileges were reciprocal: members of the IRC could be admitted to the members' enclosure at the Shanghai Race Club. This workaround enabled Chinese to gain access to SRC facilities while the SRC continued its racist membership policies.

So deeply held was the exclusion of Chinese from membership in the SRC that opponents of integrating the Hong Kong Jockey Club justified their stance by claiming that admitting Chinese members in Hong Kong would provoke Shanghai to retaliate, jeopardizing the flow of jockeys and horses into the colony.[22] In response, Hong Kong Chinese seeking admission to the jockey club pointed to the tolerance and integration on display at Jiangwan to support their view: "There is an International Race Club at Jiangwan, in Shanghai, that . . . includes among its members, members of the Shanghai Race Club as well as Chinese and . . . the Jockeys of the Shanghai Race Club habitually ride side by side with the Chinese."[23]

The SRC displayed its naive cosmopolitanism at an elaborate banquet downtown, not long after the IRC opened its new, grander, clubhouse in Jiangwan. Receiving a trophy from Zhu Baosan sponsored by Shanghai's Chinese community, H. E. Morriss implied that all China would need in order to overcome racial and national conflicts were "racecourses in various parts of China, all connected up by first-class railroads." "We have all heard and read a good deal lately about Anglo-Chinese friendship," declared Morriss, as Zhu handed him the trophy. Waiting for applause to subside, Morriss added that "it is on the racecourse that the best of both sides comes out." H. H. Read, presiding over the proceedings, proposed a toast to "Chinese friends" and said he hoped "that the good feeling and sportsmanship that has existed in the past between our Chinese friends and members of the Race Club will long be continued, and that we will all pull together and make amateur racing still more pleasant and enjoyable for all concerned." The men did not address whether these courses to be built around China would, like their own Shanghai Race Club, exclude Chinese from membership.[24]

While its patrons at the SRC may have hoped that sportsmanship and goodwill would be the IRC's main focus, the IRC was much more than that. The Jiangwan racecourse gave Shanghai a Chinese-controlled civic space at a time when national consciousness was rising (even more powerful because it had arisen from the attempt of foreigners to exclude Chinese from the SRC). Gatherings at Jiangwan were not just about racing ponies. In the 1920s, anti-Japanese and anti-British demonstrations became more and more commonplace, organized especially around the "May 30 incident" of 1925, when Shanghai Municipal Police officers shot and killed nine people, all Chinese, and injured dozens more just a few hundred yards from the Shanghai Race

The public grandstand at the Shanghai Race Club, 1927.

Club. The violence had been triggered when protestors demanded the release of Chinese workers arrested for shooting a Japanese foreman. The incident catalyzed anti-imperialist sentiment in China and, in the weeks and months that followed, boycotts and demonstrations against foreign imperialism spread across the country. Many of those protests gathered at the Jiangwan racecourse—as many as 30,000 in the case of a 1927 protest against Japanese military mobilization in China.[25]

The rise of Chinese nationalism also inspired resistance to the Shanghai Race Club. Local merchants petitioned the local Chinese government to oppose the expansion of gambling at the racecourse. At a time when China needed to strengthen itself politically and spiritually, they argued, the "gambling spirit" only weakened the country. Anecdotes like the one describing the assault of an old man by Chinese youths were linked to the fraying of society promoted by betting on horse races.[26] What's more, unlike the "sino-western harmony" that many Westerners held up as an ideal, the letter writers attacked the very premise that horse racing was good for the Chinese, asking, "Is this because racing is a part of western civilization that we welcome the practice and do nothing to suppress it—even going so far as to give it our support?"[27]

These objections notwithstanding, Chinese racing enthusiasts continued finding other ways to race when the SRC would not satisfy them. As Shanghai boomed, they planned a third track, the Chinese Jockey Club in Yangtszepoo, north and east of both the SRC and the IRC, near the mouth of the Yangtze River. Unlike the IRC, which foreigners had effectively bought out, Shanghai's foreign community looked down on this upstart. With construction of the new club's grandstand and racecourse already under way, the *North-China Herald* editorialized that this "doubtful proposition" was "not one we can recommend for public support." Illustrating the gentlemanly ethic that many foreigners trusted for their sports, the *Herald* derided that new track as "strictly a commercial affair," concluding that "there is no room in Shanghai for a third racecourse."[28]

Apparently, there was—just not for foreigners.

Rebuffed at attempts to get financing from the Shanghai Race Club, the Chinese Jockey Club turned to Chinese managers and investors. These included Du Yuesheng, head of the Green Gang, who had not been welcome in the more refined circles of the other race clubs. "Big Ears" Du and C. S. Mao were just two of Shanghai's numerous figures in organized crime who sought entry to the upper tiers of Shanghai society through the Chinese Jockey Club.[29]

T. U. Yih, one of the driving forces behind Jiangwan, became the honorary secretary, and the first racing program at Yangtszepoo was launched in March 1926. The new club accepted foreigners as associate members only. "Shanghai has had horseracing for many years, with the Shanghai Race Club [literally, "Westerners' Race Club"] and the International Recreation Club, but in these most of the control was in the hands of foreigners."[30] The new Chinese Jockey Club would address this: "The club is announced as a Chinese organization, its sole authority being vested in the hands of the Chinese."[31]

The races at Yangtszepoo succeeded despite the misgivings inside the Settlement. The *North-China Herald* ate crow about its earlier skepticism: "Whatever doubts there may have been in some people's minds," the paper reported after the first races, "there was every evidence of it being a very popular move and there was not a hitch anywhere in the arrangements." Some 5,000 people attended the first day's races, almost all of them Chinese, except for "officials and many of the best known members of the Shanghai Race Club."[32]

For its part, the Shanghai Race Club worked hard to satisfy demand for more Chinese involvement in its races without yielding to calls for membership. By the early twentieth century, Chinese were regular guests at the Club, and members at the IRC enjoyed reciprocal privileges. There was even a club of "affiliates" at the race club composed of prominent Chinese who used their station to promote understanding between Chinese and Western culture (sponsoring bridge tournaments, Chinese opera performances, mahjong, billiards, and other forms of cultural exchange).

Chinese business leaders, including Zhu Baosan, presented the Race Club with a prize in 1921, awarding the Chinese Cup for the winner of what had previously been called the Shanghai Stakes. The SRC welcomed the cup as a symbol of the cooperation between foreigners and Chinese, though the two groups may have had different ideas about what the nature of that relationship would be going forward. In what was becoming boilerplate at such events, the SRC president toasted the

Race Club's "Chinese friends" at the conclusion of his remarks, under-scoring the distinction between "Chinese friends" and "members of the Race Club."[33]

It was a golden age for racing in Shanghai. All three courses rou-tinely drew thousands of spectators, and total annual racing attendance may have approached one million. Hundreds of ponies were running at each track; most weekends during the year, at least one track was hosting races. Newspapers across the city—in Chinese, English, and French—advertised the races running on all three tracks. The opening of these new racetracks had two important consequences. The first was that racing in Shanghai expanded to include more people and animals than ever before, more than anywhere else in Asia (few cities on any continent could claim three world-class racetracks). The second was that the Shanghai Race Club was able to maintain its segregated status. Even though many of the SRC owners and jockeys raced at both Jiang-wan and Yangtszepoo, and even though many of the Chinese owners at those other clubs were regular guests at the SRC, membership at the "City Course" remained whites-only. Even Hong Kong, looked down on by Shanghailanders as parochial and stodgy, permitted Chi-nese members in its jockey club starting in 1927.

The tracks themselves competed with one another, building ever-greater facilities. In 1929, the IRC completed its new clubhouse, not at Jiangwan, where its racetrack was, but at 126 Bubbling Well Road, not far from the Shanghai Race Club in the very heart of the Settlement. At a gala in May, Chinese and foreigners crowded into the enormous, red-brick, Tudor-style building to hear speeches delivered and toasts exchanged before a table draped in the Chinese and British flags, side by side. Hosted by IRC president Brodie Clarke; its founder, T. U. Yih; and Shanghai mayor Zhang Dingfan, the ceremony just hinted at the grandeur of the clubhouse still in the final stages of decorating, but what was there was enough to whet appetites.

A 70×40-foot ballroom, with a "starlit glass ceiling" and a spring-cushioned dance floor, was one of the attractions, as were a billiard room, a gymnasium, and a coffee room decorated with the coats of arms of all the countries represented in the club.[34] "Visitors to the new club were rather more than impressed: they were almost overwhelmed," wrote the *North-China Herald*. "Other clubs have libraries, swimming baths, and racquets courts, but it was the unanimous opinion that, short of these individual particulars, the new club is beyond compare in Shanghai."[35] Shanghailanders saw the new facility as a place where they could welcome the Chinese into "foreign" territory in the settlement: "A real excuse for sportsmen of all nations getting together."[36] The *China Press* raved that the new building was "one of the finest club buildings in the Orient."[37]

The occasion and its reviews wasted no opportunity to emphasize the IRC's role in promoting cosmopolitanism and international cooperation, suggesting that like the races, the new facilities at the clubhouse would build bridges not only between people but between nations as well. "Chinese and foreigners who have struck up acquaintanceships at the course are enabled to make closer contacts. . . . Race, nationality, religion, and numerous other invisible barriers, then become lifted, and, in this melting away of prejudices a fraternity is developed of riveted cohesion so necessary for world unity and progress. Thus we can see that an institution which sets out with ponies and play [may] . . . grind away to smoothness the jagged edges of international politics and work those gigantic world-wheels into an harmonious hum."[38]

The Shanghai Race Club never did admit Chinese members.

Chinese Shanghailanders?

At the races, 1928.

IF ING TANG COULDN'T JOIN THE RACE CLUB, COULD SHE BE A
Shanghailander?

The exclusion of Chinese members from the Race Club illustrates
the discrimination woven into Shanghailander society. The complaints
against David Sassoon and his Leviathan Stables were another kind
of exclusion, but Sassoon could be admitted to the Race Club (he had
been one of the club's original voting members).[1] Because she was a
woman, this wasn't true for Ing Tang. Women were always present at

race days—the press celebrated that "the Grand Stands and the lawns were very gay with fair ladies"[2]—but club members tended to treat them as decoration.

Women could not be members at all for the first decades of racing in Shanghai, even though the number of women attending the races grew steadily. In 1920, the same year they were granted the right to vote in the United States, women were admitted to the Shanghai Race Club on a very limited basis. "Lady Racing Members" had to be "wives or lady relatives" of SRC members, and even then their access wasn't entirely free.[3] The club's coffee room, for instance, remained famously a male-only redoubt, except when it was hosting balls or other parties. And lest there be any confusion, "Lady Members," the club bylaws read, "are not entitled to ride at Race Meetings of this club."[4] But by the time Ing Tang was an adult, she certainly had the means to buy a China pony and the experience to ride one. Given her class, were she white she almost certainly would have been nominated. So, while the SRC rules were silent on the matter, what kept her from joining the Race Club was not primarily her gender, but her race.

Racial categories in Shanghai and at the Race Club were often arbitrary and sometimes fluid. David Sassoon was an outsider to both British and Chinese society, and maybe that standing could be explained because the family was from Baghdad, via Bombay. But Gussie (Augustus Victor) White (nephew of Augustus Harold White, and a horse owner and rider in his own right) was a model Shanghailander—wealthy, English, several generations lived and fortunes made on the China coast—and everyone was aware that his family was Eurasian. The Whites, in other words, weren't completely . . . white. The same was true of the Cumines. With all this in mind, again, could Ing Tang be a Shanghailander?

The story of the Tang family raises fundamental questions about who could be, in Nils Moller's phrase, a citizen of Shanghai. Ing Tang's father was born Tang Naian in Anhui province in 1873. Little is known of his childhood, but he studied English and medicine at Beiyang Medical College in Tianjin (it was probably there that he adopted the English name "Abel"). Abel Tang rose to high office in the last years of the Qing dynasty as the Manchus worked to reform and modernize their empire, putting his medical training to work as the surgeon general for the Qing Imperial Navy.[5] After the Qing collapsed in 1911, Tang worked as a medical examiner for a Hong Kong–based insurance company and moved to Shanghai, where he also ran an apothecary,[6] living the life of a Shanghailander, whether he could claim the label or not. Tang and his wife, Xu Yizhen, moved into the International Settlement, taking up residence west of the racecourse on Nanyang Road, in a neighborhood of large homes and impressively managed gardens.

It was not strange that Abel Tang was Chinese and living in the International Settlement—most of the Settlement's population was Chinese—but as a physician living in an affluent neighborhood, Tang was of a higher class than many Europeans there. (Some sources assert that Xu Yizhen was a graduate of the first class at Nanjing's prestigious Ginling Women's College, but this is not the case, although a woman with the same name was in that class.) Living in a foreign settlement with Chinese and foreign friends, Abel Tang and Xu Yizhen raised a daughter and a son between two worlds.

Many in Shanghai fancied themselves, like the city itself, bridges between West and East. The Tang family demonstrated how this characterization described not only foreigners in the city, but Chinese as well. A son, Yu-loo, was born in February 1901, and he followed a common Shanghailander career path, starting at St. John's College in Shanghai, an Anglican college and prep school founded in the late nineteenth century. After coming to the United States at the age of just fifteen, Yu-loo graduated with a degree in history and economics from Yale in 1921.[7]

China's place in the world and the relationship between China and the West were essential parts of Yu-loo Tang's upbringing. His father had been one of the first students sponsored to study abroad by the Chinese government, but that government had fallen, in part because of its inability to manage relations with Europe and the United States. The years since the 1911 revolution had shown little improvement. Fragmentation, corruption, and colonialism challenged the new republic no less than they had the Qing dynasty, while continuing to nurture foreign autonomy in Shanghai. Beyond China's borders, the Great War had shown that Europe, too, faced an uncertain future. Yu-loo Tang, raised in China and educated in the United States, was at home in both worlds and uniquely situated to help China find its place in a new, changing world.

While her brother was away, the Tangs' daughter, Ing Tang, found her own place in Shanghai society. Gender determined much about the Tang siblings' paths through the early twentieth century. Born in 1903, Ing Tang enjoyed the same privileged early-childhood education as her brother. Their father already had a successful medical practice in Shanghai, attending to prominent Chinese families and some Western ones as well. It was rumored that when Abel Tang treated patients, he asked that part of his payment be in etiquette lessons or other social training for his daughter, possibly including English lessons.[8] When she outgrew these home lessons, Ing enrolled in the McTyeire School for girls. Like so much of Shanghai, McTyeire's blended east and west (visible in the school's Chinese name, the Chinese-Western Girls' Academy). Amid gothic architecture, McTyeire's curriculum straddled linguistic boundaries. During the first two years, students learned in Mandarin and Shanghainese. English became standard in the third and fourth year, although subjects like Chinese literature and were taught in Mandarin. The result was a student body that "spoke in a lively style that blended words from several languages or dialects, within the same sentence."[9]

McTyeire and St. Mary's Hall were the two most prestigious girls' schools in the city, and McTyeire's alumnae included the illustrious Soong sisters—Ai-ling, Ching-ling, and May-ling—who would become some of the most powerful women in China and marry Finance Minister H. H. Kung, Sun Yat-sen, and Chiang Kai-shek, respectively.[10] (The People's Republic took over and merged McTyeire's and St. Mary's Hall in 1952, and they became, and remain, the Shanghai #3 Girls' Middle School.)

Ing Tang also moved between East and West, though not as literally as her brother. Even her name shifted between Chinese standards and English ones—foreign newspapers sometimes printed her family name, "Tang," first, according to Chinese usage, and other times used English style, with the family name last. After graduating from McTyeire's, Ing became a staple of the Shanghai foreign and Chinese social scenes. By age seventeen—around the time her brother was graduating from Yale—she was sought after for musical reviews, fashion shows, banquets, and other social gatherings, singing and playing the *pipa* (a Chinese string instrument similar to a lute).

By the late 1920s, Ing was a regular in the society page, and friends with Chinese artists, writers, musicians, and philosophers, including the celebrated poet Xu Zhimo. She graced the covers of magazines and newspapers across Shanghai and even beyond, including *Shanghai huabao* ("Shanghai Pictorial"), the *North-China Herald*, the *China Press*, and *Luozilun huabao* ("Violet Pictorial"). She appeared on the covers of two influential pictorial magazines: *Liangyou huabao* ("The Young Companion") and *Beiyang huabao* ("Northern Pictorial," published in Tianjin), which described her as "the most popular society lady in Shanghai."[11]

In 1930, at the age of twenty-seven, Ing Tang married Tsufa Lee, another border-crossing cosmopolitan who had been born in Shanghai, in 1893, and had recently returned to China after graduating, also from Yale, where he had earned second honors in the class of 1919. George Fitch, an American missionary who would later become famous for bearing witness to the "rape of Nanjing," officiated their marriage at Shanghai's Presbyterian church.

Ing Tang was not just a cover model and socialite; she was also a designer and a businesswoman who would parlay her celebrity into a career in music, modeling, and acting. She helped found a fashion company, *Yunshang*, along with a group of other Shanghai artists and

Miss Ing Tang, a performer and business owner in Shanghai, designed clothes worn at the Race Club's Champions Day fashion parades, before being offered a role on Broadway.

designers. Ing sold her designs, noted for combining Chinese and Western styles, in a boutique along Bubbling Well Road, between her home and the racecourse. Named "Atelier Yangkueifei" after the eighth-century imperial consort considered the standard for feminine beauty in the Tang dynasty (a golden age of Chinese culture and also the Tang family's namesake), the shop became a darling of both the Chinese and the foreign press. Chief among the designs "developed exclusively in Shanghai" at a fall 1927 fashion show, the *China Press* crowed, "will be a display from the Yangkueifei shop on Bubbling Well, where Miss Ing Tang has produced gowns of a distinctive Chinese and semi-foreign style."[12]

Those designs found their way to the racetrack. Starting in the mid-1920s, each season's Champions Day featured a "Fashion Parade," emphasizing that the day should be not just about sports but also about the Settlement's social scene of sophisticated, sometimes orientalist, styles. At the racetrack in the fall of 1926, a "lady correspondent" for the *North-China Herald* noted that "the stunning white satin mandarin-like gown worn by one Chinese young lady makes a permanent spot on the mind's eye."[13] (There's no way to know, but she may have been describing Ing Tang herself.) The models were both European and Chinese, and the parade attracted both women of all nationalities to the Race Club. The high fashion also encouraged Shanghailanders to think of their club in the company of international venues like Longchamp, Churchill Downs, Buenos Aires, and Tuxedo Park, as world centers of racing. The press emphasized the "virility of Shanghai's racing scene," which set it apart from the Paris track, where "perhaps the feminine touch is too strong."[14]

Ing Tang was, as one family friend recalled, "a very modern Shanghai lady. She played the piano . . . horseback riding . . . all the modern things."[15] As a prominent society figure, she would not have missed the most important social event of the year, likely wearing a dress of her own design. She would have stood out, but photographs and press reports confirm that in the 1930s, the great majority of spectators at the Shanghai Race Club still were Chinese. Who were these men and women who packed the grandstands to watch Shanghai's most spectacular foreign import?

Many Chinese migrants in Shanghai were poor, escaping war or other personal challenges. For them, even the $1 daily admission—let alone a wager or two—might prove out of reach, but there were tens of thousands of Chinese in Shanghai who had disposable income they might spend at the track. There were more than 300,000 "white-collar employees (*zhiyuan*)" in Shanghai in the 1930s, all of whom earned enough to attend the races.[16]

Nates Wong, the publisher and translator, was one of these. He had lived in Shanghai since at least the 1920s. We don't know exactly when he came, or where he came from, but we know he dressed well—at least when he was being photographed!—in Western-style suit and tie. He spent time at the racetrack as well, and he lived not far from the Race Club while working as writer and translator, but probably indulged in Shanghai's famous nightlife less than some, if his affiliation with the YMCA may be taken as any indication.[17]

Like Nates Wong, many Chinese at the racetrack were moderns, creating and reveling in the "Shanghai style" (*hai-pai*) that interpreted China and the West for each other while creating something entirely new. We can glimpse the racetrack's role in this style through the writings of some of Shanghai's modernist writers. In his 1932 short story "Shanghai Foxtrot (*Shanghai de hubuwu*)," Mu Shiying, for instance, uses the Race Club as a backdrop to establish the cosmopolitanism of a young Shanghai Chinese couple driving across the city, remarking on the "golden horse weathervane that seems to kick its legs toward the red moon" as they cruised past the landmarks of the International Settlement.[18]

Liu Na'ou, writing around the same time, gives even more detail about the role of the Race Club in the social lives of a certain class of Chinese, who gathered on

an elevated terrace overlooking an expansive green lawn. People swarming in the fervor of gambling made it resemble an anthill. Paper scraps, of suspense turned into disappointment, were torn up and strewn all over the cement. The breeze, turning from joyous to amorous, rustled open the green dresses of girls who leaned tightly against their lovers. . . . Dust, saliva, hidden tears, and the stench of horse manure spread in the stagnant air and formed an atmosphere saturated with people's determination, anxiety, despair, panic, surprise, and joy. But the cheerful Union Jack still fluttered in the beautiful azure sky with a crimson smile. "There, they are off!" [English in the original] Eight choice horses dashed forward, and today's last 1-¼ mile race started.[19]

For the protagonists in Liu's story, the Race Club embodies all that is modern in Shanghai. The gambling and excitement of the races transfers easily to an affair: the racetrack frames characters who, like Shanghai itself, are irresistibly exciting and modern, but also dangerous and threatening to traditional values. His characters are fictional, but Liu's description of the Race Club in the 1930s shows the racetrack to be a social center for moderns who reveled in their city's combination of the Chinese and the Western.

By the early 1930s, Ing Tang's fuchsia, green, and red designs were among the bright colors that stood out amid a grandstand packed with gray flannel suits. Annual headlines—"Elegance Marks Champions Day Feminine Parade,"[20] "Fashion Parade Gay with Color at Champions"[21]—celebrated style as an essential part of the spectacle:[22] "Feminine fashions in England have . . . the Ascot races. In New York it is the Easter Parade which brings forth new modes. But neither metropolis on its fashion day can compare in color and contrast with Shanghai's Spring Champion Day."[23]

Ing's brother, Yu-loo, was now back from America. After working briefly at the Chinese embassy in Washington, he had taken a position as a professor at Southeastern University in Nanjing but, perhaps missing the more international world where he'd grown up, soon moved back to Shanghai, as a journalist. His experience of the United States gave him unique insights into the challenges facing both sides of the Pacific. Furthermore, he had been educated in English since he was a boy; all of his formal schooling had been in English. He put this rare combination of skills to use writing about Chinese affairs in a regular *China Press* column, called "Causerie Chinoise," that tried to bridge Chinese and Western cultures using issues of interest to Shanghailanders.

Yu-loo quoted Confucius to comment on social issues of the day, and he introduced Chinese traditional music through the Tang dynasty poetry of Du Fu and Bai Juyi. Foreshadowing the wars that were to come, and commemorating those that had just recently ended, he called on Chinese and Westerners alike to reflect on the costs of war, translating a seventh-century Chinese poet Li Hua: "Clothes are of no avail; hands frost-bitten, flesh cracked. . . . Their officers have surrendered; their general is dead. The river is choked with corpses to its topmost banks; the fosses of the Great Wall are swimming over with blood. All the distinctions are obliterated in that heap of rotting bones."[24]

Yu-loo Tang tried some more optimistic authors than this, but most of his columns were somber. He was under few illusions about the challenges facing China, Shanghai, or the world, and his vision of understanding between China and the West was rarely upbeat. By contrast, from their seats at the Long Bar, the Race Club's coffee room, or walking the public gardens, Shanghailanders made their money and enjoyed spending it with few worries and little regulation or oversight. The treaties that followed the First Opium War had not just opened the ports like Shanghai as places where they could do business; they had written into law advantages of race and empire. When the Tang siblings' father, Abel, died in 1929 at just fifty-six years old, hundreds attended his funeral, including T. V. Soong (China's finance minister and Chiang Kai-shek's brother-in-law), and many prominent Shanghailanders, both Chinese and Western.[25] But while gestures like this were easy to find, substantive change was not. Shanghailanders were happy to walk on bridges spanning China and the West, but any exchange between the two would need to be on their own terms.

This condition did not go unnoticed. William Yinson Lee (Li Yuanxin) was another of the men who would have qualified as a Shanghailander, but for his race. Lee was internationally connected and opened the China branch of an American pharmaceutical firm, but he was born neither in America nor in China, but in Australia, to Chinese parents (his father was a merchant in Sydney, where Lee had been born in 1884). Because he was educated in Australia and Hong Kong—in Chinese and English—and traveled to China frequently, Lee's story underlines the complexity of racial and national identity. Lee also played a leading role in charities and hospitals, was a member of the YMCA's "Y's Men," and was a founding member of Shanghai's Masonic lodge. Befitting his prominent social station in Shanghai, Champions Day could find Lee in the members' boxes at the Race Club—not as a member in his own right, of course, but as a guest of some of Shanghai's most famous residents.[26]

Lee advocated for issues of concern to his Chinese compatriots, especially in Shanghai. When the Shanghai Municipal Council determined that Chinese residents of the International Settlement should have schools "comparable to those available outside and no more," Lee condemned the decision as wrongheaded.[27] Shanghai, Lee wrote, should "make itself a worthy model for emulation by China's educational authorities" as much for self-preservation as for noble intentions. "The prosperity of Shanghai . . . cannot be maintained without the cooperation of foreign and Chinese interests and international friendship. One is entirely dependent on the other."[28]

Against this backdrop, the exclusion of well-heeled Chinese from social and sporting clubs was a frivolous but clear illustration of the same point: Chinese in their own country were subject to foreign laws and behavior. Returning to Shanghai just a few weeks after the murders of May 30, 1925, Lee recounted his travels in Britain and contrasted the welcome he received in London with the "race discrimination" that barred him from clubs in Shanghai. "While in England," he wrote, "I had the honor and privilege of meeting socially members of the British nobility, and of the distinguished orders, merchant princes, and captains of industry, but in Shanghai I am considered not good enough to converse with junior clerks of British nationality."[29] The *China Press* replied that Shanghai society self-segregated: "Mr. Lee has been misinformed. We do not believe there is a club in Shanghai which constitutionally bars Chinese from membership." Rather, the paper rationalized, "Many foreigners [feel] that they should have social gathering places, where only foreigners are admitted to membership. The Chinese undoubtedly have similar instincts."[30]

Yu-loo Tang grappled with this same tension. Just as he was returning to Shanghai to promote the idea of a cosmopolitan city blending Chinese and Western ideals, Shanghai lost one of the most important examples of this class, Zhu Baosan, the Ningbo-born merchant and banker. Like the Tangs, he had made a career in the international milieu of Shanghai, embraced and excluded at the same time, and his work to establish the Jiangwan racetrack—the International Recreation Club—had been an important physical and symbolic link between foreigners and Chinese in Shanghai.

Zhu's funeral, in the fall of 1926, acknowledged his success as a banker—loans he had managed were critical for Chinese businesses in Shanghai—as well as his importance to the city's Chinese and foreign communities. Beginning at the Zhu family residence, where five sons (including at least one who rode and owned horses at Jiangwan) lived in the family compound, more than a thousand mourners processed with the casket north through the French Concession to the International Settlement, passing within a few blocks of the race club that had welcomed his enthusiasm but denied him membership. The procession closed streets for hours to accommodate more than five hundred soldiers representing various Chinese and foreign armies, six brass bands, and mounted Chinese, French, and Sikh policemen. (Sikhs were frequently employed as police throughout the British empire, and the informal empire of Shanghai was no exception.)

After entering the International Settlement, the funeral passed down Thibet Road, in front of the Siming native-place association's new headquarters that Zhu had helped design and finance, and down to the waterfront. There the casket, drawn by eight black horses, was placed aboard a specially chartered steamer that would take the body across Hangzhou Bay to Ningbo, where Zhu would be buried. Both the Chinese and the Western press praised Zhu as a leader in both commerce and community: the "dean of Chinese merchants"; "merchant Prince"; and "the most popular Chinese merchant."[31] These superlatives didn't change the fact that his nationality excluded him from many aspects of Shanghai elite society.

Zhu Baosan had been an example of the Chinese "comprador bourgeoisie." Compradors were Chinese go-betweens who represented Western business interests in China—a class with its origins in the days of the Canton System, when foreigners were compelled to do business through officially licensed Chinese merchant monopolies. Those restrictions were now gone, but for practical reasons many foreign businesses still relied on Chinese partners or employees, frequently prominent businessmen in their own right. The comprador bourgeoisie by the late nineteenth century were middle-class (or better) Chinese who made fortunes and lived comfortable lives directly or indirectly from the Western presence in Shanghai. This group felt the same exclusion that had driven Zhu to help organize the Jiangwan racetrack.

To address the problem of racial exclusion at the SRC, a dozen or so Chinese men formed an organization that was rendered in English as the Shanghai Race Club Staff Club. That translation, though official, was misleading: in English, the term "staff club" suggests that the members were employees of the club, of a different class than the members. Actually, though its membership did include the Chinese staff at the race club, its leaders were prominent merchants and professionals, members of the comprador bourgeoisie exemplified by Zhu Baosan, Yu-loo Tang, and others. The wealthiest members of the SRC Staff Club were as affluent as all but the richest members of the Race Club, which, of course, they could not join because of their nationality, and nationality was central to the Staff Club's identity. The club held its official opening on October 10—the "Double 10," founding holiday of the Republic of China—and the club's organizers focused on a patriotic mission to strengthen China and its institutions, both cultural and commercial.

The Staff Club members struck a conciliatory tone in their nationalism. Theirs was not the approach of the May 30 protestors, but then their concerns were not those of workers struggling for a living wage. The Staff Club members were not all wealthy—Nates Wong, for instance, was not a rich man—but they were prospering in Western-dominated Shanghai. Indeed, most of their livelihoods, including Wong's, depended directly on the Western presence in Shanghai. They lamented the inequality and discrimination facing Chinese in the city, but they did not experience daily oppression. Founding member Shen Zhirui remarked that since the opening of Shanghai as a treaty port, British and American businessmen had established clubs to serve both social and business functions, helping foreign merchants to build and develop networks. This sort of social organization, Shen felt, had given Europeans (especially the British) an advantage over the Chinese, enabling them to expand foreign commerce at the expense of Chinese merchants.[32]

Meeting in the shadow of the Race Club (and sometimes in the Race Club buildings themselves), the Staff Club and its members were, just like Nils Moller, Augustus White, and other Europeans, proud of "their" Shanghai, holding the city up as a unique blend of nations and cultures. The Staff Club celebrated the city and popular images of it, just as many foreigners did, but approached Shanghai differently. In a volume celebrating the club's anniversary, Shen Zhirui wrote that Shanghai was China's most foreign city: cosmopolitan and multicultural, yes, but also an imperial prize where foreigners lived on Chinese soil but free from Chinese law.[33] Lin Heqin—a graduate of Carnegie Institute of Technology in Pittsburgh and owner of a printing company in Shanghai[34]—agreed, asserting that institutions like the Shanghai Club and the Race Club enabled foreigners in Shanghai to expand their power and their authority and to erode Chinese sovereignty and livelihood. The Race Club Staff Club was an attempt to address that imbalance, giving Chinese of means access to the kinds of facilities that foreigners had.[35]

Shanghai was also China's most modern city—and distinguishing "Western" from "modern" was one of the most contentious debates in East Asia. For decades, reformers in China had looked to the West as a model of a modern future. Replacing the Qing monarchy with a republic was a part of China's move toward modernity and toward the West. Authors like Lu Xun parodied China's traditions with compelling, tragic allegories of the country's failures to modernize. Not everyone embraced modernity as a goal, but those Chinese who did tended to view the West as the model to emulate. Western power was not always positive, but it was effective and, it appeared, beneficial to those who could muster its support. Social Darwinist ideas were in vogue for intellectuals in China and the West, and many Chinese reformers believed that the success of Western imperialism showed that countries like China were headed for extinction if they did not adapt.[36]

But the Great War undermined Chinese faith in Western progress— faith that had been vivid in Shanghai, where cooperation between China and the West seemed tantalizingly close. In June 1918, Silas and Liza Hardoon hosted an "Anglo-Chinese Garden Party" that showed the hopes and potential for the relationship between China and the West. Surrounded by national flags moved indoors because of rain, prominent members of the British and Chinese communities celebrated Chinese support for the British war effort and spoke to the possibility of future cooperation.

On behalf of the Chinese community, Chamber of Commerce secretary Zhang Nieyun said, "We know that many of your people are fighting with the civilized world in a great war and you know that many of our labourers are over there in France doing what they can. . . . Coming closer home to Shanghai . . . there is every reason for us to shake each other's hand cordially and sincerely." Looking ahead, Zhang hinted at hopes for change in the future: "We are mindful of the protection and justice we have received at your hands," he said, aware of his audience, before adding, "[We] fervently hope that you will be able to show us increased consideration in the future in our mutual interest and the welfare of the Settlement."[37]

Zhang was speaking in the last months of a war that China had supported, hoping to gain membership in the "civilized world" that Europeans had promoted to justify their expanding empires. Instead, World War I gave the lie to the notion that Enlightenment values would ensure rationality and unending progress: science developed poison gas; industry mass-produced machine guns; democracies volunteered for war that jeopardized their very existence. China had joined the Great War on the side of the Allies, but instead of welcoming China to the family of nations, the Allies gave Germany's former colony of Qingdao to Japan. As the Republic disintegrated in the 1920s, many Chinese were less sure than before about the Western model: did it promise progress and prosperity, or was it a pathway to global, mutual destruction?

The experiences of the 1920s confounded the Chinese of the Staff Club. The West had made many of them rich, but its promise was not as pure as it had been before the war. Lin Heqin wrote about Shanghai as a modern city and the threats it posed to traditional China (whether he felt the threat was mainly to China or to tradition is hard to disentangle). Lin saw in Shanghai the dangers that came with the modern city—in his words, decadence, corruption, luxury, and romance— contrasted sharply with the romanticized simplicity of rural China. Lin proposed the club as a way to avoid the temptation and loneliness of the modern city, an antidote to the "pathological condition in modern social systems." Without these institutions, Lin lamented, many Chinese in Shanghai succumbed to temptation or, in extreme cases, even suicide.[38] (The metaphor of suicide was potent during this time, applied both to individuals struggling to cope with a rapidly changing society—one of Mao Zedong's first public essays focused on the suicide of a young girl compelled to marry against her will—but also to a country facing *national* suicide by refusing to adapt in a world of imperial conquest and social Darwinism.) For Chinese Shanghailanders—if the category can be said to exist—their city was the opportunity that made them possible, but also the obstacle that held them back from reaching their potential.

Yu-loo Tang confronted this same situation, despite the status provided by his father's social standing, his English-language ability, and his Ivy League degree. His "Causerie Chinoise" column each week was a small—some would say trivial—but appealing link between his Chinese world and his foreign one. Tang introduced his readers to the Daoist philosopher Zhuangzi by comparing him with George Bernard Shaw (Zhuangzi, Tang asserted, embodied the anarchism that Shaw promoted when he wrote that "the golden rule is that there are no golden rules."[39]) Read in the wake of the Great War, Li Hua's "On an Old Battlefield" evoked the trench poets.[40] Tang drew parallels between classical Chinese writers like statesman Ouyang Xiu, poet Su Dongpo, and writer and official Wang Daokun and contemporary Western authors.[41]

Many of Tang's comparisons were genius, decades ahead of their time, but his column's success depended not only on his own abilities but also on the willingness of Shanghai's English-speaking residents to consider Chinese ideas. Tang's mixing of Chinese and Western culture in his column fit the ideal, held by many Shanghailanders, that they were building a hybrid Chinese-Western society—under Western leadership, to be sure, but with Chinese participation. To maintain the view that they were doing something other than occupying a foreign city for their own profit and pleasure, they needed examples of cooperation and collaboration between foreigners (by which was meant western Europeans or Americans) and Chinese.

It was tempting, amid the pageantry of races, weddings, and even elaborate funeral processions, to view Shanghai as a bubble, insulated from the violence and upheaval taking place across China. The violence of May 30, 1925, showed that Shanghai was not immune, but certainly the upper classes were protected from much of the deprivation that defined the lives of many Chinese who lacked the wealth or status of the comprador bourgeoisie in Shanghai.

The Tang siblings combined the finest of China and the West. Neither Ing nor Yu-loo followed their father into medicine, but both shaped their world. Though successful as a journalist, Yu-loo saw the need to influence China's future more directly and turned to politics. He left his job writing for the *China Press* to become personal secretary to T. V. Soong, the finance minister in the new Chinese government. As assistant to one of China's most powerful (not to mention wealthiest) men, Yu-loo Tang had direct access and could influence policy at the highest level. China was trying to rebuild itself after decades of division and civil war, and men like Tang were using their Shanghai experience to do it.

The Chinese Shanghailanders struck a delicate balance from their unique position on Chinese-Western relations. They were emulating Western habits and institutions, even while working around the racism and imperialism that underlay many of them. The dual nature of their day-to-day interactions put the class in a delicately moderate role: rejecting and often criticizing the racism that excluded them from full participation, but unwilling to jeopardize the privilege (and wealth) that China's Western ties afforded them. Institutions like the International Recreation Club or the Shanghai Race Club Staff Club were appeal-

The Shanghai Bund, ca. 1936.

ing because they could maintain a structure that benefited them while retaining the rhetoric of combining East and West, ancient and modern. Shanghailanders may have felt that they lived in the most international of places and celebrated Shanghai's cosmopolitan ideal, but not everyone shared that enthusiasm.

Creating a Chinese Shanghai

"THE SHANGHAI THAT EXISTS NOW," WROTE ARCHITECT Du Yangeng, "is a foreign Shanghai, and it is an embarrassment."[1] Du described not only his own thoughts about the city where he worked, but the feelings of many Chinese in Shanghai. In the late nineteenth century, men like Zhu Baosan had objected to being excluded from the Race Club because of race or nationality, and in response they had built Chinese places, including new racetracks where they could be members. In the late 1920s, many sought ways to promote and express national pride in their "foreign" Chinese city beyond (though certainly including) its leisure activities.

Yu-loo Tang was comfortable on the campuses of elite American universities and in the members' enclosure at the Shanghai Race Club, but in both settings he was a guest. His status illustrated China's weakness. Studying abroad emphasized the importance of foreign schooling and the shortcomings of China's own educational system; back home, he was second-class in his own country.

Since the 1840s, and certainly since the creation of the International Settlement and the French Concession in the 1860s, the relationship between Chinese and foreign authority had been consistent, if not always clear in its details. Foreigners held most of the real power, although formal sovereignty resided with the Chinese. A long process finally led to the seating of the first Chinese members of the Shanghai Municipal

Council in 1928, but they remained a small minority with little influence, even though most of the Settlement's population had always been
Chinese.[2] Tang's step into the new Nanjing government was part of a
bold attempt by Chinese leaders to redress these imbalances.

The revolution that finally brought down the Qing dynasty and
initiated the Republic of China (without disrupting the horse races in
Shanghai, as Austin Coates noted)[3] swept nationalists like Sun Yat-sen
to power. Sun opposed the dynasty, in part, because it was ruled not
by Chinese but by Manchus who had conquered China two centuries
before and remained culturally distinct from their Chinese subjects.
Sun was generally friendly to Westerners and Western values, but he
was a Chinese nationalist, who wanted China to be ruled by Han Chinese (China's majority ethnicity), and this nationalism could be directed
toward Europeans as well.

Sun was abroad, raising money in the United States on October 10,
1911, when revolution broke out. Returning to China, he took leadership of the revolution. Little went right for Sun after the January day in
Nanjing when he was inaugurated provisional president of the Republic of China. Just two months later, in March 1912, he surrendered his
power to the less popular, but better armed, Yuan Shikai, a former Qing
general who had switched sides to back the rebels, bringing his troops
with him and ensuring the dynasty's defeat.

Sun had little choice but to acknowledge Yuan's military superiority,
but the decision was disastrous. Over the next few years, Yuan dissolved
the new parliament and accepted an "invitation" to do away with the
Republic and restore China to monarchy, with himself its new emperor.
Sun escaped to his home province of Guangdong while Yuan planned
an elaborate coronation with all the trappings of power. Yuan's procla-
mation was an overreach. He had now betrayed two governments, and
his allies quickly abandoned him. He canceled the new dynasty before
the ceremony could even take place, but the damage was done. China
splintered into dozens of pieces, some larger than European countries,
others as small as New England states. Whichever army occupied Beijing at any given time claimed to be China's legitimate government.
Meanwhile, the foreign concessions in Shanghai carried on as before,
even as China fell into warlordism and Europe tore itself to pieces.

From his internal exile, Sun Yat-sen continued working for republican government in China. He rebuilt his political base and—having learned the lesson of relying on men like Yuan Shikai—set about forming an army. He allied the Guomindang (Chinese Nationalist Party) with the newly created Chinese Communist Party, and in 1923 the two opened a military academy with Soviet money and advisers. Preparing for a "Northern Expedition" to reunify China, Sun traveled the country, speaking on the need to free China from both imperialism and warlordism. Before he could implement his plans, however, he fell ill and was examined by doctors who discovered he had cancer. Sun died on March 12, 1925, just two months after being diagnosed.

Sun left a fragile legacy. His followers agreed on little besides their devotion to him and a goal of unifying China under a single government. The alliance with the Soviets was especially polarizing. Some believed that Sun's Communist-Nationalist pact was a marriage of convenience, designed to acquire military and financial resources, but without a political commitment to communism or the Soviet Union. Others believed that Sun had moved ideologically to the left and was embracing socialism. Both sides had evidence to support their view, and even the Guomindang itself was divided between a Left favoring more socialist policies, and a Right advocating republicanism or even fascism, but everyone saw in Sun Yat-sen a unifying personality who carried the gravitas of thirty years as an international revolutionary.

The tensions that existed throughout the country often became visible in Shanghai. This had happened in the May 30 incident of 1925, putting a face on imperialism, and it recurred in 1927, when the divisions within the Guomindang burst violently to the surface. The Northern Expedition began in the spring of 1927 as all sides—the Right and Left wings of the Guomindang, as well as the Communists—briefly cooperated to unify the country. Until April, that is, when the Guomindang's National Revolutionary Army approached Shanghai, the only city in China with a significant Communist movement.

As part of the Northern Expedition strategy, the Communists in Shanghai seized the city from its warlord government in order to deliver it to their Nationalist allies. When the Communists arrived at the rail depot to welcome the Nationalist trains entering the city, however, instead of a celebration they found a massacre. Nationalist machine guns opened fire from railcars, initiating a slaughter that spread across

Shanghai. In the hours and days that followed, most of the Communist Party members in China were killed, and fervently anti-Communist Chiang Kai-shek established himself to be Sun's successor as leader of the Nationalists. The beleaguered Communist movement struggled just to survive, and even Guomindang members sympathetic to the Left fled into internal exile. The Nationalist Northern Expedition swept to victory and established a unified Chinese government, relocating its capital to Nanjing, less than 200 miles from Shanghai.

The massacre of 1927 played out with the highest stakes imaginable, setting China's course for decades to come. But Settlement officials fretted mainly over whether to postpone the spring race meeting, scheduled for just a few weeks after the killing had begun. In the end, "troublous conditions" canceled several races in March and April, but the Race Club's spring meeting went ahead as scheduled, and with a record number of ponies, 230, entered. The increase in entries was partly down to the occupation of the Jiangwan course by Guomindang armies on their way north: thousands of race fans packed the grandstands in the Settlement, while thousands of soldiers camped on the racetrack at Jiangwan.

Chiang Kai-shek's Northern Expedition and reunification of China had profound implications for Shanghai, even if they weren't apparent right away. For decades, extraterritorial protections and rudderless Chinese governments had kept Shanghailanders autonomous and powerful, living as they pleased. Chiang Kai-shek wanted to change that as he established his capital at Nanjing.

Chiang was himself an odd mixture of traditional and modern. He modeled himself on the Confucian ideal of a gentleman. His legendary asceticism frustrated corrupt associates, and he opposed communism largely because it sought to undo traditional hierarchies of family, class, and education that Chiang saw as essential to the Chinese character. Intensely nationalist, Chiang was not xenophobic, availing himself of foreign ideas and technologies if they could modernize and strengthen China. His studies in Japan had demonstrated the effectiveness of industrialization and military reform, and he set out to put China on a path that would free it from the encroachment of foreigners.

He employed German advisers to assist his campaigns to wipe out what remained of the Communists, and he curried favor with foreigners and foreign governments to gain support. Chiang courted American public favor, as well as his bride, when he married Wellesley College (and McTyeire) alumna Soong May-ling in a Christian ceremony in Shanghai, reprised at St. Bartholomew's Church in New York City. Chiang did not convert to Christianity (though he did not discourage the impression that he had done so), but his anticommunism and American connections made Chiang a favorite of *Time* and *Life* publisher Henry Luce, who would put Chiang and/or Soong on the cover of his magazines more than a dozen times.

Despite a pro-American stance, Chiang wanted above all a China strong enough to stand up for itself. He opposed the quasi-colonial power of foreigners in China, and he set about strengthening the Chinese government so that it could better enforce its own laws and customs. Military victories, alliances, political bargains, and concessions to regional power holders enabled Chiang to claim that he had reunified the country in 1927, but its success was far from assured. He moved the capital to Nanjing, the "southern capital." (Beijing, the imperial "northern capital" for 500 years, was demoted and officially renamed Beiping.) The Nanjing government went so far as to declare that extraterritoriality would be ended in 1930, including the concessions (though that declaration proved premature).[4]

The move to Nanjing, announced even before the Northern Expedition was complete, symbolically underscored Chiang's claims to be renewing the nation, but skepticism was widespread. For one thing, the new capital was close to Chiang's own base of support, consolidating his own power. For another, the change removed one of China's most constant symbols of legitimacy and appeared to emphasize the instability that had defined China's national politics since the start of the Republic. To reassure skeptics and confirm his status as not just another warlord but a ruler of unified China, Chiang Kai-shek set about turning his new capital into a model city and a showcase for the new government's values and development.[5]

Liu Jiwen, the mayor of Chiang's new capital, turned to an American to develop Nanjing into a city that was at once modern and traditional. Born in Connecticut, Henry K. Murphy studied architecture at Yale and then partnered with Richard Dana to establish a firm in 1908. Although their offices were on Madison Avenue, Dana and Murphy maintained close ties to New Haven: Dana taught architecture at Yale,

and Murphy commuted to Manhattan from his home on the Connecticut shoreline. They made a reputation designing private residences and
offices, but it was their work making campuses for New York and New
England colleges and prep schools that led Murphy to China.

The Yale-in-China Association, a medical and missionary organization associated with but not part of the university, commissioned
Murphy to design a medical school and hospital in Changsha. The
program, founded largely to honor Yale graduate Horace Pitkin, murdered in the Boxer Uprising of 1899–1900, had been looking to build
a campus in Changsha since 1904. After two previous architects were
found wanting, the Yale-in-China trustees contracted the firm of Murphy & Dana.[6]

Murphy first visited China in 1914, passing through Shanghai en
route to a site visit in Changsha, where he proposed blending Chinese
and American architectural elements to produce "a modern renaissance
of their ancestral heritage,"[7] but his ideas remained vague until a subsequent trip to Beijing transformed his views of Chinese architecture.
The stately lines and vast courtyards of the "Forbidden City"—the
fifteenth-century palace complex then still occupied by China's deposed
last emperor—captured Murphy's imagination. He described the palace as "the finest group of buildings in the world" and saw in this line
of Chinese architecture a legacy that rivaled European traditions as a
source for inspiration.[8] Murphy made China and Chinese architectural
opportunities and expressions "his life work—the revival of the ancient
architecture of China into a living style by adapting it to meet the needs
of modern scientific planning and construction."[9] He opened a branch
office of his firm in Shanghai in 1918.

Murphy developed his idea of "adaptive Chinese renaissance"
architecture throughout the 1920s, in projects like Yanjing University
in Beijing, Jinling Women's College in Nanjing, St. John's College in
Shanghai, and the Yale-China campus in Changsha. He followed the
same principles to be found in Gothic or Classical Revival in the West,
repurposing an older architectural style for modern use. His revival was
not just "traditional Chinese" architecture—there were and are many
types of traditional building design in China—but revival of a particular style. Murphy took his inspiration from the Ming-Qing palace
architecture that he had so admired in Beijing's Forbidden City.

It was this portfolio that drew the interest of Liu Jiwen. Nanjing's mayor named Murphy his chief architectural adviser in October 1928, heading a team of American and Chinese architects, city planners, and engineers that would design a new capital city for a new government, a new China. The plan, first unveiled in December 1929, combined "European and American principles of sciences and the advantages of aesthetics of our country."[10]

Planned around a grid with grand boulevards and plazas, this new capital followed Murphy's insistence that key design features and aesthetic elements be drawn from Chinese palace architecture. Within Murphy's master plan, dozens of mainly Chinese architects designed showcase buildings for the new capital, including a 60,000-seat national stadium, a supreme court, and a ministry of foreign affairs. Murphy personally designed the Memorial Tower and Martyrs' Cemetery— "China's Arlington" he called it—on the slopes of Purple Mountain, within sight of Sun Yat-sen's mausoleum on the outskirts of the city. The plan included a memorial hall depicting key scenes from the Nationalist revolution, a cemetery for soldiers, and a nine-story Memorial Tower inscribed with important quotations from Sun's speeches. (The tower remains one of Nanjing's most popular tourist destinations and a challenging climb during the city's devilishly hot and humid summers.)

Redesigning Nanjing, the nation's capital, was an important political statement that China was changing, but Chiang Kai-shek wanted his message to reach the world, and the place to send that message from was Shanghai. Shanghai's foreign concessions were among the most modern places in China. Electricity, telephone service, elevators, and air-conditioning were just some of the innovations that reached Shanghai before most other cities, not just in China, but anywhere in the world.

By contrast, Shanghai's original walled city (the Western press sometimes called it the "native city") was routinely held up as a place where foreigners could glimpse the "real China." Guidebooks recommended hiring a Chinese guide to "go slumming," with a mixture of curiosity and contempt. "Shanghai is not China. It is everything else under the sun and, in population at least, is mostly Chinese, but it is not the real China."[11] This was precisely why architect Du Yangeng had called it an "embarrassment," but the powerful and plentiful foreign presence in Shanghai also meant that foreigners would be immediately aware of any changes that were made. Now just a few hours away by train, Chiang could influence Shanghai in ways impossible when the capital had been nearly a thousand miles to the north in Beijing. Chiang's government would use Shanghai to declare that China was to be treated as an equal, sovereign nation, not as a possession for Western powers (and Japan) to divide among themselves.

Chiang had limited options for challenging foreign power in China. He wanted to assert Chinese authority but avoid the antiforeign sentiments that had been seen in violent extremes like the Boxer Uprising of 1900, which still worried many foreigners and their governments. Direct military or political confrontation was out of the question. Most Western governments considered China a friend, or even an ally; moreover, support from the foreign community was one of Chiang's most important political advantages, cultivated through his Christian wedding and American-educated wife. Embracing modernism and yet making it Chinese would show that Chiang's government was progressive and powerful, but also inclusive and cosmopolitan.

One of the Nanjing government's first acts was to establish Shanghai as a special municipal area, bringing all the previously separate Chinese jurisdictions (not including the foreign concessions) into a single city administered directly by the central government, not within the jurisdiction of a province or county. (This same arrangement persists to the present day in Shanghai, and the cities of Beijing, Tianjin, and Chongqing are similarly designated.) Shanghai's first mayor, Huang Fu, was put in place in July 1927.

The person who would remake Shanghai, like Chiang's Nanjing, as both Chinese and modern would need to be bilingual, conversant in both Eastern and Western architectural forms—someone like Dayu Doon, a young Chinese-born architect at Murphy & Dana. His resumé was tailor-made for Shanghai. Born in 1899 in Hangzhou, a short distance west of Shanghai, Doon spent much of his childhood abroad, in Japan and Rome. The modernist transformation of those two cities shaped Doon's opinions on architecture and design, and those influences would shape his career.

Returning to China as a teenager, Doon enrolled in prestigious Tsinghua University in Beijing, graduating in 1921. He then moved to the United States, becoming one of the first Chinese students to study

Portrait of
Dayu Doon
(Dong Dayou),
architect and
designer of the
New Shanghai
city plan.

at the University of Minnesota. After graduating in 1924 and earning a master's degree in architecture in 1925, Doon began his career at architecture firms in the Twin Cities and Chicago. After that, he moved on to New York and the Madison Avenue offices of Murphy & Dana. Working with Henry Murphy, Doon developed the synthesis of American and Chinese architectural traditions that would define his career.[12]

Dayu Doon worked at Murphy & Dana for just a few months before returning to China to practice architecture in 1928, one of dozens of American-trained Chinese architects helping to reshape the country during this period. He continued to work closely with Henry Murphy, collaborating, for instance, on the Martyrs' Cemetery in Nanjing and jointly developing " 'Chinese renaissance' style, a combination of the traditional Chinese style with modern comforts."[13]

Hoping for just such a vision, the Greater Shanghai Municipality hired Doon as chief architect. Tasked with creating a new Shanghai, Doon chose not the centuries-old walled city along the Huangpu that had become an object of derision for both Chinese and foreigners, but instead a completely new urban center. Doon and his commission selected Jiangwan—home of the International Recreation Club's racetrack—as the site of the new city. Northeast of the Bund and the rest of the International Settlement, Jiangwan was, according to Doon, the ideal location because it was geographically at the center of the

Shanghai municipality (though it was miles from the center of current development), with easy river access, flat topography, and little existing construction; no buildings would need to be demolished to create the New Shanghai.

Working closely with Doon in this effort was Dr. Shen Yi, born in Zhejiang province in 1901. Like Doon, Shen had attended university in China and pursued graduate studies abroad, earning a doctorate in engineering from Dresden University in 1925. He returned to China in 1927 and was appointed head of public works for the Shanghai municipal government. In the summer of 1929, the government formed the Greater Shanghai City Planning Commission, with Shen Yi and Dayu Doon its directors. Together, Doon and Shen planned their new city.

Writing about the project for the *China Press*, Doon assessed Shanghai frankly: "Although reputed to be the greatest port in the Orient, Shanghai by no means comes up anywhere near the standards and requirements of a modern city. The Chinese City, of course, is about a century behind time, although considerable improvements have been made." The foreign concessions were "nothing but a natural growth of a trading port" with no master plan or vision. "The ultimate purpose of this new project is," Doon wrote with no lack of ambition, "to create a new city which will not only be worthy of the name of the greatest metropolis of the East but also will eventually occupy a proper place among the great cities in the world."[14]

A draft of the city plan was made public in the fall of 1929. American city planner Asa Phillips, who had no experience of China and held much of Shanghai's cityscape in contempt, praised Doon's work: "Your plans for Greater Shanghai are broad in scope and comprehend the needs of your situation in a masterly manner," he wrote Doon in a letter. "No other city in the world has been confronted by so difficult and unique a problem, of which the plans you are developing present a singularly happy solution."[15]

Not everyone shared Phillips's enthusiasm. Many in the International Settlement saw the planned New Shanghai as an attempt to develop facilities that would bypass the docks and warehouses of the Settlement. Others feared the loss of playgrounds in Jiangwan, including the International Recreation Club and several golf courses. Much of the land in the area was held privately, and the government would pay less than market value for land needed to construct the model city. "What is still worse," opined the *North-China Herald*, "under the existing laws, the Chinese municipality can seize the land if they so wish as it is well known that no foreigners can hold title deeds on land in Chinese territory."[16]

Objections and anxieties from entrenched Shanghailanders did little to cool enthusiasm for the project. New Shanghai would rise 5 miles northeast of the International Settlement, linked by a 200-foot-wide boulevard patterned after the grand causeways of Chinese imperial architecture. The new Mayor's Building would face south, as Chinese seats of power traditionally did, but in this case the view south also asserted Chinese sovereignty by facing—challenging?—the foreign settlement. An elaborate plan evolved for an orderly street grid, a 1,500-foot reflecting pool along the main boulevard, generous parkland, and connections to rail, water, and road transport networks. Jiangwan's "spacious boulevards and landscaped areas, with arched bridges spanning pools and streams, a magnificent pai-lou and pagoda towers, is the heart of the Shanghai of tomorrow."[17]

Amid the controversy and the praise, in 1929 a call for proposals to design the new city's buildings went out. The invitation asked contestants to design "a Mayor's Office and nine bureaus, a set of ten buildings of monumental character. . . . [E]mbellished with gardens, fountains, pools, bridges, monuments, etc., the whole to form, with the future Courthouses, Museums, Art Galleries, Auditorium, Post Office, etc., a beautiful and monumental ensemble." The proposal sought not simply a new and beautiful space for the city government, but an expression of "China's national character with respect to her old traditions as well as her new spirit of progress."[18]

The contest—with a prize worth about US$100,000 in today's money to the winners—concluded in January 1930 after attracting some fifty submissions. The winners reflected the city they were designing for: The first-place design was submitted by two Chinese architects, Zhao Shen and Sun Ximing (Zhao had graduated from the University of Pennsylvania and, in 1927, had founded one of the first Chinese-owned architecture firms in Shanghai). Second prize went to American Edward Phillips, an associate in Henry Murphy's firm.

Third-place Poy Gum Lee was a Chinese American who had trained at MIT and Columbia.

Zhao and Sun's designs won the competition, but the commission determined that "none of the winning designs reached the hoped-for standard." In particular, they failed to incorporate "the full possibilities of Chinese architecture and knowledge as to how to adapt it most successfully to the practical requirements of modern planning and construction without sacrificing its essential aesthetic qualities."[19] Doon took the winning designs into account but designed the new city center and its buildings himself, with input from other prominent local architects.

The cornerstone for the civic center was laid in an elaborate ceremony on July 7, 1931, with about two thousand people in attendance. The centerpiece of the complex was the mayor's administration building: ten stories tall and more than 300 feet wide. "Modern in all respects from the utilitarian standpoint, the interior as well as the exterior of the building will retain the picturesque beauty of ancient Chinese architectural decoration. The interior will have vermillion columns, polychrome beams, coffered ceilings, wall panels, etc."[20]

Speaking to the crowd, Mayor Zhang Qun took the opportunity to emphasize the possibilities that came along with the new city center. For eighty years, Zhang said, the International Settlement has been said to be flourishing, but for China it has been "like tuberculosis infecting our lungs." This new center, he added, would bring "not only physical facilities, [but] the spirit of culture, morality, discipline, and order" that Shanghai's Chinese government needed. Concluding the ceremony, Chamber of Commerce member Wang Xiaolai exhorted the crowd that "the future is boundless [for] the greater Shanghai master plan."[21] Du Yangeng, the architect and critic who had decried Shanghai's foreign influence, went even further: the Jiangwan project was a way "of saving not only the city, but the entire country."[22] Construction was anticipated to take eighteen months.[23]

JUST TWO WEEKS AFTER the laying of the cornerstone, Yu-loo Tang arrived back in Shanghai, accompanying Finance Minister T. V. Soong.

As was their custom, they arrived on a Thursday morning, having taken the overnight train from Nanjing to Shanghai (the days of an overnight train between the two cities are long gone; high-speed rail service now takes about an hour). Tang, married just two months earlier, was walking with Soong along the platform at the Shanghai North Railway Station at about 7:15 a.m. when assassins ambushed the finance minister with machine guns. Bodyguards managed to protect Soong, but several bullets hit Tang. "Three bullets aimed at Dr. Soong on the left side, penetrated through my hat, but went astray only narrowly off the mark," Tang told his cousin in the hospital. "A fourth shot pierced into the lower part of my abdomen, where the bullet was delayed, allowing the minister enough time to go upstairs to the board room for safety."[24]

T. V. Soong survived the attempt on his life, but Yu-loo Tang did not. He died later that day in the hospital. The Chinese and English press reported his death as a loss not only for the Chinese leadership, but also for the prospects of Sino-foreign friendship—an impression reinforced by the array of some 400 prominent Chinese and Westerners who attended his funeral, presided over by George Fitch. The assailants were never caught. Theories abounded, some claiming that the target had actually been a Japanese official traveling that same day. Others blamed Chinese opium dealers upset at Soong's antidrug campaigns, or Chinese political rivals.[25] Yu-loo Tang's murder was just the most recent reminder that the world was dangerous and that Shanghai was not the invulnerable bubble it often imagined itself to be. Still, the violence targeted mainly Chinese; few foreigners were even inconvenienced.

As Dayu Doon's designs emerged from the marshes of Jiangwan, it was easy to imagine Shanghai divided between two worlds—one foreign, the other Chinese. But of all the foreign powers in Shanghai, it was Japan that would most directly shape the city's fate in the 1930s. After rapidly modernizing in the late nineteenth century, Japan surprised many observers when it defeated China in an 1894–95 war, proving it was the strongest military power in East Asia.

Japan confirmed its membership in the Western imperialist club in 1900 when it joined the United States, Germany, Britain, and France in an expeditionary force to free foreign diplomats and missionaries besieged in Beijing and put down the Boxer Uprising. The "Allies" (the first time this now familiar label would be applied) broke the siege after fifty-five days and left troops behind to protect their embassies and other assets. Japan interpreted this right more broadly than did most other powers, stationing garrisons to advance its interests in China more generally, particularly in port cities and near mines, factories, railroads, and other economic assets controlled by the Japanese. The largest of these garrisons, with several thousand soldiers, was in Tianjin, the port city near Beijing.

Japan continually expanded its interests in China, particularly Manchuria, over the next few decades, finally invading and occupying Manchuria in 1931. In March 1932, Japan established the state of Manchukuo—nominally independent but directed by Japan—and installed the Manchu former Qing emperor as chief executive. The invasion took an enormous piece of China's territory—Manchukuo was as big as Germany and France combined—but it did not lead immediately to war. Chinese delegates instead appealed to the League of Nations, which, after investigating Chinese claims, declared Japan's invasion and the state it had spawned illegal under international law. Japan withdrew from the league in protest, but it didn't even need to; with no enforcement powers, the league could do little. Manchukuo remained, a Japanese proxy on China's border.

Though Manchuria was far away, the fighting there raised tensions in Shanghai too. More than thirty Japanese military vessels assembled on the Huangpu River, anticipating conflict. It came on January 18, 1932, when a Chinese crowd attacked five Japanese Buddhist monks, members of an aggressively nationalist sect, outside a Shanghai factory. Accounts differ over exactly what started the incident, but one monk died and the factory burned down. A policeman was also killed, while attempting to quell the riot that ensued. Protests against Japanese aggression spread around the city, and on January 28, Japan responded by attacking Shanghai (except the foreign concessions) with artillery, infantry, and one of the first large-scale aerial bombings of civilians. By the end of February, more than 50,000 Chinese troops and 100,000 Japanese troops were fighting, and casualties exceeded 10,000 on both sides. So serious was the situation that Chiang Kai-shek ordered the Chinese government evacuated from Nanjing to Luoyang out of fear that the fighting would spread to the capital. In early March, the League of Nations imposed a ceasefire, although fighting continued sporadically until a treaty was signed in May.

This "Shanghai War" also reshaped the International Settlement. Previously, the Settlement had administered areas north of Suzhou Creek, in the region known as Hongkou (or Hongkew). The Astor House Hotel—the oldest Western hotel in China—was located there, just across the Garden Bridge from the Bund. Japanese troops, though, expanded into all of Hongkou during the fighting of 1932 and never left. Although the borders never technically changed, in practice the International Settlement after 1932 ended at Suzhou Creek, with de facto Japanese jurisdiction in Hongkou.

Shortly after the ceasefire, a press tour of foreign journalists assessed the damage in Jiangwan. The *North-China Herald* detailed the destruction: "As we neared the station and the racecourse we could see shell holes in the ground and many traces of houses having been struck by shells. Some dead bodies. . . . The station building was in ruins. What had been a new railway coach . . . a charred skeleton. In the station compound, the Statue of Sun Yat-sen with the neck and face blown off stood amidst piles of wreckage." The party toured the entire area, describing bodies and parts of bodies strewn across the ground, unburied corpses in coffins alongside burial parties, themselves killed before they could inter their comrade. Wrecked temples, homes, and roads. "One wonders why," the *Herald* concluded with heartbreaking naivete, "in the twentieth century such methods should be necessary to settle differences."[26]

Dayu Doon's Jiangwan Civic Center somehow escaped with little harm, despite heavy fighting nearby. Only the roof had been left to finish when combat suspended work on the new city, and by mid-June, Doon reported that only tiling remained to complete. Once that was done, the model city would rise up behind it, including a 3,000-seat auditorium, municipal museum, art gallery, and library, as well as courthouses and other public buildings. At the center, a 700-acre plaza would surround a statue of Sun Yat-sen to accommodate rallies and ceremonies. A reflecting pool, some 600 meters long, would frame the entire campus, approached through a five-story traditional Chinese ceremonial gate.[27]

The human tragedy of the 1932 Shanghai War was widely understood. The graphic description of charred bodies and wrecked villages personalized the tens of thousands of casualties the war had inflicted. Some, though, showed less empathy: What about their entertainment? The *China Press* lamented that because of Japan "putting Prussianism into practice," the Jiangwan racetrack had been transformed into a "no-man's-land," and that the races scheduled for Jiangwan beginning in February were postponed indefinitely; Yangtszepoo, it was reported, was even worse. Not to worry, however, about the club's horses, because "the hundreds of ponies that have given local race-goers many a thrill in these two suburban courses were removed to safety in the Settlement."[28]

The spring races couldn't be held at Jiangwan or Yangtszepoo, but that didn't stop their members from racing. Owners, including gangster C. S. Mao, who had more than thirty ponies in his "Merry" stable by this time, had their ponies transported to safety at the so-called City Course—the Shanghai Race Club.[29] Jiangwan repaired and rebuilt its facilities and reopened for racing in September, but war had shown just how precarious Shanghai was, and why, despite attempts to recover and reassert Chinese sovereignty and strength, the International Settlement remained a safer choice than the rest of Shanghai. The world-class facilities at the Jiangwan Civic Center and the International Recreation Club were still at the mercy of geopolitics. Dayu Doon, Ing Tang, and other Chinese cosmopolitans chose to live in the foreign concessions rather than outside the protection of foreign powers.

Shanghai Races

Spectators in the grandstand at the Shanghai Race Club,
November 1, 1927. British troops were on high alert given
the recent massacre of Communists by Nationalists.

THE 1932 SHANGHAI WAR DEALT A BLOW TO AMBITIONS FOR a more Chinese Shanghai, but most Shanghailanders were unfazed. They defined their city through institutions like the Shanghai Club, the Race Club, and Champions Day, and the 1932 war affected them little. The fighting that had killed thousands just a few miles from the downtown grandstand was for club members mainly a diversion from the seasonal pageantry of the races. Even outside the International Settlement, Shanghai moved on quickly from the events of 1932. Speedy repairs at Jiangwan and Yangtszepoo enabled racing to resume there in the fall. By 1933, more than sixty racing days were scheduled annually, and three tracks were racing.

The lesson that many Shanghailanders took from the events of 1932 was neither their city's vulnerability nor the potential dangers facing China, but the need for a new playground. The Shanghai Race Club was the pride of the Settlement, but it was by far the oldest of Shanghai's racetracks, threadbare after sixty years in service. Many members of the SRC had recognized for some time that its rival in Jiangwan was better appointed, but change came slowly. It took a partial ceiling collapse—a section of the clubhouse ceiling narrowly missed one of the senior members—to finally convince the SRC membership to invest in a new, grander structure, but even then plans advanced slowly. The club first proposed a new clubhouse in 1920, but plans languished, with few tangible results. The relocation of International Recreation Club races to the City Course in the fall of 1932 put spurs to the renovation project, and within a year of those races, the SRC broke ground. Just ten months after the cornerstone was laid on May 20, 1933, the Race Club building that now stands in People's Park opened its doors.

The British ambassador, scheduled to open the building, was unavailable because of mourning for the recently deceased king of Belgium, but club chairman A. W. "Bertie" Burkill took the gold keys from the architect and crowed that the SRC clubhouse was ushering in "a new epoch" in Shanghai racing, praising the construction firm Ah Hong for its record-setting pace (aided, it was said, by a windstorm that knocked down the construction scaffolding the day after work was done, saving the time and expense of dismantling it).¹ With much of the world mired in the deepening Depression, the clubhouse bragged on the Settlement's prosperity; many considered this the grandest racetrack in Asia, its grandstand rivaling the world's largest, in Buenos Aires.²

Attending the ceremony opening the new SRC clubhouse in 1934 would have been all of the members who would take part in the Champions Day of November 1941, including the seven owners: Cornell Franklin, Arthur Henchman, Robert Aitkenhead, Eric Moller, Gussie White, Vera McBain, and Leslie Hutton. They fell into two broad categories. The first—of which White, Moller, and McBain were good examples—descended from families who had come to Shanghai in the nineteenth century. Unlike their forbears, who had been adventurers and entrepreneurs in a remote city where creature comforts were scarce and society was small, the new generations of these families were well established, born in China, often of mixed European and Chinese parentage, into comfort if not luxury. These families were "Settlers"; Shanghai was their home. Shanghailanders in the fullest sense, they were loyal to Shanghai before, perhaps, even to England.

The second category—men like Franklin, Henchman, and Aitkenhead—had come to the banks of the Huangpu to join the capitalist frenzy of a metropolis, not an outpost. Historian Robert Bickers distinguishes these "expatriates" from Settlers and excludes them from the narrowest definition of "Shanghailanders," arguing that for expatriates, "Shanghai was incidental; they might have been sent anywhere in China, or wherever their employers operated."³ Bickers makes clear the many divisions between "Settlers" and "expatriates," but viewed from outside, they were all Shanghailanders.⁴

Fortune magazine observed these foreigners on the China coast and devoted the better part of an issue to the "Shanghai Boom," promoting the city as the place where you "might have trebled your money between '27 and '34," inauspicious years in many places. *Fortune* profiled the men, and some women, who had taken advantage of the opportunity.⁵ Whether new arrivals or old China hands, these Shanghailanders were, according to *Fortune*,

A small, snotty, fast-moving club of white people who consider the Mistress of Cathay their own particular preserve. Shanghailander incomes vary from the hundred thousands down to stenographic salaries, but Shanghailanders themselves act as one classless social group. The distinction between taipan and wage earner, old family and upstart, is lost in the glaring fact of their common race. . . . He is generically loose in his sexual morals. He is apt to be a sportsman—golf, tennis, cricket, bowling, paper chasing, horse racing, and dog racing. And he will gamble on anything under the sun, from the New York Stock Exchange to Manchu ponies.[6]

The center of the Shanghailanders' world was the new Shanghai Race Club, its hallmark clock tower rising above the International Settlement. The orientalist art deco spire housed 13-foot-diameter "Big Bertie," named after club secretary Burkill, as well as the secretary's penthouse apartment. Invitingly breezy during stifling Shanghai summers, the tower's veranda opened onto the grandest views of the city below, down Nanking Road past the remnants of former racecourses to the Huangpu waterfront, where international Shanghai had begun.

Members entered the clubhouse from Bubbling Well Road, at the tower's base, through a pillared entry hall. From there they could walk directly to the pari-mutuel rooms, though most members would head upstairs, via a sweeping staircase with wrought-iron railings adorned with horseheads, to the mezzanine (for those not wanting to walk, the entry hall also featured an elevator). There, a bar and lounge, as well as a wine cellar, reading room, billiard room, and card room, waited, along with six bowling alleys—four American-style and two (20 feet longer) English-style—all soundproofed to be inaudible to floors above or below.[7] The centerpiece was the so-called coffee room: nearly 5,000 square feet, detailed with teak and an oak parquet floor. The coffee room was capable of hosting the Settlement's most lavish parties—and those parties were the only time women were permitted inside.

The elevator or the horsehead stairs took members from the mezzanine to the second and third floors, where they could reserve tiffin rooms for private parties during race days ("tiffin," derived from an Indian word, had by the 1930s in Shanghai come to mean an often elaborate midday meal). These rooms were grand spaces "decorated in various national styles,"[8] with balconies overlooking either the racecourse

The Race Club's clock tower was an important landmark for Shanghai residents, including Isabel Sun Chao, author of Remembering Shanghai: A Memoir of Socialites, Scholars and Scoundrels, *shown in this 1949 photo.*

or the paddock area, depending on which side of the building they faced. A central private elevator went directly from these two dozen private rooms to the pari-mutuel hall on the first floor, but dedicated phone lines also connected them to the betting windows, so that members could place wagers without ever leaving the suites. The 350-foot-long grandstand was accessible directly from the members' rooms, its entire length covered by a glass roof with retractable sunshades, and linked to a 500-foot-long guest grandstand with teak-paneled suites. Behind the grandstand were the betting halls—one for members and one for guests.[9]

IN THE RACE CLUB, members did their best to uphold Shanghai's reputation as, in the words of *China Press* editors, "the most drinkingest city in the world."[10] Cocktail parties drove the Settlement's social calendar, and Saturday evenings at the Race Club were especially famous for their "social glow," generating a healthy trade in the science and lore of hangover cures and prevention.[11] (The club's Turkish baths were trendy therapy for the overindulgent, though Mr. Jerome Ephraim, who assessed the various options available, warned that "the cure is probably worse than the disease," if one tried to sweat out the previous night's revelries.)[12]

Before his murder in 1931, Yu-loo Tang had closely observed Shang-hai society, and—inevitably?—some of his first and strongest impressions were of alcohol. "If persons congregate together in drink," Tang wrote in his first "Causerie Chinoise" column, in 1926, "let them all be seized and brought to me in the capital. I will put them to death."[13]

Tang was quoting King Wen, cited by the twelfth-century BCE Duke of Zhou, for commentary on the problems of his day. The Duke of Zhou was the classical model for Chinese rulers, revered by Confucius as the moral polestar around which ethics should revolve, and Tang had looked to him to find precedents for Prohibition in the United States, wondering whether Andrew Volstead was aware of the Duke of Zhou's 1115 BCE "Edict against Drunkenness," in which he observed that when states have gone into decline, "misuse of wine has always been the cause of their downfall." Or maybe he offered the Zhou leader's advice as a warning to what must surely have seemed a profoundly dissolute place. There was, of course, no Prohibition in intemperate Shanghai. Booze seemed as essential as money. *Fortune* made the point plainly: "The Shanghailander drinks too much (his definition of a drunkard pivots around the presence or absence of a drink at breakfast)."[14]

If Yu-loo Tang, or *Fortune*, had anyone in mind when railing against the influence of drink, it may well have been the Franklins. Cornell and Estelle Franklin left the United States within months after the Volstead Act came into effect; perhaps the timing was coincidence, but their lifestyle abroad took full advantage of it. "I don't think I took a sober breath for three years," Estelle wrote of her time in Shanghai. "It started at about eleven in the morning and ended about three or four the next morning. There was nothing else to do—no housework, no anything, and in the American and British communities it was expected . . . to do a certain amount of entertaining. And you never declined an invitation so that it was literally non-stop."[15]

The Franklins' path to Shanghai began in unlikely fashion, deep in the American South. "Born and reared in the quaint old town of Columbus, Mississippi," near the border with Alabama,[16] Cornell

Franklin had deep roots in this small town, but his father died before he was even born, leaving him little property to inherit.[17] Cornell worked his way through the University of Mississippi, becoming class president, and then on to law school there, where his classmates voted him "most likely to become a millionaire."

Despite his peers' endorsement, Franklin was no millionaire yet at the time, and he was eager to earn a fortune. He had been courting Estelle Oldham, an Ole Miss undergraduate, for three years, and he had reason to believe that she would marry him if he had more money, so Franklin set out to improve his prospects. A law degree—and some family and political favors—took him to Hawai'i, not yet a state, where he joined a prominent law firm. Three years later he resigned that position to become deputy attorney general for the territory, and two years after that, President Woodrow Wilson appointed him a US circuit judge for Hawai'i. His prospects secured, Franklin returned to Mississippi, and in April 1918 he and Estelle were married. They spent their wedding night at Memphis's famous Peabody Hotel, traveled for a month visiting friends and relatives on the East Coast (it was Cornell's first time on the mainland in nearly four years), and by June had arrived in Honolulu to begin their life together.[18]

Nothing about the move to Hawai'i went as expected. Estelle had never lived outside of Mississippi, aside from four years at finishing school in Virginia, and Hawai'i could scarcely have been less familiar. Complicating their plans even further, Cornell enlisted in the army. He was already in the National Guard, and with the United States now in World War I, enlisting enabled him to avoid deployment to Europe. He was assigned to Camp Schofield in Honolulu, where Estelle lived as a guest with army wives whom she had never met, and soon discovered she was pregnant. Their daughter, Cho-cho—their Japanese nanny gave Victoria the nickname—was born in February 1919.

The three years in Hawai'i foreshadowed much about their lives in China, once Cornell got out of the army and the family set up its own house. Like Shanghai, Honolulu was a semicolonial city built on a racial hierarchy (in that way, both cities resembled the Jim Crow Mississippi where the Franklins had grown up). Cornell traveled frequently for his work as a judge, but when he was in Honolulu, the social calendar was packed with polo matches, dinner parties, luncheons, and even—

twice!—balls for the visiting Prince of Wales. As in Shanghai, liquor sustained the top levels of society, but even by the standards of Honolulu's semicolonial community, the Franklins drank to excess. Eventually, they found themselves socially exiled after "a scene between Cornell and Estelle that even their hard-drinking guests found beyond the pale."[19]

Estelle was tiring of the scene as well. She and Cho-cho began returning home to Mississippi regularly, spending time not only with her parents, but with friends she had made before her marriage. They were away during the summer of 1921 when Cornell took a three-week tour of East Asia, visiting Tokyo, Beijing, and, finally, Shanghai. The Shanghailanders convinced him that his lawyering could be more lucrative if he represented American interests amid the legal complexities of their burgeoning treaty port. When Estelle and Cho-cho returned to Honolulu in November, he informed them that they would be leaving Hawai'i for China. On New Year's Eve 1921, they arrived at the Customs Jetty in Shanghai.[20]

Cornell cashed in on the opportunities he had scouted the previous summer. He made the fortune that his Ole Miss classmates had predicted, representing Standard Oil, Liggett & Myers Tobacco, and other American corporations doing business in China. At home, he was less successful. During their first months in Shanghai, Estelle and Cornell hosted parties and dominated society pages. Glimpses of their life in Shanghai emerge through Estelle's fiction; an unpublished short story titled "Star-Spangled Banner Stuff" survives in typescripts.

Estelle's is a tense, multinational Shanghai where divisions between Britons and Americans appear nearly as wide as those separating whites from Chinese. Liquor is an essential character in her fiction, as Shanghailanders and their servants move from the Shanghai Club to the Astor House to the various nightclubs throughout the Settlement, each stop seemingly requiring a new set of cocktail recipes. The climactic scene is a capsule of Shanghailand: midnight at the Carlton Ballroom, with Brits, Americans, Russians, and Chinese, all drunk or well on their way, dancing to jazz, hiding in the shadows before playing out private dramas in public.[21]

We can surmise that this portrayal reflects at least some of the Franklins' time in Shanghai, but the entertaining diminished as Estelle became more disenchanted with life abroad. She continued to take the children—a son, Malcolm, was born in 1923—to Mississippi, sometimes for months at a time. When she was in Shanghai, she wanted to be somewhere else. In 1924, less than three years after arriving in Shanghai, Estelle and her two children left, bound for America and not intending to return.

Soon after she left, an awkwardly timed package arrived at the Franklins' Shanghai address: a copy of William Faulkner's newly published collection of poems, *The Marble Faun*, inscribed to Estelle from the author. Faulkner, a fellow Mississippian, was Estelle's first love. Her parents hadn't approved, and the relationship's formal prospects seemed to end when she went away to prep school and then accepted— at her parents' insistence—Franklin's proposal of marriage. But the relationship between Faulkner and Estelle had persisted. They corresponded while she was in Shanghai; Estelle shared "Star-Spangled Banner Stuff," with Faulkner, beginning a collaboration that was to last decades. ("Star-Spangled Banner Stuff" is one of just a few of Estelle Oldham's manuscripts to survive. Faulkner commented on it and at least three others and played a role pitching them to publishers.)[22]

When Estelle arrived back in her hometown of Oxford, Mississippi, in late 1924, Faulkner called on her regularly from his home in New Orleans. Cornell brought Estelle back to Shanghai with him, but only a few months later she left China for good, in the spring of 1925. For the next four years, stop-and-go divorce proceedings dragged on while she lived with her parents. When the split finally became official, in the spring of 1929, Estelle and Faulkner married immediately. "I did not marry who I wanted the first time, but I will do it the second," she wrote to her friend Katherine Andrews. Estelle and William Faulkner remained married until his death thirty-three years later.[23]

In Shanghai, Cornell Franklin also remarried quickly, wedding Dallas Chesterman Lee, a Richmond debutante and direct descendant of Robert E. Lee, in September 1929. Dallas, whom Franklin had met when he represented her in her own divorce[24] several years earlier, was the society wife that Franklin had hoped to find in Estelle. The couple became a fixture in the Settlement. Cornell and Dallas moved into the antebellum-style mansion that Cornell had been building even before Estelle left, at 200 Avenue Jordan, west of the city center and just outside the technical boundaries of the International Settlement. There, the Franklins hosted cocktail parties, dinner parties, and luncheons. Their annual Fourth of July party was a highlight of the calendar for Americans in Shanghai from the 1930s until everything changed in the fall of 1941.

Franklin had been around horses in Shanghai before he even lived there. On the 1921 trip that convinced him to relocate to Asia, he had organized a polo match between Shanghai and Honolulu teams. Once he was established in Shanghai, everyone agreed that he was one of the city's very best players, once scoring ten goals in a single match. (When he left Shanghai for a trip to the United States in 1925, the local press lamented, "He will be much missed on the polo field, where he has been playing a splendid game."[25]) But Franklin turned forty in 1932 and began to focus on owning horses more than riding them.

Franklin's first pony, Bunny, won Shanghai's top steeplechase— a race that includes jumps over hedges, rails, and water—at both the spring and fall meetings in 1932, and finished as runner-up twice more. But steeplechases and owner-riders were the stuff of amateurs and hobbyists. Judge Franklin liked money; he had turned down an early chance at a judicial appointment because the salary was too low, and the move to Shanghai was based on the belief (justified, as it turned out)

Horses approaching the finish line at the Shanghai Race Club, 1928.

that Shanghai was a lucrative market for lawyers. The high stakes and big money were in flat races. That was the way to the Champions', and Franklin started looking for faster horses.

ARTHUR AND MARY HENCHMAN arrived from London around the same time that Franklin came from Hawai'i, and they were an institution in Shanghai. No one better represented what the city had become in the twentieth century. Hench, tall and fit, with deep-set eyes and an aquiline nose, was still an impressive athlete at sixty years old, excitable and passionate. Born in 1880, he had grown up in the North London suburbs, with two older brothers and a servant but without his father, who died while Arthur was still in primary school. Before he was twenty, Henchman began working for the Hongkong and Shanghai Bank and eventually moved to London's Highgate section, though he barely saw the place after the bank "sent him East" to Singapore, Dalian, and Hong Kong, before spending seven years in Manila.

Henchman left the Philippines in 1922 and returned to London just long enough to marry Mary Annie Cook that same year. Hench and Mary left almost immediately for Asia. At the end of September, the P&O steamer *Karmala* took them from Southampton to Gibraltar, Marseilles, Port Said, Aden, Bombay, Colombo, Singapore, Hong Kong, and, finally, Shanghai, where passengers disembarked at the Customs Jetty, at the center of the Bund. Awaiting Henchman as he came ashore was his employer's home, a granite and marble neoclassical structure so new that scaffolding still encased it.

The Shanghai office was technically just a branch, but the amount and importance of the business it conducted made it every bit as significant as the company headquarters in Hong Kong. The Bank—what today is HSBC was then often known as simply "the Bank" or else by its name in Chinese, Wayfoong—had occupied this spot since the 1870s and in 1919 acquired two adjacent properties, eventually razing all three for their new building that would dominate the Bund. The entire construction took place in just two years, and when Hench arrived, the branch where he would soon begin working was three-fourths complete.

Hench and Mary were married to the Bank as much as to each other for the next decade. They didn't stay long after their first arrival in Shanghai, traveling across East Asia to climb the corporate ladder, first to Qingdao, then Bangkok, then Kobe, Japan. The Bank was grooming Henchman for one of its most important positions—he had narrowly missed appointment as manager in Hong Kong—and his work in Japan demonstrated that he was ready for a more important post. He came back to Shanghai as submanager in 1929, and two years later Hench was managing the Shanghai branch. He was now one of the most powerful men in all of China, with a corner office at Shanghai's most prestigious address.[26]

The building that was still going up when Hench arrived in 1922 was now finished, the second-largest bank building in the world (after the Bank of Scotland in Edinburgh). Two bronze lions—named Stephen and Stitt after two of the Bank's directors, both owners of successful stables at the Race Club—guarded the doorway. Placid Stitt projected stability amid chaos, while Stephen roared, dominating his realm, the paws of both already beginning to polish as passersby rubbed them for good luck. (The two lions are now on display in the former Race Club building, welcoming visitors to the Shanghai History Museum, while replicas take their former spots on the Bund.)

Inside, the lobby celebrated the Bank's global reach, and even in Shanghai's notorious summer heat it did so comfortably: the building was one of the first in the world to have central air-conditioning. Even grander than the marble floors and fixtures was the ceiling mosaic: eight panels depicting the Bank's most important offices—in Bangkok, Calcutta, Hong Kong, London, New York, Paris, Tokyo, and, of course, Shanghai. Rich in symbolism and style, they told the story and the mythology of the Bank in elegant detail. Up the elevator on the second floor, the manager's office looked out over the Bund and the Huangpu River.

It was from his desk in that corner office that Henchman cemented his reputation. The Crash of 1929 did not affect China or Shanghai to the extent it did the United States or Europe—*Fortune*, after all, had touted Shanghai as the place to triple your money in the early 1930s—and although China's GDP and industrial output both fell after 1931, they recovered within just a few years. Shanghailanders worried little about the Depression as the city continued a boom that had begun during World War I, but the new Chinese government at Nanjing was asserting its authority and sometimes butting heads with the Settlement authorities.

After the Nationalist government's 1935 decision to take over China's currency and move away from the silver standard, China's currency foundered, losing value rapidly and threatening to scuttle China's economic development, especially in the treaty ports and, most of all, Shanghai. According to a leading economic historian of the era, "In the end, stabilization on minimal funds was achieved through the technical brilliance of A. S. Henchman."[27] Some called him a "wizard" for the way he calculated, pleaded, coerced, bluffed, and compromised Shanghai through the crisis. The Chinese government awarded him the Order of the Brilliant Jade (and a gold wristwatch).

There were problems to sort out—there always were in Shanghai— but the future seemed bright, especially seen from within a society of symphonies, cinemas, cabarets, and dance halls. The Henchmans were on all the right guest lists, attending every party that mattered, feting diplomats, dignitaries, and celebrities who passed through Shanghai. Their Christmas Day ball began as an office event for a few dozen Bank staff, but grew to become the unofficial Christmas Party for British Shanghailanders. By the early 1930s, a hundred people or more were celebrating at the Henchman house at 1185 Bubbling Well Road, a short distance west of the racetrack.[28]

And it was the racetrack, more than the dancers and the dinners, and sometimes even work, that occupied Arthur Henchman's attention. Hench had come to Shanghai to profit from the fortunes being made there, but the city's reputation as a place to spend money more than matched its reputation as a place to make it. "Money is apparently quickly earned in Shanghai," wrote a visitor from Calcutta, "and is often as quickly dissipated."[29]

Jai alai, a fast-paced Basque sport with rules similar to those of squash, was popular with bettors. So was dog racing. But horses were the most popular way to try one's luck, and it was the one that best suited Shanghailanders of a certain class. Henchman arrived at the Race Club just as the new clubhouse was opening, now one of the world's grandest settings for racing horses, surrounded by art deco skyscrapers and the unblinking neon of Nanking Road. Hench was never much for

Arthur and Mary Henchman leading their pony outside the
Shanghai Race Club, 1941.

riding, but now, as one of Shanghai's most powerful men, he followed
the path of generations of Shanghailanders and tried his hand at racing.

Hench's focus was not just the races but the Champions'; winning
that race was the way to gain bragging rights in the International Settlement, and for a relative newcomer like Henchman, it could make all
the difference. The potential winnings were worthwhile too: the winner would take home $5,000 (about US$83,000 in today's money), the
largest purse at the track. And others could share in the success. Altogether, bettors would put down close to a million in today's dollars on
the outcome of the Champions'. For the gamblers, the winnings could
be a ticket to a new life (or a way out of an old one). For the scions of
Shanghai, rulers of a world that seemed simultaneously timeless and
doomed, with unique rules and standards, the claim to be champion—
crowned "King of the Turf"—was as great an attraction as the money.

Hench wanted to be Champion.

IF HENCHMAN WERE GOING to be Champion, he would have to get
by Robert Aitkenhead.

At first glance, this appeared an unlikely rivalry. For one thing, about the time that Henchman was starting his job in Shanghai, Bob Aitkenhead was deciding to leave. It was 1932. He'd been in China for twenty-five years, and his friends gathered to celebrate his time in Shanghai with a "smoking and supper concert": an evening of "songs and humorous Scottish sketches."[30] Bob was a "tower of strength a good friend to all," and his friends would raise a glass—or several—to wish him well in his new home, back in Scotland.

A Glaswegian born just three months after Henchman, Aitkenhead was also Shanghailander elite, but with quite different roots. He was the son of a railroad clerk, the oldest of eight children and apprenticed as a naval engineer. His path out of Scotland was a job with the China Merchants Steam Navigation Company, the first Chinese-owned steamship company, founded by Li Hongzhang, a polymath who was central to China's nineteenth-century reform movement. Arriving in 1907, Aitkenhead, like many British expatriates, reinvented himself in Shanghai. His name was soon familiar to every reader of the sports and society pages, as he excelled at golf, lawn bowling, and tennis especially. His name spread beyond just Shanghai: in Hong Kong, lawn-bowling teams played for the "Aitkenhead Shield."

Bob Aitkenhead and Jean Ramsay Allan married in 1912 at the Anglican Holy Trinity Cathedral in Shanghai, a mainstay of expatriate society a few blocks from the racecourse, after a civil ceremony at the British consulate.[31] Although Shanghailanders prided themselves on having a classless society (they relied on race more than class to segregate themselves), the Aitkenheads had neither the connections nor the wealth to be social fixtures like the Henchmans. Jean, like Robert, was a Shanghailander via Scotland. She had grown up in China, in Hong Kong first, before accompanying her father to Shanghai, where he took a job as an engineer in 1910.

The Aitkenheads were a sporting couple, collecting tennis and golf trophies even as they raised two children (a daughter born in 1914, and a son born a year later). They were also travelers; their lifestyle saw the husband and wife less and less frequently in Shanghai at the same time. Jean usually returned to Britain in the springtime, taking the children with her. Bob traveled even more often, usually by himself or with business partners, to Japan and other East Asian ports, to Europe, and to North America (the fastest route from Shanghai to London was via Canada and the Canadian Pacific Railway).

Although Aitkenhead was prominent—by 1930 he had become the manager of the Blue Star Line shipping company's Far Eastern service—he did not have Henchman's status. He made friends more easily than Henchman, though, especially in sporting circles, as shown by the festive send-off he received at the Yangtszepoo Bowling Club. One of those who toasted his farewell recalled that just three years before, the club had given a similar send-off to another one of their members, but had been happy to welcome him back just a few years later. The anecdote proved prescient.

Aitkenhead traded Shanghai for the idyllic Scottish village of Clunie, on the loch of the same name. The wooded hills could scarcely be more different from the marshy plains of the Yangtze delta. The warmest days of the Scottish summer felt like Shanghai's spring, the oppressive humidity of Shanghai summers nowhere to be found. The waters of the River Tay sparkled with a clarity unknown to murky Suzhou Creek, and the clear Lowland skies contrasted sharply with Shanghai's haze. From one of the world's great modern cities, focused on constant renewal, Aitkenhead had moved to a tiny village that wore its ancient past on its sleeve, with twelfth-century ruins at the town's center and a thousand-year-old hunting lodge linked to the first king of Scotland. Nearly 6 million people from all around the world lived in Shanghai in the 1930s; in Clunie, there were just a few hundred Scots.

Perhaps Aitkenhead had been in Shanghai too long to make Scotland home again. Maybe a need for money lured him back. Or perhaps he just missed the friends he had made in a quarter century on the China coast. Whatever the reasons, the steamer *Corfu* brought Aitkenhead back to Shanghai in February 1933, just seven months after he had left.[32] Once again he was a Shanghailander; really, he could not be otherwise.

Aitkenhead's reputation suggests that he was one of the "quiet conservatives," of which *Fortune* assured its readers there were plenty in Shanghai, though they were "not typical . . . a smaller percentage of the resident population than in the average metropolis."[33] That speculation notwithstanding, Aitkenhead certainly fit the description of a sportsman and a gambler. Like Hench and Franklin, Aitkenhead had his eyes on the Champions', but he had a long way to go. None of his horses had even entered one of the Shanghai classics.

ERIC MOLLER HAD INHERITED his business from his father, "Captain Nils" Moller, who decades earlier had ineffectively declared himself beyond the jurisdiction of any country, particularly those whose courts were hearing lawsuits against him for breach of contract and other claims. Whatever his citizenship, Nils Moller died in 1903. His will was not without controversy; he had married twice in Shanghai and had been less than forthcoming with his families about the nature and disposition of his assets, but once his estate was resolved, his sons Eric (formally Nils Eric) and John emerged to run the business.

The brothers moved aggressively to modernize their fleet, selling the company's sailing vessels and buying their first steamship (the *Canton*, built in 1885). Eric took over sole ownership in 1910, and his timing could not have been better. The Great War devastated Europe, including, for a time, its ability to participate in the global marketplace. China's coastal economy was one of the great beneficiaries. Moller took full advantage, buying eighteen vessels, though German torpedoes sank at least four of them.

When the war ended, China was both a manufacturing center and an important import-export market; more than a dozen ships featuring the navy-blue "M"-emblazoned funnels of the Moller line carried the growing trade. The Great Depression drove competitors toward bankruptcy, and Moller purchased their ships for pennies on the dollar, adding them to his fleet. Moller's shipping line in the 1930s was the largest on the China coast, comprising not only oceangoing vessels, but also steam ferries on the Yangtze River. His business interests extended to insurance, finance, and real estate.

Eric Moller was also a fixture on the racecourse. His father had taken a passive interest in racing (he presented the "Anchor Flag Cup" at the Tianjin races for several years during the 1890s), but Eric went all in, riding horses at the racetrack as early as 1898, when he was twenty-three years old. He became one of the most successful jockeys in both Shanghai and Hong Kong. When he came into his inheritance, Eric began buying horses, as well as riding them, partnering with John Wingard in 1905 to found the Cire stable, liveried, like his ships, with a blue anchor motif. (Originally blue and red, Moller later changed his colors to the chocolate and gold that would become the signature of the stable in both Hong Kong and Shanghai.) By the 1930s, his stable of some sixty ponies was the largest in Shanghai.

His father had claimed to be a citizen of Shanghai, but Eric Moller was Shanghai nobility, and appropriately enough he lived in a castle. His "Moller Villa," completed around the same time as the new SRC clubhouse, stands out even in Shanghai for its mix of styles: Gothic, Tudor, and Scandinavian are easiest to spot, but there are Islamic and Chinese elements too, and nautical motifs throughout. (The building is today a boutique hotel: with "brooding, Gothic spires that look like witches' hats, grafted onto a grand Tudor facade, Moller Villa looks like something from a Hans Christian Andersen fairytale—not quite real, and not quite of this world."[34])

Eric Moller's work in shipping brought him frequently to Hong Kong, the center of British power on China's coast and (probably) the first racetrack in China. He also maintained a stable there of a dozen horses, but he made his reputation with just one race, one that many "China Hands" considered the most important horse race on the coast: the 1938 Hong Kong Champions' Cup. For years, a horse named Liberty Bay had dominated Hong Kong racing, winning every race he started in from 1932 to 1935. Liberty Bay was so overwhelming that his owner agreed to withhold the horse's name from the racing form when he ran: winning odds would go to the second favorite. With this arrangement, Liberty Bay continued to win all the major races, until the spring of 1938. In that year, Eric Moller entered a dark-gray pony, Silkylight, ridden by his son, Ralph, in the Hong Kong spring race meeting, that won both the Maidens' Cup (for first-time competitors) and then, as a long shot, the Hong Kong Derby.

When, a day later, Silkylight faced Liberty Bay in the Hong Kong Champions', Liberty Bay had not lost for six years. The spectators in the packed grandstand at Happy Valley racetrack, in the center of Hong Kong Island, rose to their feet as Silkylight broke from the gate two lengths ahead, but they sat back down, bored, when Liberty Bay overcame the poor start to take a ten-length lead by the halfway point. As the horses turned for home, the lead was still nine lengths, but then Eric Moller, from his vantage point atop the grandstand, saw Silkylight leap forward "like an arrow." The two horses battled side by side toward the wire, but Silkylight surged forward at the finish, winning by a length and a half. No one was more stunned than Liberty Bay's owner, Lambert Dunbar, who refused ever to race the pony again.[35]

WHITE WAS A NAME that rivaled Moller when it came to Shanghai aristocracy in the early twentieth century.

Augustus Victor (A. V., or "Gussie") White—was the great-nephew of the banker who had come from Hong Kong with Sewey Hong. By the early twentieth century, the family was established as one of the most important in Shanghai finance. Gussie White's father, William, worked as a broker and lived in the heart of the International Settlement two blocks from the river, behind the Bund. William White's Szechuan Road home was less elaborate than the Clatterhouse estate of his brother Augustus Harold, but it still illustrated the privilege that Shanghailanders enjoyed: "a cook and a second cook; a coolie; a boy and a second boy; two amahs and a house tailor." These circumstances, which White considered "a fairly average number of servants" meant that the family "never lifted a finger."[36]

After finishing school, Gussie White worked as a broker in a family firm. His wedding in 1921 to Katherine Godsil was society-page news, and why not? White was a society mainstay, joining the Race Club in 1918, and was soon one of its most prominent and successful riders and owners.[37] Throughout the 1920s, Gussie White contended in classics at both Jiangwan and the City Course. His gray pony Pat won the Champions' in 1929, in what seemed would be the first of many wins. But White's fortunes turned.

By the time Franklin and Henchman arrived, Gussie White was still racing but hadn't won the Champions' again, and he was less often among the contenders in the classics. He was in the headlines for other reasons, however: rumors of scandal. White was said to have been carrying on an affair with Louisa Brand—not only a married woman, but a woman at whose wedding he had been the best man![38] Brand divorced in the summer of 1936, and White, named as a codefendant in the suit, soon divorced as well.[39] Gussie and Louise married in Hong Kong the following winter.[40] Getting back to the Champions' would be a good tonic for a chaotic personal life.

MOST OF THE HORSE owners in this new generation were men, but not all. Katherine Godsil, for instance, before her divorce from Gussie White, was prominent at the Race Club, co-owning horses with her husband, including Champion Pat. Women who partnered with their husbands to own successful horses had some precedent, but it was not until 1920 that women owned horses in their own right. Vera McBain was one example. Born in England, she had played mainly small roles (under the name Vera Davis) at the Gaiety Theatre near Covent Garden in London's West End.[41] It was there that she had met her husband, William McBain, marrying in 1918 and moving full-time to Shanghai a few years later. William was from another prominent Shanghailander family, which had first come to the city in the nineteenth century.

A newcomer to the city, Vera McBain was a trailblazer, becoming the first woman to own a winning horse in her own right, doing so in her first meeting at the Jiangwan Stakes of 1920, and then partnering with Billie Coutts, one of the most established women at the Race Club, to form a new stable called We Two.

Billie Coutts—she was born Mary Grace but seems to have always been called Billie—was from a family with nearly fifty years of history in Shanghai, but she was cut from different cloth. Born in 1900 and growing up around the racetrack, Billie was a trainer and rider even before women were permitted to be members of the Race Club. She regularly won the Shanghai Paper Hunt, a cross-country race that was a sort of foxhunt crossed with a scavenger hunt, with riders following clues written on pieces of paper strewn across the countryside. (The paper hunt and the steeplechase were opened to women, though no women were ever allowed to ride in "flat races" on the turf.)

Billie Coutts was the first woman to train a winning horse, in 1924. Contemporaries described her as "the best dressed woman on the China coast," with a "rapier wit."[42] Vera McBain and Billie Coutts were among the most prominent female members of the SRC, and they rarely failed to cause a commotion. "An invasion by women," wrote the *North-China*

Herald, "of all that has hitherto been regarded as man's sacred ground is the score of this generation."[43]

Billie Coutts married John (Jack) Liddell in Shanghai in 1927, after a courtship that the local press described as "from bridle path to bridal veil."[44] Jack Liddell and William McBain were rivals on the racetrack and in commerce, but the two women remained fast friends, maintaining We Two and, it seems, enjoying the partnership all the more because it tweaked their husbands. Whether the stable started as a lark or with more serious intentions, they found great success. We Two fielded fast horses from the very start, and had won the Shanghai Champions' in 1932 with Mister Cinders. Since that time, although they contended regularly, Billie and Vera had yet to return to the Champions' winner's circle, either separately or as partners.

ERIC CUMINE WAS THE son of Henry Monsel Cumine and Winifred Greaves, among the first Shanghailanders to establish themselves in the city. Unlike his parents, both born in Shanghai to Scottish fathers and Chinese mothers, Eric was a Shanghai native, born in 1905 at his parents' home in the International Settlement. With two Chinese grandmothers, he grew up speaking English, Mandarin, and Cantonese. Although he enjoyed a lifestyle far beyond what most Chinese in Shanghai could aspire to, Eric was not "fully" European by the standards of the day; he was thought of as Eurasian, and he never shied away from this background. Associates later in life considered him half-Chinese.[45]

Eric Cumine's mixed identity limited his educational opportunities in Shanghai. He was unable to attend the prestigious Cathedral School because it did not admit Eurasians, but he attended the Shanghai Public School—founded by Britons and run along the lines of an English boarding school—and excelled as an athlete (taking extra delight when defeating the Cathedral School in cricket) before he left for London to continue his education at the Architectural Association School of Architecture, Britain's first independent school of architecture and one of the most prestigious in the world. Cumine graduated from the school at age twenty, in 1926, and won several national prizes for his work. In December 1927 he married Emma (Gladys) Williams, and a month later the couple boarded the Blue Funnel line's steamer *Aeneas*, bound for

Shanghai via Port Said and the Straits Settlements. Eric was welcomed into his father's firm, Cumine and Associates, shortly after arriving back in China.[46]

Eric Cumine designed some of the most prominent buildings of Shanghai's art deco heyday, including the Denis Apartments, just west of the racetrack on Bubbling Well Road. Anticipating the building's completion in 1930, the *China Press* praised its numerous modern features, thereby affirming Shanghai's self-appointed role as a forerunner of all things modern. The tallest building in the western part of the city, the Denis was nearly twelve stories high and equipped with four Otis elevators, rare in East Asia. Adorning the facade (devoid of balconies because "no one uses balconies except for cigarette ends") were statues representing the values of modernity, including *Progress* and *Harmony*. The Denis boasted of its location "in the heart of Clubland" with easy access to the racetrack, Country Club, YMCA, and shopping districts.[47]

Yet, Cumine's Denis Apartments undermined that purported cosmopolitanism. Cumine's design made clear the social structure of the International Settlement: "All flats larger than the one-roomed ones have servant quarters attached to them," the *China Press* bragged, "yet it is so planned that the servants do not live in too close proximity to their employers." Having servants close enough to be constantly available, yet not so close as to be underfoot, was a feature that would appeal to Shanghailanders. The layout was furthermore meant to prevent the gathering of servants' housing on the upper floors, as was the case in most high-rise apartments in Shanghai, which had the undesired effect of disturbing tenants by "small hours of the morning enlivened with spirited games of mah jongg or poker."[48] The design not only showcased how central servants were for many Shanghailanders but also denigrated the social habits of working Chinese (not that all the Denis's residents were white: Ing Tang was one Chinese who would later live there).

HENCHMAN, AITKENHEAD, FRANKLIN, WHITE, McBain, Liddell, Cumine—all of them had ambitions to be Champion, but if they were going to challenge for the Champions' Stakes, it seemed they would have to go through the Sassoons.

Scene at the Shanghai Race Club—
probably the members' enclosure—1928.

David Sassoon had been absent from Shanghai for thirty years, selling most of his horses and taking a select few with him to Hong Kong,
after the death of Hero in 1893. He had transformed racing in Shanghai,
changing a club of amateurs into a professional racing organization in
ten years, by his commitment to winning and his refusal to compro-
mise. The success of the Sassoon stables, powered by wealth and guided
by incomparable skill at choosing, training, and riding, had beaten the
rest of the SRC at their own game. The club resented David Sassoon
because he was young—not yet thirty when he began winning Champions' Stakes—and because he was Jewish, but he had almost single-
handedly raised the standards of racing in Shanghai before vanishing.

Then, as quietly and mysteriously as he had left, a sixty-something
David Sassoon returned in 1926, around the same time as Franklin,
Aitkenhead, and Henchman, determined to pick up where he had
left off. No longer the counterculture youth who had so aggravated
his rivals in the 1880s and 1890s, he was more likely to be known as
"Nunky." That was because there were now two Sassoon stables on
Mohawk Road: Morn, belonging to David; and Eve, belonging to his
nephew, Sir Victor (who inherited the title Baronet of Bombay when his
father died in 1924).

Raised in England, Victor Sassoon had come to Shanghai after the Great War; he had served in the flying corps and survived a plane crash in 1916. The wreck left him with a noticeable limp for the rest of his life but did little else to deter him. He built a real-estate and commercial empire unrivaled in Shanghai, symbolized by the Sassoon House hotel—later the Cathay and now the Peace Hotel—at the corner of Nanking Road and the Bund. Sir Victor's themed parties—among them famous "circus parties" in which he dressed as a ringmaster—were highlights of Settlement social calendars.

When the Race Club's new clubhouse opened in the spring of 1934, the Sassoons dominated the races, as if on cue. Of the ten Champions' Stakes run between 1933 and 1938, Sassoon horses won all but one, the sole exception being the fall of 1934, when Sir Victor's Opera Eve was upset on a muddy track. Henchman, Aitkenhead, and Franklin were frustrated that they had been unable to claim the Champions' Cup, but to live as a Shanghailander in the 1930s may have been prize enough.

Cosmopolitans

Many shanghailanders felt that they lived atop a society that combined "West and East," but while their city buzzed with dozens of nationalities and languages, inequality remained dyed-in-the-wool, thanks to the extraterritoriality. Shanghai's many communities followed different laws and remained largely separate. Still, segregation diminished somewhat after the Guomindang's rise to power in the 1920s and more spaces opened to both Chinese and foreigners. These were the spaces where, for instance, Nates Wong and the Race Club Staff Club promoted cross-cultural understanding through theater, concerts, and sports tournaments, or where Chinese and Westerners could sit alongside one another at the Jiangwan races. The idealized form of this elite cosmopolitanism might have been Hardoon Gardens, the 40-acre estate on Bubbling Well Road, about a mile west of the racecourse. This was the home of Liza and Silas Hardoon and their expansive family that blurred and crossed racial and national lines, and where they entertained elites from many different Shanghai social circles.

Liza Hardoon lived her entire life between worlds. She was born in Shanghai in 1864, in the midst of the Taiping war that tore China apart and gave birth to Shanghai's International Settlement. Both her Chinese mother and her French father were recent arrivals. Liza's mother, Shen Yi, came from Fujian, several hundred miles down the coast (a reminder that most migrants to Shanghai came from within China). Drawn by the economic opportunities of the treaty ports, Shen Yi worked as a tailor and seamstress in Shanghai's French Concession, where most of her customers were the foreigners streaming into Shanghai, seemingly by the hundreds every day.

Among those foreigners was a Frenchman named Isaac Roos. Born a world away from swampy Shanghai, in the alpine foothills of Alsace, Roos made his way to China from Neuwiller, near Basel, Switzerland, in his twenties. He bounced from job to job, working for the French Concession police force in 1863 and trying his hand in several business ventures, with little success.[1] Though he was neither wealthy nor politically connected, Roos's race and nationality still conferred on him extraordinary privilege. Protected by French courts and French laws, he enjoyed a lifestyle far beyond what he could have expected in Europe.

We don't know exactly when Isaac Roos met Shen Yi, but their daughter, Liza, was born in 1864. As we have already seen, relationships between Chinese and foreigners were common, but marriage was not; elaborate schemes were often constructed to maintain appearances. Shen Yi and Isaac Roos lived together for many years but never married, pretending that Roos employed Shen as his housekeeper, even after Liza was born. Shen Yi continued her work as a seamstress and tailor. Roos accumulated debts rather than savings, and abandoned the family altogether when Liza was about three years old, although he remained in China until at least 1873.[2]

Only six years after Roos disappeared from her life, Liza's mother died, leaving Liza, nine years old, with no formal education and few prospects. Her mother's extended family took Liza in and moved across the river to Pudong, today Shanghai's financial district of towering skyscrapers, but then a rural area worlds away from the foreign concessions of Shanghai where Liza had been born.[3]

Raised by her mother's family, Liza identified as Chinese. She spoke Shanghainese as her native language, learning English only after her marriage, and Mandarin not until she was in her fifties![4] Contemporary observers, both Chinese and foreign, considered her Chinese. She was known in English primarily as Liza Hardoon (after her marriage), and acquired notoriety and fame by that name. As a girl, she was called Luosi Lirui ("Luosi" was a transliteration of her father's surname,

"Roos") and later by her Buddhist name, Luo Jialing. As a teenager, she worked in the same way her mother had, mending and washing clothes in Shanghai. She also worked—some sources say as a maid, others as a wet nurse—for several households, including some in the French Concession, where she learned some basic French and also pidgin, the English-Chinese hybrid language that facilitated trade in the treaty ports.

Rumors and speculation surround Luo Jialing's early life. She herself wrote that she worked "selling flowers"—a common Chinese euphemism for prostitution—when she was young. Some accounts confirm that she had indeed worked as a prostitute; others disagree. It is clear that Luo Jialing worked in some capacity in the foreign concessions of Shanghai, but she was neither wealthy nor famous and did not stand out among the hundreds, perhaps thousands, of young Chinese women working in service jobs in foreign Shanghai. All of that changed fundamentally through her relationship with Silas Aaron Hardoon, which began in the 1870s. It was through that partnership that she became a celebrity, so much so that her funeral, some sixty years later, would attract thousands of people, including hundreds of Buddhist monks, to one of the most elaborate homes in all of Shanghai.

The Hardoons, like the Sassoons, highlight the Jewish thread in Shanghai's fabric—not Chinese, but not fully accepted by many Shanghailanders.[5] Jewish merchants came with the influx of Europeans after the First Opium War. The two families had been connected since Bombay, where the elder David Sassoon had moved from Baghdad and where he had opened his first business in 1832. As the Sassoons flourished, the Hardoon—then spelled Hadun—family arrived, also from Baghdad, during the boom of the 1850s. Silas Aaron Hardoon was six years old.

Silas worked for the Sassoons as a teenager in Bombay before going to Hong Kong in the early 1870s, where he had failed in his first attempt to strike out on his own. Around 1874 he made his way to Shanghai, where David Sassoon, Nils Moller, and Augustus White were making their fortunes. Silas persuaded the Sassoons to give their former employee a job, but it was the slenderest of lifelines: a warehouse watchman. He supposedly earned 12 shillings and saved one each week, but whether this legend was exactly true or not, Silas Hardoon did rise from humble beginnings, and the Sassoons were instrumental in helping him get his start.[6]

By about 1880, Hardoon was working as a manager for David Sassoon's company and buying real estate, both for Sassoon and, it seems, for himself. It was around this time that he met Luo Jialing. Silas Hardoon's public and legal acknowledgment of Luo Jialing as a partner was rare. The couple did not register their marriage at the British consulate in Shanghai until 1928, but they were first married in 1886, in both Jewish and Chinese ceremonies.[7]

Hardoon took an interest in Luo Jialing's (now Liza's) Buddhism, and those connections brought him into contact with Chinese business networks that were inaccessible to most foreigners. Rumor had it that Liza advised Silas to invest in real estate rather than in some of the many get-rich-quick schemes that abounded in nineteenth-century Shanghai. Whether that was true or not, Silas Hardoon's business thrived and the family's wealth grew. The first real-estate transaction for which records survive was from 1895, when he purchased a large tract of land in central Shanghai, near Nanking Road.[8]

By this time Silas Hardoon was one of the wealthiest men in Shanghai, with an office on the Bund and the beginnings of an elaborate estate. Part of the Hardoons' fortune, immense even by Shanghai standards (as much as US$15 billion in today's dollars when he died), derived from the (legal) opium trade—an association that defined Hardoon in much of the scholarship about him published in China.[9] Central to the Hardoon's legend and to their place in Shanghai was their home. The gardens, named Aili in honor of Liza (*ai*, meaning "love"; and *li*, the first character of Liza's given name), were a fantastic landscape that could have existed in few places other than Shanghai. Designed by a Buddhist monk Liza commissioned, the gardens contrasted, or perhaps complemented, the Jewish and Buddhist elements inside the home. Buddhist pagodas and a temple, an artificial stream, Chinese theater, pavilions, and scenic spots for meditation dotted the garden.[10]

Silas and Liza Hardoon were central to many different aspects of Shanghai society, but they challenged many of their peers' prejudices. Some of the projects they supported were Jewish: The Beth Aharon synagogue (Shanghai's largest until it was demolished in the 1980s) was "the gift of Mr. and Mrs. S. A. Hardoon to the Shanghai community."[11] Others were Buddhist: Liza sponsored the publication of a complete edition of the Buddhist scriptures (which the press reported reduced their cost to potential readers by more than 90 percent, from $3,000 to $240), as well as renovations to the Jing'an Temple on Bubbling Well Road.[12] (Some, too, supported the Christian community, like opening the garden for church picnics.)[13]

The Hardoons crossed national divisions as well as religious ones. They paved Nanking Road, and also hosted fund-raising garden parties for the Allied relief effort during the Great War,[14] like the "Anglo-Chinese Garden Party" that had brought Chinese and Britons together to celebrate their common cause.[15] Even as the war was going on, the Hardoons turned their annual fall "Chrysanthemum Party" into a fund-raiser for famine relief in North China.[16] (This was itself in keeping with family tradition: a decade earlier, Liza Hardoon was one of just three women to be awarded the Qing dynasty's Order of the Golden Crop for her charitable donations for famine relief.[17])

Enormous wealth could overcome pervasive Shanghailander anti-Semitism, at least publicly, in cases like Sassoon and Hardoon (the paving on Nanking Road was supposedly in exchange for a seat on the Shanghai Municipal Council, to which Silas Hardoon was elected in 1900, the "payment" being necessary to placate opposition to a Jewish member on the International Settlement's governing body).[18] Examples like the Cumine and White families make clear that the divisions between races were not as stark as might be imagined. Nonetheless, it was exceptional for a Westerner to embrace Chinese culture to the extent that Silas Hardoon did. Even within the Baghdadi Jewish community, however, Hardoon was unusual, and many in Shanghai's Jewish community (about a thousand strong at the turn of the twentieth century) questioned both Silas Hardoon's marriage and his embrace of Chinese culture at the expense, it seemed to many, of Judaism. For that matter, it was unusual for a Chinese—especially a Chinese woman—to assume a prominent role in international society as Liza did.

The couple adopted eleven European or Eurasian children—Nora, George, Rubin, Madeline, Louis, Philip, Daphne, Maple, Emile, Leo, and Eva—who Liza agreed would be raised as Jews. Liza adopted nine Chinese children as well; they had the surname Luo (Liza's family name) were much older than the "Hardoon" children, and had their own children, who were also part of the extended family. The Chinese and European children lived separately, though they spent much time together,[19] in a melding of cultures rare even in Shanghai. Silas Hardoon observed Jewish holidays and attended synagogue regularly, while the "European" Hardoon children also celebrated Christian and Chinese holidays.[20]

The rare mingling of cultures challenged attempts to categorize the Hardoons. Was he "Baghdad Caliph of the Far East," or "Western Buddha" (both titles were applied to him in Shanghai)[21]? Was he a full-fledged Shanghailander, as his membership at the Race Club and on the Shanghai Municipal Council implied? Did Liza Hardoon become Jewish? Did Silas Hardoon embrace Buddhism? These questions mattered not only because the Hardoons were curiosities in Shanghai's segregated multicultural society, but because great sums would be gained or lost, depending on how they were answered.

When Silas Hardoon died in 1931, he left his entire fortune to Liza. Predictably, claimants emerged to challenge the will in Shanghai's British court. Shanghai's Jewish newspaper, *Israel's Messenger*, described Hardoon's exclusion of the Jewish community as a selfish tragedy.[22] Hardoon relatives from Baghdad questioned the legitimacy of the marriage altogether, backed by some in Shanghai's Jewish community, claiming that a wedding between a Jew and non-Jew was invalid and thus no basis for the inheritance existed. Others challenged the jurisdiction of the British, arguing that neither Silas nor Liza was a British subject. Some claimed that Iraqi law was in force, since Sassoon had been born there. Others invoked Jewish law. (Notably, no one in the case argued that Chinese law was relevant, even though the British consul affirmed that the court was best understood as a Chinese court that had been established with the consent of the Chinese government to administer British law in Shanghai.)[23] The court found in Liza Hardoon's favor, and she became one of the wealthiest women in the world, and one of the richest people in Shanghai, regardless of gender.

Established now in her own right as one of the wealthiest people in Shanghai, Liza Hardoon continued to dazzle—still an idiosyncratic blend of East and West, though less connected to her husband's Judaism, now that he was gone. At her seventieth birthday party, in August 1933, "streams of local residents, including many leading Chinese and foreigners, visited the garden . . . scores of Buddhist priests participated in the celebrations . . . theatrical performances . . . thousands of firecrackers."[24]

The centerpiece of the celebration was Silas Hardoon's sarcophagus, unveiled to the public for the first time. Macabre for a birthday party, but an impressive monument to the Hardoon's multiculturalism, the black-and-white marble structure was marked in English, Hebrew, and Chinese, with Silas Hardoon's biography inscribed, in gold-leaf Chinese characters, on the surrounding walls.[25] In 1935, Liza hosted a party for one of her adopted children that the English-language press found "most spectacular": "Chinese in the main, but quite a sprinkling of Mrs. Hardoon's foreign friends attended as well."[26]

The border crossing of the Hardoons was especially complex, but all of these events took place amid a burst of sinophilia that briefly captured Western arts and imagination. Shanghai—defying global depression—embodied the movement. Silas Hardoon's funeral, in 1931, had fed the West's fascination with things Chinese; descriptions of the orthodox rabbis alongside Buddhist monks at his funeral appeared in newspapers as far away as New York and Los Angeles, feeding exotic images of Shanghai as a fusion of East and West, exemplifying a hopeful cosmopolitanism that many wanted to believe in.[27]

While racist caricatures like the 1932 film *The Mask of Fu Manchu*, or more benign but still demeaning stereotypes like Charlie Chan, dominated Western views of China, there was a countercurrent. Pearl Buck's *The Good Earth* depicted proud, hardworking villagers in rural China and was the bestselling novel in the United States for two years, winning a 1932 Pulitzer Prize. The book was a sensation not just in the United States, and Buck later won the Nobel Prize in Literature. Lin Yutang's *My Country and My People* was also a bestseller. These books (and a film adaptation of *The Good Earth*) cultivated American sympathy and admiration for China at a time when planners in both countries were preparing for the possibility of war in the Pacific and a Sino-American alliance. These factors mattered in Shanghai, but there was more to it there.

Enter *Lady Precious Stream*.

Its obscurity today makes it hard to comprehend the extent of *Lady Precious Stream*'s popularity or influence throughout the English-speaking world in the 1930s. The playwright, S. I. Hsiung, studied

English at university in Beijing, graduated in the early 1920s, and moved to Shanghai, where the international environment helped him develop his skills in writing, theater, and English. Working for the Commercial Press, one of China's most important publishing houses, he translated English-language authors into Chinese (George Bernard Shaw, John Barrie, and Benjamin Franklin, to name a few), but he needed a foreign degree to land the university teaching position he coveted. In 1932, Hsiung's wife and five young children saw him off as he boarded a train that would take him to a steamer bound for Britain, where he enrolled in University College London.[28]

Hsiung went to England to study English literature, but his familiarity with China's literary past and facility with English gave him unique potential to adapt and translate works from Chinese literature. He chose as his first subject a Peking opera, *Wang Baochuan*, which was, at the time, in the repertoire of Mei Lan-fang, the most famous actor on the Chinese stage. Hsiung completed his adaptation, which became *Lady Precious Stream*, in just a few weeks in the spring of 1933.

The actress Louise Hampton in costume as Madame Wang in Lady Precious Stream, *on a cigarette card, evidence of both the popularity of the "ancient Chinese play," and of the orientalism and racism that led to white actors playing Chinese roles in yellowface.*

OGDEN'S CIGARETTES

LOUISE HAMPTON

It was quickly picked up by a producer and began a run in Birmingham in April 1934.

The Shanghai papers followed *Lady Precious Stream* from the very beginning. The same month it opened, the *China Press* wrote about "an old Chinese play" that had been translated into English and would soon open in Birmingham. The column speculated that although most parts would be played by English actors, the lead role would go to a Chinese performer.[29] This turned out not to be the case, at least in London, where the show had an entirely white cast except for one role, the "Honorable Reader," who acted as a narrator to provide context that might not be apparent to an English audience.[30]

On November 27, 1934, *Lady Precious Stream* opened at London's Little Theatre, beginning a three-year run that attracted the praise of H. G. Wells and George Bernard Shaw, among others, and earned a private performance for the Chinese legation that included as guests Wells, the Lord Mayor of London, and several British cabinet members. Queen Mary enjoyed a subsequent performance. Shanghai papers credited the play with creating "a vogue for things Chinese" in London, including art exhibitions, curio shops, and plans for a new play.[31]

Shanghailanders were both proud and envious of the play's success, sensing above all that *Lady Precious Stream* belonged there. Its author, after all, had gone to England from Shanghai, and the play's themes included a love affair between a Chinese man and a red-haired, green-eyed woman from the "Western regions" (in the original, these were the realms of central Asia, but Hsiung's version left it ambiguous). Plans for a Shanghai production of the play emerged in September 1934, just as *Lady Precious Stream* was preparing its London run.

It wasn't just white Shanghai that invested in *Lady Precious Stream*. Financial backing in Shanghai came from diverse sources. Victor Sassoon was a patron, as were author Lin Yutang and Sun Fo, the president of the Chinese legislature (and son of Sun Yat-sen). Strikingly, Shanghailander newspapers noted another advantage for Shanghai's production of the play: Chinese actors. "As everyone knows," wrote the *China Press*, "the play was first produced in London last year and is having an outstandingly successful run there. Here in Shanghai, 'Lady Precious Stream' should have much additional interest, for the first advantage over the London production is the all Chinese cast in the Shanghai version."[32]

That the English-language press promoted an all-Chinese cast as one of Shanghai's advantages relative to London was an unusual dynamic, and it underscores two aspects of *Lady Precious Stream*'s appeal: for white Shanghailanders, the play was a chance to prove their cosmopolitanism; for Chinese elites, it validated their culture. Theater in Shanghai was a common leisure activity, but the offerings were typically very English; amateur productions—frequently Shakespeare or Gilbert and Sullivan—were common. Chinese drama was rare.

Having expanded and built upon her repertoire in the 1920s from music and dress to acting, Ing Tang, now usually known as Mrs. Tsufa Lee or sometimes Ing Tang-Lee, earned the lead role, Precious Stream herself. The convergence of Ing Tang and *Lady Precious Stream* was fitting. Both existed in a mixed Chinese-British society and suggested at least the possibility of cultural fusion. The play—like Shanghai itself—was in some aspects essentially Chinese, but it was also a product of foreign influence and desire.

The source for the play was traditional—though not "thousands of years old," as some promotions claimed—but Hsiung's English-language version made changes to the story. In the original, Precious

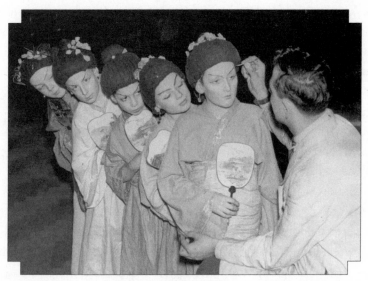

Schoolboys during a rehearsal of Lady Precious Stream.
London, 1937. The many productions of S. I. Hsiung's play hint at the West's fascination with Chinese culture in the 1930s.

Stream is forced to marry against her will, resigning herself to her fate by bowing to the wishes of her father rather than pursuing a match he deemed inappropriate. In Hsiung's version, the title character defies her father and deceives the family, enabling her to marry her true love, the family gardener (and subverting the emphasis on filial piety essential to the original). Hsiung also altered the characters' names in ways he thought would appeal to his English audience.

The theater company that would first perform *Lady Precious Stream* in Shanghai was a unique institution, the International Arts Theatre Studio. This assemblage of Chinese and foreigners had been established in the spring of 1935, the press reporting its first performances, alongside news of one of Liza Hardoon's parties, as an "amusing evening."[33] The IATS first claimed space in a renovated warehouse on Nanking Road before moving a short distance to Yuenmingyuen Road, both locations within a few blocks of the racecourse.

In terms of class, if not size, the studio matched the Race Club, though its membership was much more diverse, including avant-garde intellectuals, progressives, and artists who produced concerts, lectures, and plays. *Lady Precious Stream* was exactly what a cross-cultural troupe like IATS was seeking, and they began rehearsing the show that same spring at the Carlton Theatre, one of Shanghai's showpieces, opposite the racetrack at the intersection of Bubbling Well and Park Roads. The Carlton showed both films and stage plays, and hosted lectures as well (Jane Addams drew a large crowd shortly after the theater opened in 1923, "notwithstanding," the *North-China Herald* noted, "Champions' Day").[34]

On an especially hot July night, Shanghailanders like Arthur Henchman, Robert Aitkenhead, and Gussie White were among those in the audience when the International Arts Theatre Studio put on *Lady Precious Stream* as its inaugural production, with Ing Tang as its star (Nates Wong, one of the founders of the Staff Club, was also in the cast). "Mrs. Lee performed before a large and somewhat dubious audience . . . and completely won [them] over," reported the *China Press*.[35] The *North-China Herald* heaped praise on her performance as acted "with a great amount of charm and absolutely to the manner born."[36] The Chinese press, too, took note of the performance, praising Tang in particular for her ability to bring the Chinese play to the stage in English.[37]

The play was a smashing success. "The social world of Shanghai was completely wrapped up in the first night production of 'Lady Precious Stream,' " observed the *China Press*. "The Carlton Theater was quite the most fashionable place . . . leaders of society, government and diplomatic officials, and prominent residents, as well as near-prominent people."[38] Victor Sassoon and the wife of Wellington Koo, Chinese ambassador to the United States, were just two of the many celebrities that the press reported in the audience. "Last night at the Carlton Theater," the *China Press* went on, " 'Lady Precious Stream' became Lady Precious Shanghai."

The IATS production of *Lady Precious Stream* succeeded far beyond Shanghai. The play was going to Broadway, and Shanghai buzzed with the rumor that S. I. Hsiung himself wanted Ing Tang to play the lead role when it opened there. In December 1935, producer Morris Gest, who had acquired the right to stage the play in New York, sent a telex asking her to reprise the title role in his American production. Both Gest and Hsiung traveled to Shanghai to try to persuade Ing Tang to come to America. "Tang Ying will go to the United States to play Lady Precious Stream!" blared the Chinese-language *Tiebao*.[39]

The chance to play Precious Stream on Broadway was more than just a business offer. It showed, the *China Press* suggested, how "Shanghai seemed to gain in proximity to the Occident through one cultural endeavor or another." The Shanghai papers urged Ing Tang to take the role as much for the city's reputation as for her own career. Comparing her work to the writings of Pearl Buck and Lin Yutang, the *Press* saw Ing Tang with an even greater opportunity to bridge China and the West: "In her, one finds Chinese culture in a living being. . . . She is in and of the best Chinese society. In her are embodied the traditions of old Cathay and the ideals of contemporary China. Her education in Chinese and English has minutely qualified her as the beloved heroine . . . her success is more than certain." And to underscore the reasons for her to go, the paper concluded that if she were not persuaded to go for her own career, "there should finally prevail her sense of duty to make China better understood abroad."[40]

Shanghai's newspapers—English and Chinese—sparked with excitement. Ing Tang's invitation to New York dominated the press for some weeks, as rumors and reports of meetings, telephone calls,

Playwright S. I. Hsiung (right), with actors Mei Lan-fang (left) and Carol Coombe, at lunch in London, 1937.

and telegraphs flew. There was no resolution, though. Ing Tang never appeared on Broadway. She faded from the headlines in January and next appeared in the news in the summer of 1936, announcing that she had married H. L. Yung, an insurance executive (and another Yale graduate) in Singapore that July.[41] The couple's elaborate welcome-home party cum wedding reception helped open Victor Sassoon's nightclub, Ciro's, across the street from the Race Club and soon to be the most fashionable club in the city.[42]

It's not clear what happened to the Broadway role. Some reports suggest that the terms offered were not sufficient to lure Tang to New York.[43] It's likely that as a Chinese woman, Tang would have been offered substantially less than she might have expected for the role. It's also possible that Tang's divorce from Tsufa Lee, which took place sometime in the fall of 1935, scandalized the producers just at the time the Broadway offer was being negotiated. Whatever the case, Ing Tang did not go to Broadway with *Lady Precious Stream*. The show opened to mixed reviews in New York on January 27, 1936, with Helen Kimm in the lead role, the only Asian cast member besides the "honorable narrator." The show closed after just 105 performances.

The Chinese press in Shanghai was quick to blame the show's failure on Ing Tang's absence from the title role on Broadway, and also on a cultural divide. The *Tiebao* spent a full page reporting that "Americans don't like Lady Precious Stream," blaming their response on a failure to understand the conventions of Chinese drama, and on the absence of a star who could measure up to Ing Tang.[44]

Ing Tang was the most recognizable public face of the International Arts Theatre Studio, but she was not its only prominent member.[45] White Shanghailanders like Emily Hahn and Victor Sassoon attended the group's performances, but most of the performers on the stage of this unusual cultural conduit were Chinese. George Hardoon, one of Liza Hardoon's many children, performed in an evening of one-act plays in Chinese, drawing on his bilingual upbringing.

George, whom Liza Hardoon had adopted as an infant from a foundling hospital in Shanghai, was rumored to be half-Russian, and the press always described him as "Eurasian."[46] He was a staple of the society pages, and sometimes the front page too, for various performances as a roué offstage. About a month after his debut at the IATS, local papers reported on an escapade at Shanghai's new beach resort, Kaochiao. Along with three friends—two women and another man—George had hired two bungalows and spent a weekend at the beach, but apparently beyond his means. Presented with a $250 bill for drinks and food, George had found himself detained by the café owner while the young girls (the press reported that they were Russian but identified them only as "Joan" and "Mary") disappeared, leaving their parents to search for them in the Shanghai streets.[47]

Over the next few days, George was allowed back to Shanghai to ask his mother for money to settle the bill, but he returned to Kaochiao several times empty-handed. Liza Hardoon went so far as to publish notices in the local Chinese papers disowning George, stating that he was a fraud and that she was not responsible for any debts or bills that he incurred. Apparently, George changed her mind, and Liza paid the $250.[48] Just two weeks later, George made the papers again for trying to bribe the judges of a beauty pageant in hopes of impressing one of the contestants.[49]

PROMINENT EURASIANS LIKE THE Whites, Cumines, and Hardoons confounded many of the racial hierarchies in the city and challenged the self-image many Shanghailanders embraced that their city was a model of cosmopolitanism. As early as the 1920s, Herbert Day Lamson, an American sociologist working in Shanghai, observed the limits of Shanghai's tolerance as he studied the place of Eurasians there. "Whatever the degree of 'cosmopolitanism' in Shanghai," Lamson wrote in 1936, "it is insufficient as yet to have overcome the antipathies on both sides, native and alien, against miscegenation."[50]

Though rooted in the scientific racism of his era, Lamson's work challenged the strictly biological approach to the mixing of peoples that characterized the conventional wisdom of the time. Many scholars accepted as given that children of mixed parentage were intellectually superior to their nonwhite parent but inferior to their white one, pointing as evidence to the fact that mixed-race people gained leadership positions in much higher proportion than did nonwhites.[51] Lamson observed that in the Shanghai of the 1920s and 1930s, this wasn't the case; few Eurasians achieved much status. Lamson attributed that to several factors, including the disdain that both white and Chinese society held for racial mixing, and the "poor biological start" that "casual unions" of lower-class parents gave their offspring.

Lamson was not the only one studying the role of Eurasians in mixed-race societies. C. C. Wu, another sociologist, focused on American Chinatowns, and came to see the Eurasian as a tragic "marginal man" that both sides excluded and discriminated against. The Eurasian had extraordinary potential, Wu argued, because he—Wu focused on men—was more sensitive to cultural differences, more "cosmopolitan" and "civilized" than his peers. But this exceptionalism came at a price: Wu observed Eurasians to be vulnerable to "spiritual malaise" and "restlessness" that in extreme cases led to suicidal tendencies. Wu believed that in American Chinatowns, Eurasians—"hybrids"—were essential parts of assimilating Chinese culture into the dominant American culture, but their position left them as vulnerable as they were important.[52]

In Shanghai, Lamson saw something different. Part of the difference had to do with the reversal of the power relationships between racial groups: In the United States, the minority population was expected to assimilate into the majority. In Shanghai, it was the opposite: white foreigners were a tiny minority of the population even in the International Settlement, but they expected to keep their cultural identity and political power, while Chinese residents, it was assumed, aspired to become more culturally European.

In Lamson's view, this expectation diminished Eurasians' class status. Observing the streets of Shanghai, Lamson concluded that because the minority class (white Europeans) was the object of admiration rather than assimilation, both Chinese and Europeans looked down upon the intermediary race: the Eurasian. "The mixed blood has no prestige for either group, native or alien," Lamson wrote. There was no need for an intermediary when Chinese could aspire to emulate Western colonizers directly. Lamson pointed to "modernized pure-blood Chinese such as returned students, American-born Chinese, and those students in Chinese colleges who adopt foreign fashions" as stronger influences on Shanghai's cosmopolitanism than "the despised Eurasians."[53] Eric Cumine and Gussie White were not despised, Eurasian heritage or not, because, in Lamson's analysis: "Wealth creates prestige, and few Eurasians have any Wealth."[54] Even if not the richest of Shanghailanders, Cumine and White were among those wealthy few.

Cases like the Whites and Cumines demonstrate how the opportunities and limitations of being Eurasian varied greatly from case to case. Eric Cumine and Gussie White found that being culturally English dominated other influences. The situation was far different for others, even for those who, like Cumine and White, were members of the Race Club. Silas Hardoon, born in Baghdad to Jewish parents, was admitted to the Race Club. His wife, Liza, could attend only as her husband's guest. This distinction highlighted the arbitrary nature of race: Silas Hardoon born in Baghdad, was admitted to the club as an Englishman. The Race Club excluded Liza Hardoon on the basis of her Chinese heritage, but she was half French.

Shanghai was less colonial in the twentieth century than in the nineteenth. Still, the change was often superficial and must not be overstated; even Anna May Wong, the American Hollywood actress, was excluded from the American Columbia Country Club when a friend brought her there during her 1936 visit to Shanghai.[55] The racism of Shanghai club land was clear: appearances were what mattered, and Chinese members were not allowed.

New Shanghai

WHILE NATES WONG, ING TANG, AND GEORGE HARDOON grappled with colonial attitudes, and Arthur Henchman, Cornell Franklin, Vera McBain, and Robert Aitkenhead looked for faster horses, Dayu Doon and others continued building, literally, a Chinese Shanghai in other parts of the city. Shanghai style already combined Chinese and European architectural elements, but the Chinese elements were usually ornaments. Buildings that looked "Chinese" were viewed as "old and oriental," the antithesis of modern, international Shanghai. Doon's new Shanghai Civic Center challenged that image.

While Renaissance, neoclassical, art deco, or Beaux-Arts structures with dragons or peonies added as grace notes abounded in Shanghai, Dayu Doon's new civic center in Jiangwan displayed something different when its first elements began opening in the fall of 1933. Underneath its half-hipped, half-gabled roof—typical of Chinese official buildings for generations—the Mayor's Building was thoroughly modern in its amenities and construction. Western observers, who thought of Shanghai as an essentially European creation, felt that Doon had created a "happy combination of the East and the West, its fashioning Chinese and method of construction western. In its architectural style, the best of the East comes into a delightful intermingling with the essence of the West. China one hundred per cent Chinese from the modern point of view."[1] The Chinese press also praised Doon for "taking advantage

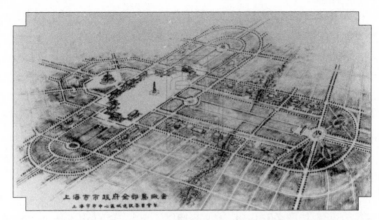

*Dayu Doon's grand 1935 plan for a New Shanghai in Jiangwan
district, several miles north of the International Settlement.*

of the best of Chinese and Western style";[2] *Shenbao* thoroughly analyzed the extensive plans for housing and an economic base for the new
district—aspects that the Western press, which focused primarily on
the aesthetics of the main buildings, paid little mind.[3]

The Shanghai government dedicated the first of the civic center's
buildings on the October 10 national holiday, and it was no coincidence that the ceremony resembled a national pageant. Airplanes cir-
cling overhead dropped patriotic leaflets on the crowd: Jiangwan was
not just a city government center, it was a point of national pride.[4] At
10:00 a.m., shouts of "Long live the Republic of China!" "Long live
Greater Shanghai!" and "Long live the Guomindang!" filled the plaza
as Mayor Wu Tiecheng prepared to address the crowd and present this
rebirth of the Chinese nation through the construction of a thoroughly
modern yet thoroughly Chinese Shanghai. The colonial presence of the
European concessions still rankled, and extraterritoriality constantly
reminded Chinese that their European and American counterparts considered them second-class citizens in their own country.

Wu had invited representatives of the foreign consular community
and military forces to bear witness to the creation of a new Shanghai.
The results impressed the foreign press: "Perhaps, before long, the
wealthy Chinese citizen may contemplate the transfer of his favor to
the Garden City of which the bare outlines now stand revealed."[5] It
is unclear why the writer suggested that only Chinese might move to
Jiangwan. Perhaps the Chinese city was still deemed beneath the inter-

ests of foreigners. Maybe it was too far away—about 5 miles—from the Bund for foreigners to find it desirable. Or perhaps its goal was segregation, a place for Chinese who would otherwise live in the Settlement. Whatever the case, Jiangwan showed at least the beginning of a Chinese Shanghai that could challenge foreign Shanghai.

A month later, on November 12, tens of thousands gathered in the plaza to celebrate Sun Yat-sen's birthday.[6] With the magnificent, Chinese-style Mayor's Building as a backdrop, Wu Tiecheng unveiled a bronze statue of Sun, the centerpiece of the celebration. Towering above the plaza at the center of Jiangwan's government district, behind the administration building, the larger-than-life statue was mounted on a platform so that Sun could survey the city's progress from more than 30 feet in the air. (This was the second Sun statue in Jiangwan, after the 1932 Shanghai War destroyed a first, which had been placed outside the North Railway Station, where Sun could welcome new arrivals.)[7]

This new statue showed Sun with a hat in one hand and a walking stick in the other, wearing a long Chinese scholar's gown underneath a short "makwa" jacket. Sculptor Jiang Xiaojian, who had trained in France in the years leading up to World War I, based the likeness on a photograph of Sun taken in Tianjin in 1924, a year before his death.

In front of this new statue, foreign and Chinese dignitaries gathered to honor Sun's memory.[8] Mayor Wu called upon the people of Shanghai to recognize the many threats facing their nation, and to honor Sun not just through ceremony but through action: "We must not limit our commemoration to erecting statues and holding meetings, but by refusing to retreat, resisting the enemy, and defending the nation."[9]

Despite the rhetoric of unity, the ceremony barely concealed deep political fissures. Out of view, machine gun posts monitored the proceedings. Motorcycle patrols increased around Shanghai, including in Jiangwan, the French Concession, and the International Settlement. Their primary concern was "Communist radicals" who were suspected of plotting to disrupt the ceremonies, but the only disturbances of the day came from the Right, not the Left. Unidentified men worked the crowd at the unveiling, distributing leaflets urging, "Only fascism can bring about national unification!" At the same time across town, members of a "Federation of Film Company Employees for the Extermination of Communists" vandalized a movie studio accused of promoting Communism, smashing windows and furniture but injuring no one.[10]

"I have served the cause of the People's Revolution for forty years, during which time my object has consistently been to secure liberty and equality for our country." These words, from Sun Yat-sen's 1925 will, were routinely read at annual national holidays commemorating the day of his death (March 12), the revolution that brought about the Republic he led (October 10), and his birthday (November 12). They rang out repeatedly in the Jiangwan Civic Center during the 1930s, echoing off of the statue's bronze features year after year as new buildings rose all around. Each time Sun's will was read, Dayu Doon's vision for the new Shanghai was closer to realization, reinforcing the connection between modern design and nationalism.

These words were read in October 1934, as the new civic center was dedicated, and again in December, as builders laid the cornerstones for the new municipal museum and library, each one evoking Beijing's Forbidden City just as Henry Murphy would have liked.[11] The 40,000-seat stadium—"largest in the Orient"—opened in the summer of 1935, part of a complex that included basketball, tennis, and volleyball courts; an Olympic-sized swimming pool; and accommodations for athletes taking part in national or international competitions.[12] Sun's words again filled the plaza in May of 1936, when the government's China National Aviation Association building—an art deco gem built in the shape of an airplane—opened, and again when the municipal library and then the art museum opened.[13] In the fall of 1936, on National Day, the chairman of the central government presided at celebrations in Jiangwan.

The city plans, and the progress made realizing them, were ambitious, but Jiangwan was still not the Shanghai of most people's imaginations. The International Settlement had grown organically, squeezed by competing jurisdictions amid land speculation, war, and migration. There was a hint of a grid in its layout—most of the downtown area was right angles and regular blocks—but plenty of exceptions revealed a lack of central planning. Some of the variations were natural, like the bends in the Huangpu River or Suzhou Creek. Others were imposed, like the shadows of previous racecourses that left roads with unexpected curves and breaks. The rush to settle and the scarcity of real estate produced dense apartment blocks and crowded alleys, even while the enormous profits to be made in the city led to lavish estates and mansions, not to mention golf courses, country clubs, and, of course, the racecourse.

Jiangwan, in contrast, was drawn on a clean sheet of paper. One of the site's attractions was its lack of development. Virtually nothing had to be torn down to accommodate the city's design, professionally conceived by urban planners trained in Chicago, New York, Philadelphia, Berlin, and Tokyo. Jiangwan was less crowded and less diverse than the alleys and avenues of the International Settlement. It lacked the extremes of wealth and poverty that made Shanghai both loved and loathed. Most fundamentally, though, Jiangwan was not administered in any way by foreign powers or people. It was Chinese sovereign territory without any impingement from concessions or settlements, and an example of what many in China hoped their nation could and would be.

Although Dayu Doon reveled in the chance to design updated homages to China's imperial past at places like the Jiangwan Civic Center, symbolically establishing China's sovereignty, he made different choices for himself. In 1935 he designed and constructed a new private home that was just what one might expect of an architect, though perhaps not of one who based his career on "Chinese revival." Doon's new home in the western outskirts of the French Concession was stunningly modernist: geometrical and bold, with flat roofs, portholes, chrome railings, and catwalks.[14] In the context of his international upbringing, in Italy, Japan, the United States, and China, the home makes sense. Doon envisioned a modern China that would take its place among the world's great nations. The home also illustrates the standards enjoyed by members of his class. A rooftop swimming pool, a horse stable, and a tennis court offered the leisure pursuits ascribed often to foreigners, but less often to Chinese.

By the summer of 1937, Jiangwan seemed finally to have arrived. The model city was nearly complete, with most of its facilities open, and it would host a celebration of China's emergence from the humiliation and colonialism that had defined much of the previous century. The new Chinese government in Nanjing, led by Chiang Kai-shek, was observing its tenth anniversary, as was the Shanghai city government that knitted together the various Chinese jurisdictions surrounding the International Settlement.

Jiangwan was the ideal spot to mark these twin occasions. Not only did it represent the modern, progressive future that many held up as China's ideal, but it did so at the doorstep of foreign power in China. The Chinese authorities put on a show, making the civic center into a fairgrounds for the celebration, with temporary stages, pavilions, restaurants, and exhibition halls arranged in its plazas and boulevards to both celebrate the tenth anniversary and announce the country's arrival as a new, modern nation.

More than 100,000 people—one report exaggerated that it was "practically the whole of the Chinese population of Shanghai"—crowded into Jiangwan[15] for twelve days of exhibitions, movie stars, boxing matches, political speeches, brass bands, and fireworks. Chinese and foreigners mingled at a grand "Monte Carlo night" at the Jiangwan race club, and of course there were races. Political instability had canceled the entire Jiangwan racing program in 1936, but the races had resumed with great fanfare in the spring of 1937, and now a special race meeting celebrated the anniversaries. The best ponies in Shanghai did not race—the event was too late in the calendar to fit the schedules of Champions' contenders—but David Sassoon, Gussie White, and Eric Cumine were among those appearing at the International Recreational Club for the event.

On the evening of July 6, the night before the festivities were officially to begin, a parade of cars, trucks, brass bands, and other marchers "almost hidden under effigies of lions, dragons, and other fantastical beasts" made its way from Jiangwan along the boundaries of the International Settlement, drawing crowds reminiscent of the throngs on Nanking Road celebrating the coronation of Britain's new King, George VI, two months earlier. The parade route, along the border of the French Concession and the International Settlement, was determined by those boundaries—Settlement authorities weren't likely to grant permission for such a display through the streets of their territory—but it also made clear the divided and colonial nature of the city. To help underscore the point, organizers erected lantern towers at key intersections along the parade route, and calls for more lanterns to line the route circulated in the Chinese press.[16]

Chinese-owned businesses throughout the Settlement advertised the parade and the celebrations in their storefronts, and in response, tens of thousands of people lined the parade route, literally outlining the extent of the foreign incursion. As daylight faded, lanterns made the procession even more spectacular, illuminating the demonstrators as they passed through normally quiet residential areas (including some of the stately suburbs where Cornell Franklin and Abel Tang had made their homes), marking their presence with music, fireworks, and headlights.[17] The procession took more than two hours to pass a single point, and 200,000 people watched it make its way from Jiangwan to the "Chinese City" south of the French Concession, where it arrived around midnight.[18]

Back at the civic center the next morning, the city's acting mayor, Yu Hongjun, stood in front of Sun's statue and waited for the strains of the national anthem to subside before formally opening the festivities. "The spontaneous enthusiasm with which the citizens demonstrate their loyalty to the city has filled our hearts not only with fresh hopes for the future of this great cosmopolitan city, but also with an added sense of responsibility towards the public" proclaimed Yu.[19] Local and national officials took the podium one after another to reiterate the same points: celebrating the anniversary of the new Chinese national government and Shanghai city government was appropriate because of Shanghai's importance to China as a gateway.

Was this the moment to start reconsidering the foreign concessions themselves? Wu Tiecheng (now the former mayor of Shanghai, having recently left the post for the Guangdong provincial administration) made bold suggestions that if China were truly to recover its national dignity, the concessions would need to go. The previous night's parade route had illustrated how the Settlement carved up China's territory. Wu was careful not to antagonize the foreigners in Shanghai, calling friendship between Chinese and foreigners (and within the foreign community too) essential to Shanghai's success and China's prosperity. But even so, Wu insisted, the Shanghai city government (that is, the Chinese government centered in Jiangwan) was the "fundamental" government of the city. Foreigners needed to be recognized as city residents, but Wu clearly saw the concessions as temporary—needing the protection of the Chinese government until "they could be recovered."[20]

Wu's successor, Yu Hongjun, called on those assembled—including invited foreign dignitaries like Cornell Franklin, the newly elected chairman of the Shanghai Municipal Council—to see the ceremonies as a pivot: a celebration that looked back on the successes of past, while working toward the goal of a stronger China in the future. Yu emphasized that this new Shanghai was an essential part of the new nation, the completion of the new Shanghai complementing the strengthening of China's republic.[21] At least some in the foreign community agreed. In its editorial praising the Jiangwan celebrations, the *China Press* argued that "the Shanghai of tomorrow must be conceived of as a single unit rather than as a group of three municipalities. While the pioneering work was performed by the foreign municipal councils . . . the future destiny of this metropolis must rest with the Chinese, largely if not entirely."[22]

Wu Tiecheng's implication that the concessions remained at the pleasure of the Chinese government was good propaganda, well received by a mostly Chinese crowd. This was a moment to celebrate Chinese sovereignty, even though the offending concessions offered the people of Shanghai more protection than could a still-weak Chinese state. Wu and other speakers on July 7, 1937, acknowledged the Japanese threat that left Jiangwan vulnerable. The Chinese state was more powerful and unified than it had been for some time, but it could not match the force that either Europe, the United States or—most crucially—Japan could project. The Shanghai War of 1932 had demonstrated this weakness, but the city had since recovered.

As part of the street fair in Jiangwan, two plays were put on. *A City Fragment* and *A Home in the North-East* were both anti-Japanese plays, calling attention to Japan's encroachment on Shanghai in the first, and to its invasion of Manchuria in the second. Settlement authorities had banned both plays to comply with Japanese protests and avoid conflict, but in Jiangwan, outside the Settlement's jurisdiction, the plays were produced, leading to a formal complaint from Shanghai's Japanese consul. But controversial theater was just a start in a conflict that would soon consume all of East Asia sooner than anyone expected.[23]

While the Shanghai government planned celebrations in the spring and summer of 1937, tensions between Chinese and Japanese troops around Beijing (then known as Beiping) had been high for some time. Several thousand Japanese soldiers were manning the garrison based in nearby Tianjin. Even though leaders on each side were reluctant to go to war, Japanese and Chinese troops were nervous, and dangerously close to one another. Commanders imposed curfews to keep people off the streets and limit chances for violence.

On the night of July 7—while celebrations in Shanghai were ongoing—a missing Japanese soldier in the vicinity of the Marco Polo Bridge near Beijing tipped the situation over the edge. By the time he turned up (apparently he had made an unauthorized visit to a brothel and missed his muster), fighting had begun; no one knows for sure who fired first. After a few days of negotiating a doomed truce, Japanese reinforcements arrived and attacked Chinese positions surrounding Beijing. By August, North China was in flames.[24]

PART TWO

A LONE ISLAND

(1937–1941)

If this state of affairs is allowed to continue, Shanghai will eventually become a "dead island."

— *CROSSROADS* MAGAZINE,
JULY 6, 1938

. . .

Beginning the End

THE FIRST AMERICANS TO DIE IN WORLD WAR II WERE NOT killed in Europe, or at Pearl Harbor, but in Shanghai.

Since opening as a treaty port in 1842, Shanghai had flourished, accessible and independent. That changed fundamentally in 1937, when war isolated the city and it became, for four years, a "lone island."

World War II in the Pacific emerged in stages over several years. Many Americans think of Pearl Harbor as its beginning, but that attack occurred more than a decade after Japan invaded Manchuria—part of a move to acquire resources and territory on the Asian mainland that had started even earlier in Korea and had sought to take advantage of China's internal division and weakness. It is more common in the West to consider the Marco Polo Bridge incident of July 1937 as the start of the Pacific War, but even after that it was unclear that the fighting near Beijing meant no turning back.

The Japanese commanders paused, assessing their options and the implications of a wider war. North China was close to Japan and its puppet state in Manchuria, making reinforcement easy and supply lines short. Limiting military action to that region could expand Japanese interests without overextending their forces. Tactical considerations were important too: troops, tanks, and other vehicles could move easily across the arid North China Plain. Farther south, marshes and creeks would slow troop movements.

While the Japanese hesitated, Chiang Kai-shek decided to act. For years, Chiang had refused to engage the Japanese, trading land for time—first in Manchuria and then in North China. Besides delaying so that he could better prepare to confront the Japanese threat, Chiang insisted that the Chinese Communists were the greater long-term threat. (His reluctance so frustrated his subordinates that one of them kidnapped Chiang in December 1936 and compelled him to ally with the Communists to fight the Japanese.) Chiang continued to believe that China needed more time to modernize and train its armies, but he decided that the actions at Marco Polo Bridge had crossed a line. With high stakes, it was time to fight, but where? Chiang wanted to push the Japanese out of North China, but counterattacking there was risky. The fighting around Beijing and Tianjin in late July had eliminated virtually all of the Chinese forces in the region; new troops would have to be moved in. Japan held a clear advantage in men and armor, and reinforcements were coming.

Aware of these challenges, Chiang and his generals decided on Shanghai. The marshy terrain mitigated some of Japan's materiel advantages. Shanghai was also close to the Chinese capital, Nanjing, and nearer Chiang's base of support. The large community of Japanese civilians at Shanghai might become a negotiating chip, and the fact that few expected Shanghai to be the starting point for Chiang's counterattack might help tactically.[1] But most of all, Chiang was counting on foreign witnesses. International opinion had played a role in settling the brief Shanghai War of 1932, and Chiang hoped to repeat that dynamic and gain sympathy for China. What Chiang needed now was a Japanese provocation to ensure that international public opinion would support China.

Early impressions suggested that Chiang's plan might work. On August 12, the *China Press*'s front page showed fourteen Japanese warships steaming up the Huangpu River above the caption "Nippon War Dogs." The accompanying story described Japanese demands that China abandon all defenses of Shanghai as 2,000 new Japanese troops moved into the city.[2] Shanghai's mayor protested the encroachments to Japanese consular and naval officials, but the invasion gave Chiang his opportunity. Chinese troops—many of them veterans of the 1932 Shanghai War—moved quickly into positions surrounding Shanghai's

"Little Tokyo." Both sides continued negotiating for a truce, but the only thing either wanted was to avoid appearing as if they had been the one to abandon talks. On the evening of August 13—Friday the thirteenth—shots fired in Shanghai ushered in a new phase of war.

The next morning, Chinese forces took the fight to the Japanese. Chinese planes flew toward the cruiser *Izumo*, moored in the Huangpu River in front of the Japanese consulate, just a few steps from the Garden Bridge, which crossed Suzhou Creek where it flowed into the Huangpu. The Chinese were eager to destroy or disable the *Izumo*'s 8- and 6-inch guns, but a first attack, at about 11:00 a.m., had missed the target, partly because of low clouds and high winds from a typhoon passing nearby. A second sortie approached a few minutes later, passing low over the towers of the International Settlement, drawing fire from guns at the consulate and on board the *Izumo*.

The battle drew the attention of Settlement residents, who had heard sporadic gunfire in the distance—most of the fighting the first night took place in Chapei, a mile or more north of the Bund—but now they saw Chinese bombers and Japanese warships just yards away. Crowds gathered on the rooftops of hotels, banks, and office buildings to watch the spectacle. Geysers erupted from the river as bombs missed their targets and black antiaircraft smoke filled a sky already shredded by the storm. Shrapnel occasionally reminded the viewers that this was the real thing and not a newsreel. There was a sense of the surreal. Many of the foreigners viewed Shanghai as an opportunity for adventure, and this might be the greatest adventure yet. The spectators gazed at the unfolding war as entertainment, "with the amused aloofness of onlookers forced to witness a drunken bar brawl."[3]

The drone of more planes, this time around 4:00 p.m., attracted spectators back to the viewing posts they had given up during a midday lull, often on the rooftops that, for someone like Arthur Henchman, were just a short flight of stairs away.[4] Hench was in his office on the Bund that day, writing nervously to his colleagues at other bank branches as the bombs fell. The situation in Shanghai was likely to become impossible, he wrote to HSBC chief manager Vandeleur Grayburn. "Chinese aircraft have just bombarded river within few hundred yards of H.S.B.C. and entire place is panic stricken."[5]

What happened next made August 14, 1937, "Bloody Saturday" or "Black Saturday" in Shanghai's International Settlement. Resuming their attacks on the *Izumo*, Chinese bombers again missed their target, but this time, instead of overshooting into the Huangpu River, their bombs fell short, setting off "a screaming hell to hundreds of Chinese and foreign civilians such as has not been seen nor scarcely imagined in this city."[6]

Five bombs fell near the intersection of Nanking Road and the Bund. One tore through the roof of the Palace Hotel. Two others damaged Victor Sassoon's Cathay Hotel—one at the main entrance, on Nanking Road, the other striking a roof cornice. Hundreds—hotel guests and workers, pedestrians, rickshaw pullers, and street vendors—were killed instantly, and many more lay dying, mutilated. Two more bombs fell just off the wharf; geysers of river water shot into the air. The Palace Hotel lobby became an emergency room and a morgue. "Children without parents and parents without children wandered helplessly over and through the maze of bomb mangled Chinese bodies."[7]

Fifteen minutes later, another Chinese plane, this one apparently

Although unoccupied and neutral until December 1941, the International Settlement was not always safe. More than a thousand people died in the bombings of August 14, 1937 (Bloody Saturday), including many here, in front of Victor Sassoon's Cathay Hotel.

damaged by antiaircraft fire and struggling to return to its airfield, made for the racecourse to drop its payload on the empty infield. The pilot missed. Instead, two bombs fell near the corner of Avenue Edward VII and Yu Ya Ching Road, about a block from the track. The crowds there were even denser than at the Bund, and the consequences were devastating. John Hammond wrote in the *North-China Herald* that he "had to walk with care to avoid stepping on a severed foot or a half-mangled head cast some distance from its torso." "Expressions on the faces of the majority of the killed," he went on, "were those of people having met an almost instantaneous death. Blood was splattered everywhere, indiscriminately mingled with articles of blown-off clothing, broken glass from shattered windows . . . pieces of brick and concrete."[8]

These bombs fell right outside the Great World Amusement Center, a pleasure palace designated, with grim irony on this day, as a relief distribution area for refugees seeking shelter in the Settlement. Within seconds, thousands of those who had gathered in hopes of finding help were dead. "Bodies were scrambled in a confusion of blood, dirt and debris," Hammond wrote. "At the entrance of the amusement center there were upwards to 200 bodies in such confusion that it resembled a human wood pile, blood spattered, maimed."[9]

Other horrors of World War II have come to overshadow Bloody Saturday, but it should not be underestimated in its own right. An accurate count of casualties is impossible, partly because so many of those killed and wounded were newly arrived and scarcely documented refugees, but at least two thousand people died and another two thousand or more were injured.[10] Most of the casualties, by far, were Chinese, but men and women of a dozen nationalities died, among them the first Americans killed in World War II. (Four Americans died that day: Robert Reischauer, a political scientist at Princeton on an academic study tour; Christian missionary Frank Rawlinson; and husband and wife Hubert and Eugenia Honigsberg.)[11]

Hench wrote from his office that "the Bund resembles a battlefield and it is only through mere good fortune that some of the banks have not been destroyed." One of the Chinese workers at his HSBC office died in the attacks.[12] This new turn challenged even Henchman's optimism. "I am informed the British Commander-in-chief regards the situation as very grave," he wrote to his superiors in Hong Kong.[13] The

British military in Shanghai, he went on, had "almost certainly decided on total evacuation," an idea that Henchman strongly opposed as "lamentably defeatist and disastrous to all our interests and would lead to serious Chinese panic and riots."[14] Hench urged his superiors to pressure London not to order the evacuation. By late August, Henchman was drafting language for London to send to Japanese diplomats assuring them of Britain's commitment to the International Settlement.[15]

Henchman succeeded; the International Settlement remained. None of the European powers in the foreign concessions, or the United States, were at war in 1937. Japan's generals were still seeking a limited war in China, preferring to restrict their operations to coastal cities and strategic centers, and hoping to avoid antagonizing the United States. For now, the foreign concessions remained neutral. Refugees still made their way in if they could. Uncertainty, sometimes panic, and increasing isolation typified the International Settlement, but it was not, usually, a war zone. Bloody Saturday, and a Japanese bomb that killed 200 people on Nanking Road ten days later, had been mistakes.

Just 5 miles away, in Jiangwan, there was no mistake; there was war. On Friday the thirteenth, the guns from Japanese warships on the Huangpu began shelling the Jiangwan Civic Center (anticipating this action, the Chinese city government had fled Jiangwan the night before). The Jiangwan racecourse was likewise abandoned, soon to be occupied by Japanese soldiers.[16] As Chinese and Japanese troops vied for control, renewed destruction and displacement accompanied each advance and retreat.

Within weeks, Dayu Doon's creation was shattered. Just a month earlier, Jiangwan had celebrated Chinese sovereignty and this new model city with a street festival. Now, those streets were battlefields where Shanghai fought for survival. Journalists invited to tour the civic center in late August painted a dreadful scene that recalled the First World War and foreshadowed the Second. "Four weeks of incessant bombardment by Japanese planes, warships, and artillery has converted the city hall, the library, the museum, the stadium, and the hospital into charred and broken monuments to the fury, the futility, and the fanaticism of war," wrote James Mills of the *Chicago Tribune*, comparing the scene to Belgian cities bombarded during World War I.[17]

Shanghai's mayor pledged to rebuild, but such promises were little more than hopes, with the city's very survival in doubt.[18] "Kwangyin, Goddess of Mercy," wrote the *North-China Herald* in mid-September, "smashed from her pedestal and lying amid the interior ruins of the Museum; smoke streams still blackening the gorgeously decorated facade of the Administration Building and whirling out of the gaping holes in its green roof; flames crackling like gunfire as they have consumed lesser structures of the young city that was to have grown into the Chinese cultural interpretation of Greater Shanghai."[19] Chinese observers, seeing their hopes for a Chinese Shanghai now a smoking ruin, described the transformation of the civic center into a battlefield as "the lost dream of our Jiangwan (*wo Jiangwan zhi mimeng*)."[20]

By late October, Japanese forces controlled Jiangwan securely enough to invite foreign observers to inspect the former city capital. "Not a single undamaged building was seen" as the caravan of reporters moved up Kiangwan Road. "Most of the buildings lacked roofs. . . . All bridges on roads leading to the Civic Centre and the Kiangwan Race Course were blown up."[21]

At the civic center itself, the roof of the Mayor's Building remained, but pockmarked with craters. The walls were blown out of the grand entryway, its once-colorful beams charred. The wings of the building where the mayor's offices had been located fared even worse. On one end, a fractured marble facade only partially covered an interior gutted by artillery and fire. At the other end, just a scorched frame outlined the remnants of Dayu Doon's monumental Chinese renaissance structure. "Here," wrote the *North-China Herald*, "in shattered beauty, we have the most direct example to date of 'man's inhumanity to man,' and thinking people are wondering how the world ever deserves to progress when warlike genius can devise such hellish treatment for some of the most intelligent works of man."[22] In three months of fighting there were 250,000 Chinese casualties.

More than a million refugees crowded into the Settlement, fleeing Japanese guns, many across the Garden Bridge to the Bund. The migration included an elite crowd who, along with themselves, relocated hundreds of horses from the International Recreation Club at Jiangwan, now in Japanese-occupied territory, to the Shanghai Race Club downtown. Among these, of course, were Chinese owners who were still technically barred from membership in the SRC, but who were granted "reciprocal privileges" because of the circumstances. By October, land mines blocked the entrance to the IRC's racecourse, which had previously been plagued by traffic jams. Artillery shells had destroyed the art deco tower that overlooked the field, which itself was cratered from shells. The entrance pavilion had been obliterated. The press declared that the damage was "not irreparable," but it was clear that Jiangwan would not host racing anytime soon.[23]

For many millions, of course, the consequences were much greater. The Battle of Shanghai that began in August lasted until November 1937. Believing their own propaganda that the Chinese forces were poorly equipped and undisciplined, the Japanese had expected a brief battle with few casualties. Instead, 100,000 Japanese troops fell in three months of house-to-house fighting, the next stage in a conflict that was engulfing all of China and much of the world. From Shanghai, the Japanese armies marched toward Nanjing, arriving at the Chinese capital on December 1. One hundred thousand Chinese soldiers defended the city, outnumbered three to one by the advancing Japanese. Within two weeks, Chiang Kai-shek ordered Nanjing abandoned and fled with his government up the Yangtze to the city of Chongqing in Sichuan province, leaving behind thousands of Chinese troops with no support or means of retreat. Imperial Japanese troops entered Nanjing.

The grandstand at the Jiangwan racecourse, considered one of the world's finest, was all but destroyed in the fighting between China and Japan in 1937.

What followed defies description. Tasked first with apprehending Chinese troops, who tried to melt into the city's civilian population to escape, Japanese soldiers soon turned to a binge of sadism that lasted six weeks. Writing for the *New York Times* in a report that was picked up by Shanghai newspapers, F. Tillman Durdin described Nanjing as "a city of terror" filled with "wholesale looting, the violation of women, the murder of civilians, the eviction of Chinese from their homes, mass executions of war prisoners, and the impressing of able-bodied men."[24]

Japanese soldiers killed as many as 400,000 civilians and raped Chinese women and girls in untold numbers. A small contingent of Westerners—mostly American, but also British and German—recorded what went on in diaries and letters. Motion-picture films smuggled out of a "safe zone" established by foreigners in the city center horrified audiences when they were shown. Durdin concluded his report with this: "[Nanjing] today is housing a terrorized population. . . . The graveyard of tens of thousands of Chinese soldiers may also be the graveyard of all Chinese hopes of resisting conquest by Japan."[25]

Rumors of atrocities in nearby Nanjing filtered into Shanghai. As the rumors gained authority, stories in the foreign press, published in the last days of 1937, showed the divide between Chinese and foreigners in Shanghai. Some, like one printed on Christmas Day, validated reports of the atrocities in Nanjing under the headline "Wild Acts of Nippon Army Confirmed." The *China Press* corroborated gruesome rumors that had circulated around Shanghai for days. "Recent reports of the wholesale massacre and rape of Chinese civilians," the story began, "and the systematic destruction and looting of property at Nanjing by Japanese soldiers who ran amok upon their entrance to the recent capital have been fully substantiated from foreign sources."[26]

Observers described being unable to walk a single city block without encountering at least one body, and being nauseated by the massacre of Chinese soldiers taken prisoner, as well as civilians being abducted and raped at bayonet point while their homes were plundered or burned. The Japanese empire, one informant wrote, had debased itself with its indescribable and inhumane actions. Shanghai newspapers collected reports from around the world—the *New York Times*, *Chicago Daily News*, Associated Press, Reuters, and even Japanese newspapers (which published, for instance, the now-infamous story of two Japanese officers in a race to kill 100 Chinese first—then extended to 150 when the first competition was deemed a tie). Newspapers welcomed Shanghailanders to 1938 with reports of "the orgy of looting, murder, and rape that took place following the entrance of Japanese soldiers into the Chinese capital."[27]

Other stories—some printed on the same day and in the very same newspapers—portrayed a very different attitude toward Japan's war on China. When Japan lifted restrictions on entering the former conflict zones, foreigners streamed across the bridge to see what had happened. The crowd was almost entirely foreign: Chinese were not permitted into the area without special passes from the Japanese military authorities, while foreigners required no documentation (unless they wished to take photographs). Some of the foreigners visiting Hongkou and Jiangwan came to survey the damage and, in some cases, tend to damaged or lost property. But others had different concerns: "Sukiyaki houses were crowded with foreigners who had not tasted bona fide Japanese dishes for more than four months."[28] Food was also on the mind of Shanghailanders who wanted seafood; shrimp, in particular, but also fish, veal, and pork, dropped in price when the Hongkou markets reopened.[29] What it meant to be foreign in China—and especially in Shanghai— was never so clearly, or so disturbingly, demonstrated.

The Battle of Shanghai and subsequent destruction of Nanjing proved that a wider war was under way, and the Japanese strategists who had paused in North China now proceeded with their plans. Japanese forces had invaded almost every major coastal city in China by the spring of 1938, and all of eastern China north of the Yangtze River. Shanghai—more specifically the International Settlement and the French Concession—was a Lone Island.

FROM THE FALL OF 1937 until December 8, 1941, the distinction between the concessions and the rest of Shanghai became sharper and clearer. The term *gudao*—"lone island" is one translation, but "isolated," "lonely," or "solitary" are used as well—was coined to describe this city within a city. During the Lone Island period, both parts of Shanghai—one foreign-controlled and the other foreign-occupied—

changed. The foreign concessions' population surged. The International Settlement doubled, from 1.5 million to 3 million, after 1937 as refugees seeking the safety of the Settlement poured in from surrounding areas. Most of these migrants were poor, but not all of them; Chinese of means also relocated to the Settlement. Inflation, driven by scarcity and demand, affected the two groups very differently, as those without much to start with found themselves in increasingly desperate circumstances.

Outside of the International Settlement, within weeks of the Chinese withdrawal Japanese officials began renaming streets in Jiangwan "in line with the postbellum situation," replacing names like "Minzhu" (Democracy) or "Zhongshan" (Sun Yat-sen's name in Mandarin) with the names of Japanese cities, military officers, or royalty.[30] In March, the wreck of Dayu Doon's Mayor's Building (the mayor's administration building) framed a military parade as Japanese commander in chief in China General Shunroku Hata reviewed his victorious troops. For nearly two hours, columns of soldiers filed past the bombed-out frame that had been the seat of Chinese government in Shanghai. Japanese planes maneuvered overhead, "nearly touching the shell-torn dragon atop the Administration Building."[31]

Jiang Xiaojian's statue of Sun Yat-sen that had been erected in 1933 came down in the first weeks of the war. Several photographs show the empty pedestal, surrounded by celebrating Japanese soldiers; another shows the statue lying on the ground in September, surrounded by Japanese soldiers draping it with a Nationalist flag while the caption is clear in claiming that Chinese, not Japanese, fire had brought it down.[32] At some point in the fall, the statue was replaced with a new memorial. The replacement was not a statue and did not celebrate the Chinese revolution or its leader, but was instead a plaque emblazoned with characters honoring the Japanese soldiers who had died in the fighting. The statue of Sun Yat-sen disappeared, its fate unknown. (The pedestal remained empty until 2009, when a new statue of Dr. Sun was erected.)

The statue gone, the plaza gutted, and the buildings burned, there were no national celebrations in Jiangwan that autumn. For the first time in a decade, the October 10 National Day and Sun's November 12 birthday went unobserved in 1938. The same would hold true in 1939,

Arthur Henchman in his HSBC office.

and again in 1940. The lack of a celebration was unsurprising: What was being celebrated? Who would celebrate it? Jiangwan had been meant to mark a revival of Chinese nationalism, but now the Nationalist government was on the run, its New Shanghai all but destroyed. Just months earlier, Nationalist officials had looked forward—naively?—to a bright future, maybe even one in which the foreign concessions would be returned to Chinese control. No longer. (Ironically, the war *would* ultimately end extraterritoriality in China, but it would doom Chiang's Guomindang too.)

Instead of a national celebration that fall, the Jiangwan Civic Center—still being rebuilt—saw the inauguration of Fu Xiaoan, a sixty-seven-year-old banker, as the new mayor of Shanghai.[33] In a place known for complicated and overlapping jurisdictions, this may have been the most fraught. Chiang Kai-shek's government had created the office that Fu held in 1927 to demonstrate China's renewed sovereignty and to challenge the foreign powers that dominated Shanghai. Now, the office would be filled by a foreign power that was not just dominating Shanghai economically, but occupying it militarily. (Fu Xiaoan wasn't even Japan's first choice in Shanghai: an odd figure named Su Xiwen, who spoke little Chinese after being raised and educated in Japan, had been "mayor" since December, but Su's desire for autonomy had annoyed the Japanese, who edged him out.)[34] Now, to consolidate their power, and with Chiang's government in exile, the Japanese installed Fu Xiaoan, a collaborator occupying an office created to bolster patriotism. It is little wonder that Shanghai's foreign press called Fu the "so-called 'mayor.' "[35]

CHAPTER

I I

· · · ·

Crossroads

*When the Japanese occupied Shanghai outside the International
Settlement, hundreds of thousands of refugees streamed into the
Settlement, seeking protection from the war.*

THE TITLE OF NATES WONG'S MAGAZINE REFLECTED THE
realities of his life in Shanghai after 1937: *Crossroads* (in Chinese, *Shizi
jietou*). Shanghai had long been a commercial meeting point, but Wong
may have had the city's new political circumstances in mind. Shanghai
was a complex and dangerous junction of powerful forces pulling all of
China in different directions.

Wong wasn't the first to apply the term to Shanghai. A left-wing magazine by the same name had ceased publication in 1932. A film called *Crossroads* was released in Shanghai just months before the Japanese invasion in 1937. Shen Xiling's romantic comedy told the story of four recent college graduates, all coming to Shanghai to look for work, and was a huge success, weaving together themes of patriotism and modernization amid economic uncertainty.[1]

In the film *Crossroads*, a young woman answers her landlady's questions about her plans by explaining, "I just graduated. I came to Shanghai to do things." The older woman nods with a mixture of concern and understanding, repeating under her breath, "A young woman, coming to Shanghai to do things."[2] Tens of thousands—mostly young men and women—had come to Shanghai from all across China to do things, taking part in a flowering of literary culture that exemplified China's "New Culture" era. Dozens of China's most important writers lived in Shanghai at the time, often in the International Settlement or the French Concession.

Nates Wong was not famous, like Lu Xun or Mao Dun, but we can imagine that he spent his time like many who lived in the International Settlement, with modest means but expansive ambitions, in "alleyway-house neighborhoods—where working-class types rubbed shoulders with teachers, artists, writers, shop clerks, officer workers, small business owners, prostitutes, and priests."[3]

One former writer, who shared Nates Wong's age and occupation, described passing long evenings with friends in "pavilion rooms" in traditional courtyards, smoking cigarettes, discussing national and world politics, wondering about what life had in store for them next, or where they would go from the crossroads where they found themselves.[4]

It's not clear that Wong had either the earlier journal or the movie in mind when he started his magazine, but "crossroads" fit the city, especially at this moment. For the graduates in the film, Shanghai was a place of optimism and opportunity, but after 1937, political and military circumstances made it one of confusion more than optimism, and danger more than opportunity.

To begin, there was not just one China at this time, but at least three. Most of coastal China—including Shanghai outside the International

Settlement and the French Concession—was occupied by Japan. The process of occupation was complicated and varied greatly within this region. In Shanghai, the Japanese first established a puppet government called the Reformed Government of the Republic of China, which was run, in name, by Chinese collaborators (the first of which was assassinated). That regime became part of a new "Reorganized National Government" (RNG) in the spring of 1940 under the nominal leadership of Wang Jingwei (the man Arthur Henchman would see called out in pamphlets and posters as a "puppet" and a "traitor" as he made his way to Champions Day 1941). Wang's colorful and eventful career in twentieth-century Chinese politics appeared to have ended when he lost out to Chiang Kai-shek during the Guomindang's struggles over Sun Yat-sen's legacy. Relegated to the sidelines during the Guomindang's "Nanjing Decade," he saw an opportunity for power in the Japanese invasion, and became head of a "peace movement" and then of his own "Republic of China," even if it was one that existed only at the pleasure of an occupying army.

Chiang Kai-shek's government—also called the Republic of China—claimed legitimacy while fighting for its life. From its wartime capital in Chongqing, "Free China" would go on to be one of the Big Five powers in World War II and eventually to become one of the five permanent members of the United Nations Security Council, but all that was in the future. Until the United States and Britain entered the war with Japan, in December 1941, the Nationalists controlled little territory and few resources as they struggled desperately just to survive against the Japanese. But the powers whose nationals ran the International Settlement still recognized Chiang's government.

The third division was the Communists' "Red China," based in the distant northwest. The Communist Party had started in Shanghai, opening its first congress in the International Settlement in 1921. Barely surviving the massacre of 1927, the party had narrowly eluded destruction through a yearlong retreat, starting in the fall of 1934, called the Long March. Covering many thousands of miles from the mountains of southeast China to the deserts of the northwest, the Long March enabled the rise of Mao Zedong as party leader and became a foundation myth for the Communist Party, although fewer than 10,000 of the 100,000 soldiers who had begun the march remained. In the hills of

Shaanxi, Mao solidified his leadership and began building popular support and a cult of personality, both of which would emerge into public after 1949, when he founded the People's Republic.

All three Chinas collided in Shanghai, the crossroads. The Japanese sponsored Wang Jingwei's regime in most of the city. Meanwhile, the International Settlement provided cover for supporters of both the Nationalist and Communist movements. Just a few months earlier, at the ten-year anniversary celebrations for the Shanghai municipality, Chinese and foreign officials had talked publicly about doing away with the foreign concessions. The Japanese invasion had removed this idea from anyone's agenda, and now the concessions' existence was the only thing protecting the center of Shanghai from invasion.

For Shanghailanders, the war so far was mostly a nuisance, sometimes affecting business (Eric Moller couldn't import steel to repair his ships because of American embargoes) or daily life (inflation became a persistent threat). In isolated cases, like Bloody Saturday, Shanghai was dangerous and even deadly, but for the most part, elite lives went on as before. This was not the case for the many refugees—Russian, Chinese, and Jewish especially—who fled to Shanghai to escape revolution, war, and persecution. Their lives had been utterly disrupted, yet the Settlement offered at least a temporary reprieve.

But Chinese like Nates Wong were in a different category. Wong lived in the International Settlement, on Yates Road, not far from the racecourse. He acted in the International Arts Theatre Studio, in front of Victor Sassoon and Gussie White, and performed alongside Ing Tang when she was scouted to appear on Broadway. Dressed in Western-style suits and living comfortably, Wong did not enjoy the extraterritorial protections that foreigners did, but the foreign presence shielded him from the war all around. China was his native country, but in many ways he was an alien in Shanghai.

In the Race Club Staff Club album, Wong had written optimistically about cooperation between Chinese and foreigners just a year earlier, in 1937. This had long been a topic of interest; he had published an article on "the history of inequality between China and the West" in the YMCA journal, *Shanghai qingnian* (literally, "Shanghai Youth," but rendered in English as "Shanghai Young Men," to match the YMCA's name).[5] Wong celebrated the club as a way to help people in need, but also as a way to promote friendship and understanding, not only between foreigners and Chinese but also within the Chinese community itself. That had changed. In the summer of 1938—less than a year into the Lone Island period—Wong began publishing *Crossroads*, even though its commentary on Chinese-foreign relations in Shanghai did not make the Settlement's foreign administrators happy.

Their displeasure was, at first blush, puzzling. *Crossroads* regularly attacked Japan and its occupation but had little bad to say about Britain. Still, the Brits and Americans who ran the Settlement knew how vulnerable their oasis was. After 1937, the boundaries of the International Settlement existed only because the Japanese army chose to respect them. Japan's reluctance to invade was all that stood between the Settlement and the war outside. Local Japanese authorities pressured the Shanghai Municipal Police to enforce their policies with the thinly veiled threat of what was to come if the SMP did not comply. That's why Detective Chief Inspector David Bannerman Ross, of the SMP's Special Branch, was not pleased with *Crossroads* and wanted to speak with its editor in July 1938.

On Ross's desk was a translation of an article from Wong's magazine, blaming "subjects of a certain nation" for a string of fatal hit-and-run accidents in the Settlement, including one that had killed five people (police could find no evidence to support these allegations). The article described Shanghai's streets as "the mouth of a tiger" and implied that the Japanese were responsible for the threat to public safety. Publications like this could provoke the Japanese to claim "anti-Japanese agitation" in the Settlement and erode its autonomy, and that was exactly what the SMP wanted to avoid.

The article had no byline, so Ross called in the magazine's editor to account for what his magazine had printed. On June 20, at the Shanghai Municipal Police station on Foochow Road, Nates Wong was warned against printing anti-Japanese sentiments. DCI Ross would suspend the magazine, he told Wong, if the warning was not heeded. Wong replied that both the author of the article and the editor of the issue in question had already been fired, and efforts to locate either of them had failed.[6]

Ross was likely not gentle with Nates Wong. An artillery veteran of World War I, Ross was well known in the police force for his rough attitude, and sometimes actions, toward both the public and his fellow officers. Questioning Wong had been a nuisance, so when another article caused Ross to summon Wong again to the station, just a few weeks later, the inspector's patience was already stretched thin. This time, the subject was an article printed in Chinese under the pseudonym Dian Chun, a nonsensical name in Chinese, but a very common surname when pronounced in Japanese: Tanaka. (There's no way to know whether Ross recognized the name's unusual nature.) The first article, about traffic accidents, implied that Japan was a threat to the Chinese people, but this second one could not have been more explicit:

AN APPEAL TO CHINESE IN SHANGHAI

After the withdrawal of the Chinese forces from Shanghai, all the districts around this city were occupied by our enemy. Ostensibly, we are leading a life of peace and tranquility in the Foreign Settlements, but actually we are living under a yoke of strong oppression.

In former times, we were at liberty to walk about in the streets of the Foreign Settlements, but now conditions are totally different for we are liable to meet with any kind of unpleasant experiences at all times and places. Take, for instance, the occurrence of the numerous bombing incidents and the discovery of human heads and arms, etc. This alone is sufficient proof that this isolated island is now a centre of terrorism.

If this state of affairs is allowed to continue, then Shanghai will eventually become a **"dead island" wherein our fellow countrymen will very likely become slaves, because the island is now completely surrounded by "devils." If the Chinese residents still maintain an indifferent attitude and fail to take any action to deal with these "devils," they will meet with more oppression** when more strange reports will appear in local papers and cases of terrorism will be so numerous as to be beyond endurance. We should intensify our struggle against these "devils" and at once reveal our real strength and courage so as to drive away these "devils" from our soil.[7]

Nates Wong told Ross that he agreed the article was unacceptable. He explained that he had rejected it initially, returning it for revision, but that the author "did not take my hint" and resubmitted the article with only minor revisions. Wong blamed an error in the production process for allowing the article to make its way into publication. He promised to reprimand the author and his editorial staff and to make changes to the process that would ensure such a mistake would not happen again.[8]

Crossroads soon ceased publication, though there is no record to indicate whether that was the result of police action.

The pressure on Nates Wong points out, again, the different standards facing Chinese and foreigners in Shanghai, and the tension surrounding both during the Lone Island period. The Japanese and the British-run police considered Chinese patriotism or resistance to occupation to be provocative. Nates Wong had lived for decades in an environment of imperfect cooperation between Chinese and foreigners, run through with condescension and racism, to be sure, but aspiring to a cosmopolitan ideal. This new environment, with a hostile army at his door and intimidation from former allies, represented a new challenge.

Ironically, Wong and David Ross agreed more than either knew. Although he had forced Wong to comply, Ross disagreed with the SMP policy and would eventually leave Shanghai to join the Royal Australian Air Force. He wrote in July 1940 that Britain was "fighting for her life. It is undesirable for British staff members of the SMC to maintain the status quo in Shanghai. We should return to [Britain] to rescue her in her crisis." (Ross, under pressure, denied having said what the newspapers printed, but many officers in the SMP felt guilty about remaining in Shanghai while Britain fought for survival.)[9]

Ross's concerns notwithstanding, few in the Settlement were committed to resisting Japan. Censorship cases like Nates Wong's led not to resistance, but to more censorship. In the summer of 1941, the Municipal Council banned words and phrases that might offend Japan and distributed a list of these to all newspapers in the Settlement. Insults like "Japanese devils" were obviously rejected, as were phrases like "concerning the honor of the Japanese army." The proscription included vocabulary that evoked the allegations (or documentation) of Japanese atrocities like those at Nanjing and other Chinese cities: "indiscriminate bomb-

David Bannerman Ross of the Shanghai Municipal Police questioned Nates Wong about the provocative anti-Japanese articles published in his magazine but later resigned the force in protest over the SMP's solicitous attitude toward the Japanese.

ing," "use of poison gas," "cruel treatment of Chinese people," "raping of Chinese women," "field of corpses," or "ruthless burning of Chinese homes." Any incitement to violence was to be avoided, including most broadly, "news or statements which can have a detrimental effect on the local situation or can disturb peace and order."[10]

THE LONE ISLAND PERIOD challenged all of Shanghai's residents as they tried to make sense of the new realities. The International Settlement and the French Concession had always been unusual places, but now they were even stranger, surrounded by hostile soldiers who could overrun the Settlement at will if they chose to. Much depended on citizenship, and with so many nationalities packed into a small area, dozens of national flags flew around the city as people proclaimed their national affiliations. If the Settlement police feared that accusations of hit-and-run drivers could upset the fragile balance, it's not surprising that flags worried them.

When the International Settlement was first established, there was no Chinese flag, making the flying of a Settlement flag less of an affront to Chinese sovereignty. Though standard to European systems of state-craft and diplomacy, flags were not common in East Asia. China (which is to say, the Qing dynasty) did not have an official flag until 1862, and even that—a triangular ensign featuring a blue dragon embroidered on a yellow background—flew only at sea, to identify Qing vessels for enforcement of the treaties that had ended the Opium Wars. Not until 1889 did the Qing adopt an imperial flag, a rectangular version of the naval flag.

Ever since the establishment of a treaty port at Shanghai, a series of different national flags had flown over it. The Qing dragon flag was replaced by the first flag of the Republic of China in 1912. This "five-color flag," with horizontal stripes of (from top to bottom) red, yellow, blue, white, and black, was China's national flag until 1928, when the reunified Republic under Chiang Kai-shek adopted a new flag based on the Nationalist Party emblem. The Guomindang's white sun on a blue field became the upper left quadrant of a new national flag, the rest of it red (this flag remains in use on Taiwan as the flag of the Republic of China). It flew over Shanghai until the autumn of 1937, when Japanese armies invaded.

After 1937, and including the Lone Island period, several flags were flown by the Japanese-backed "Chinese" governments in Shanghai. From 1938 to 1940, the Reformed Government adopted a modified version of the Republic's old five-color flag, adding a torch in the center above the Chinese characters for "peace" and "national reconstruction." When that government was absorbed into the new Reorganized National Government in March 1940, the regime headed by Wang Jingwei adopted a variant of the Guomindang's Republican flag, using the same red flag with blue field and white sun as before, with the addition of a yellow triangle at the top left, on which were printed six Chinese characters spelling "peace," and "national construction" like the previous flag, but adding "anticommunism."

The Republican flag *without* the yellow pennant remained the flag of the Free China government in Chongqing that foreign powers other than the Axis recognized. In most of Shanghai, nominally controlled by Wang's Republic, Japanese police enforced the law, and the flag of Free China—a government at war with Japan—was illegal. Any displays of the Free China flag there were swiftly and severely punished, by order of the mayor of the city, Fu Xiaoan. Yet in the Settlement, Chiang's government was seen as legitimate, and its flag, in theory, was welcome.

The flagpole at the racetrack (formerly the mast of a British warship) flew the colors of the Shanghai Municipal Council. Appropriately, the flag combined many different ideas and nationalities, not always in ways that made sense. The background was the British cross of Saint Patrick, diagonal red on a white field. A ring, with the words "Shanghai Municipality" written at top and bottom, occupied the flag's center. Inside that outer ring was the Latin motto of the SMC: *Omnia Juncto in Uno* ("all joined as one") as well as the Chinese characters 工部局 (*gongbuju*). The Chinese text literally means something like "public works department," perhaps derived as a translation of London's "Metropolitan Board of Works." Converging at the flag's center were three shields, each divided into the flags of the countries represented in the Settlement. The arrangement is haphazard: there were eleven treaty powers at the time of the flag's adoption in 1868, and eleven nations are represented, but the lists don't quite match (Belgium had a treaty but is not represented, and the reverse is true of Austria and Portugal).

The French Concession, formally a part of France, followed different rules from either the International Settlement or the Shanghai municipality, further complicated when France fell to Nazi Germany in the spring of 1940. From this time forward, France was an ally of Japan, but even before this the French authorities in Shanghai were vulnerable to Japanese pressure. At Japan's insistence, the French Concession agreed to break with decades of precedent and suppress displays of the Chinese flag during national holidays. The French concession's municipal council justified its decision by saying that flying the flag was objectionable only when connected to "political activities." Chinese newspapers scoffed at the justification, noting that national flags were essentially political symbols and displaying them—or prohibiting their display—was always a political act. The paper protested that "the order for the removal of the Chinese flags was carried out closely following the local puppet mayor's demands."[11]

The authorities of the International Settlement faced the same pressure from the Japanese as those in the French Concession, and the man who had to deal with the pressure was Cornell Franklin, as chairman of the Shanghai Municipal Council. In 1939 Mayor Fu Xiaoan insisted that the International Settlement ban all displays of the Chinese national flag and the Guomindang flag, as had been done in the French Concession.[12]

The ban, according to the Japanese, was necessary to safeguard "peace and good order" throughout the city. Without it, the Japanese navy and army ministers warned, the International Settlement would be considered an ally of the exiled Nationalist government in Chongqing.

Franklin's response satisfied neither side. Asked if the Settlement would ban displays of the Chinese flag, as the Japanese demanded, Franklin replied that it was beyond the SMC's legal power to do so. However, he did oversee regulations that would forbid display of the flag "in connection with political campaigns." To enact this policy, Franklin met with influential Chinese leaders in the Settlement and requested that the flag be flown on only the eight officially designated Chinese national holidays, one of which was Sun Yat-sen's birthday: November 12.[13]

The first test of the policy came just a week after it was announced. May 6, 1939, was the anniversary of Sun Yat-sen's election as president of the Republic in 1921, one of the eight holidays designated for flying the flag. In anticipation, Chinese shopkeepers on Yates Road (where both Nates Wong and Gussie White lived) raised the national flag the day before. The Japanese consulate complained, and the Settlement police arrived immediately to confiscate the flags. In response, more than 150 Chinese flags emerged from surrounding and nearby businesses, leading to an unlikely spectacle: Yates Road was the place to buy lingerie in Shanghai, and shop windows were now filled with lace and satin fluttering alongside rows of Chinese flags. Crowds and still more police arrived. By day's end, all the flags had been taken down and order maintained. The following day, national flags flew from nearly every Chinese-owned store in the Settlement, lining Nanking Road as it ran from the Bund to the racetrack. Anti-Japanese graffiti and leaflets appeared as well, but no organized protests or demonstrations took place.

Even though the Settlement police had enforced their regulations, Japanese officials and newspapers howled in protest at the appearance of the Guomindang flag. "We the Japanese are continuing the hard struggle of 'iron and blood' for the construction of a new order in East Asia," wrote one newspaper, which went on to protest that seeing the national flag, even for eight days a year, was like "being told not to interfere with neighbours who, hidden in sheltered places, abuse us."[14]

The Japanese consistently pressured Settlement officials to clamp down on any indication of Chinese nationalism, and they demanded that all displays of the Chinese flag be banned. The Settlement resisted this requirement, and Franklin, who would have preferred to worry about his horses or his law practice, found it increasingly easier to accommodate Japanese demands than to resist them.

Races Renewed

ARTHUR HENCHMAN, CORNELL FRANKLIN, AND ROBERT Aitkenhead also found themselves at a crossroads. It was not that same one facing Nates Wong or Dayu Doon. Their nations were not (yet) under threat in the way that China was, even though their livelihoods were in danger. Extraterritoriality still protected them from Chinese law, but even more important, their status as foreigners kept them—and their ponies—safe from the Japanese, for now at least. The stakes

Arthur Henchman leading one of his horses at the Shanghai Race Club. This is probably Northwood, whose best Champions' finish was third, in the fall of 1940.

for the Chinese were their very survival; the Shanghailanders were concerned with a different sort of stakes.

The races that had provided diversion for Shanghailanders with too much time on their hands now offered distraction for a community trying to ignore its predicament. Refugees and blockades led to shortages; scarcity and profiteering drove prices of food and other essentials ever higher. Japanese soldiers policed large areas of the city as British and Japanese officials negotiated whose police would patrol which sections of the city's western "Badlands." From the Race Club's rooftop garden high above the track, Henchman, Franklin, Aitkenhead, and the rest could see the gun placements and sentries that guarded the entrances to the International Settlement. For anyone with a knowledge of international affairs, the situation appeared dire. To those who knew less, it may have seemed even worse.

Like Nero, they played on.

The smoke from the 1937 Battle of Shanghai had barely cleared when racing resumed. Despite rumors that war would cancel Champions Day for the first time, it delayed the autumn races only a few weeks. David Sassoon's Radiant Morn won his fourth Champions' on December 8, in front of a small crowd of 4,000 spectators. A Sassoon pony at the front of the field suggested that little had changed, but the Settlement's status quo had been shaken, and those changes were coming to the races too.

While refugees streamed into the relative security of the International Settlement, those who could considered whether it was time to get out of China. Sir Victor Sassoon had started hedging his bets on Shanghai in the early 1930s, convinced that Japan's imperial expansion would not end with Manchuria. Sir Victor publicly discounted the threat of a wider war, but privately he began to plan for the end to Shanghai's foreign enclave. He had been spending more time away from Shanghai, starting in the summer of 1937—just weeks before the war would begin—and he steadily reduced his holdings in the city, including selling off his stables. Sir Victor ran ponies from his Eve stable in Shanghai for the last time in 1937 (a few continued to race for new owners), though he maintained a string of ponies in Hong Kong.

Sir Victor Sassoon was still away for the next Champions Day, in May 1938. Surrounded by war, Shanghailanders could no longer travel around China. The vacations to the mountains or up the Yangtze by houseboat were now impossible, as were business trips to other Chinese ports. Overseas travel—back home to Britain or America, for instance—could still be managed, but Shanghai under siege was hardly attracting newcomers. The Japanese encirclement of the Settlement was in its sixth month. Foreign consulates were advising their nationals to leave, but many Shanghailanders ignored these warnings and instead threw their resources and time even more aggressively into the racetrack. Crowds that had diminished in the mid-1930s rebounded to record levels. With the Jiangwan and Yangtszepoo tracks now closed by war, the Shanghai Race Club was the only game in town.[1]

"Armies come and go," wrote the *China Press*. "Depressions lay their icy fingers on trade and commerce, the Dollar performs its daily dozen to the great dejection of those who are not 'in the know,' but the Champions go on for ever."[2] Little was stable about Shanghai in 1938, but at least the Sassoon horses could be counted on. Radiant Morn, owned by David Sassoon (Sir Victor's uncle), was the favorite to win a fifth Champions'—one short of David's own legendary Hero. Henchman hoped to spoil Radiant Morn's run with Roehampton, who contended all the way but faded down the stretch to lose by a length and a half. It was Hench's second runner-up finish in a year. Radiant Morn confirmed his place as one of Shanghai's best ponies ever. But the performances on the track were almost beside the point. Shanghai had shown it could continue even under siege, thanks to this race "that cracked the city's wartime blues wide-open."[3]

But the blues soon returned. Just ten days after Radiant Morn won his fifth Champions', David Sassoon passed away at the age of seventy-three, never fully recovered from the double pneumonia he had contracted two years earlier.[4] The success of the spring 1938 Champions Day tempted Shanghailanders to think that their world might not be in jeopardy after all, but David Sassoon's death symbolized the sweeping changes that were under way, and reminded Shanghailanders that the world they had known was changed. Radiant Morn's win would be the last Sassoon race in Shanghai: Sir Victor had almost entirely relocated his Eve stable to Hong Kong. Now, David's unexpected passing shut down the Morn stable.

Grief over "Nunky," as everyone now called him, was widespread.

Few seemed to remember the venom that had driven him out of Shanghai in the 1880s when rival owners complained that his dominance at the track was draining the drama and fun from Shanghai's racing. Almost all of Shanghai's prominent racing figures—though not David's nephew Victor, who was in North America—attended the funeral at the Jewish cemetery on Mohawk Road, a few short yards from the finish line that Radiant Morn had just crossed. Mourners crowded into the graveyard, a tiny patch of grass and headstones overshadowed, literally, by the Race Club, to observe the simple ceremony. As the crowd fell silent to let the rabbi offer his closing prayer, a racehorse in the nearby stables whinnied.[5]

It seemed obvious that the races couldn't continue—how could racing go on in the midst of a war?—yet continue they did. The following fall marked a year since the Battle of Shanghai and his consulate wanted him to leave, but Henchman was all in on the city. He had confidence in the Settlement and in the safety net his connections provided, but what he really wanted to justify his commitment was his first Champions' win. The Autumn Race Meeting of 1938 seemed a golden opportunity.

For a decade, a Sassoon pony had been favored to win every Champions'. This time, there were no Sassoon entries at all. The owners who remained reveled in the new opportunity. "For a long time," wrote the *China Press*, "Shanghai has not seen such an open Champions as it will today in the absence of Radiant Morn."[6] Henchman's Roehampton had twice finished runner-up, but neither of those horses was running on this day. Radiant Morn was, like his owner, gone from the Shanghai races, and Henchman's stables had a new top pony, Bagshot. Vera McBain had bought Sparkling Morn, the only other horse to win the Champions' in three years, and renamed him Magic Circle. Billie Liddell and Vera McBain's We Two stable, Eric Moller, Henchman, and Gussie White were poised to fill the void left by the Sassoons' absence. Billie Liddell's Cordon Rouge attracted most of the money, though there was also buzz in the grandstands over Moller's Cire stable because of what had happened in Hong Kong that spring, when Silkylight had taken down the legendary Liberty Bay.

The wide-open field encouraged the participants, but so much was new about the fall 1938 Champions' that it made fans and bettors nervous. There were no previous Champions' winners in the field—a rare occurrence in Shanghai—and that would make race strategy unpredictable. The Sassoon style had been to go strong from the start and lead wire to wire. (That habit lived on in a handful of former Morn ponies acquired by other owners, including a gray, named Phantom Morn, that Cornell Franklin bought and renamed simply Phantom.) Without the fast-starting Eve and Morn horses, owners, riders, and bettors wondered who would set the pace.

Pace is an inexact science in racing, often distinguishing the best jockeys from their competition. Going out too quickly might exhaust a horse before the finish, but too deliberate a pace can allow slower horses to stay with the leaders and lead to a sprint to the finish. Luck—a stumble or a collision—could be decisive. To avoid these pacing pitfalls, stables with more than one horse to run sometimes employ a "rabbit," or a pacesetter: a horse that is fast, but not expected to contend, perhaps because of a lack of experience or stamina. The quick early pace will encourage horses to run faster than they might like, just to stay in contention, tiring weaker rivals. In the fall 1938 Champions', both the White and Moller stables sent out rabbits.

At the start, White's White Major and Moller's Flyinglight burst from the gate and went straight to the front, as planned. The two pacesetters led, but not by much—Flyinglight in the lead, White Major half a length behind. Bagshot and Cordon Rouge, the favorite, followed close behind. At the ¾-mile pole, White Parade—Gussie White's lead horse—moved to the front and stayed there until the field entered the final turn. With a quarter mile to go, Merrylight moved to the outside, taking Moller's chocolate-and-gold silks from fifth to second in just a few strides, then rocketing past White Parade to lead by a length at the top of the stretch. He pushed that lead to three lengths before White Parade began to close as they approached the finish, but it was too late. Eric Moller had his first Champions' win. We Two's Gold Vase finished second. White Parade settled for third.

Moller's win was popular; he had been running in Shanghai for decades, but this top prize had eluded him until now, and newspapers ran pictures of the Mollers beaming across their front pages. Shanghailanders reveled in the spectacle; the crowds were the largest in seven years, according to David Zentner in the *China Press*.[7] Billie Liddell's Cordon Rouge had been the bettors' favorite before disappointing and finishing fifth, but she was just three lengths from winning a second Champions'. Top competition, burgeoning crowds—maybe the party wasn't about to end?

For Henchman, though, the Champions' Stakes in fall 1938 was a discouraging missed opportunity. After two second-place finishes and the Sassoons out of the picture, Hench expected great things, not last place. Hench and Mary were fixtures in the owners' boxes, and their horses had won a lot of races, but they continued to fall short in the biggest race of all.

Bagshot didn't get a chance to redeem himself, because Henchman brought a new pony to the races in the spring of 1939. Hindhead— named, per Henchman's custom, after one of his favorite British golf courses—was probably not from China. Few China ponies were. He had been born in Mongolia, somewhere in the grasslands northwest of the Chinese provinces of Hebei or Shaanxi, sometime in the mid-1930s, and driven in a herd—or "mob"—to Shanghai for auction.

Since the 1860s, ponies had been sold at the Shanghai Horse Bazaar, following the spring race meeting, at a stable adjacent to the race-course. These auctions had expanded to twice—sometimes more— per year and continued into the early 1930s, though the horse bazaar company had changed its name to the Shanghai Horse Bazaar and Motor Company two decades earlier, reflecting the rise of the auto-mobile.[8] Each auction would put some two dozen China ponies, and occasional Thoroughbreds from Australia, on the block. After the last horse bazaar a Chinese firm, Loong Fei, carried on with the auctions for another few years, until the Japanese invasion in the summer of 1937 cut Shanghai off from its supply of horses. Loong Fei's last auc-tion, with fifty-two ponies up for sale, was held in May 1937, just six weeks before war began.[9]

China ponies were generally not named before they were sold; Hindhead would have been designated just "brown griffin" like doz-ens of others. ("Griffin" was a term for a first-year pony, but as slang it was applied broadly, and even people newly arrived in the city could be labeled griffins.) Hindhead was likely purchased between 1935 and 1937—maybe at the very last Loong Fei auction—for a few hundred dollars (between US$1,000 and US$2,000 in today's money). The pony was a winner from the start, qualifying for the Champions' in his very first season. The competition was strong: Eric Moller's Merrylight was back to defend his crown in the spring of 1939, and so was Gussie White's White Parade, third place the fall before. Billie Liddell—who, as half of We Two with Vera McBain, had finished second in the fall with Gold Vase—this time entered Rain.

At the start, Night Express, a consistently good horse belonging to newspaper publisher Roy McNair and Hungarian Gabor Renner (who doubled as jockey) set the pace. Rain followed him down the backstretch while Merrylight hung back, just as he had the fall before, along with White Parade and Hindhead. At the end of the backstretch, the favorites took their cue and went to the front.

But Merrylight, the defending champion, missed his entrance. In his first Champions', Hindhead surged, reeling in the leader as he rounded the last turn. Watching from his owner's box, Henchman could see his opportunity coming into focus. Jockey Nobby Clark took Hindhead on the outside, while Rain and Night Express held the rail. Clark's longer outside line was a risk, but Hindhead seemed to have the stamina and speed to pay it off. Rounding into the final straight, Rain and Hindhead strained toward the finish while Night Express, between horses, faded. Twenty thousand spectators came to their feet as two of Shanghai's most experienced jockeys—Peanut Marshall and Clark—raced side

Original caption: "A good example of a China pony, brought over from the Mongolian steppes: Applejack, one of the spring winners." Shanghai Race Club, 1939.

by side. At the wire, Rain gave Billie Liddell her second Champions' (her first as solo owner). Hindhead was second, just half a length from bringing Henchman his long coveted Champions'. But Hindhead was named Griffin of the Year and was considered a favorite for the next Champions' as a muggy summer spread across Shanghai.

WHILE HENCHMAN WAITED FOR his next opportunity, news from Europe dominated the summer of 1939. Germany invaded Poland in September, and Shanghai could no longer dismiss the war as a dispute between China and Japan. The United States remained neutral, but Britain was now besieged and at war. France's defeat by the Nazis meant that French overseas territories—including the French Concession in Shanghai—were now technically allies of the Germans and also the Japanese. Though no territory in Shanghai changed hands, and the French Concession continued to operate as it had before, many wondered whether the new war would affect Japan's plans for China, and perhaps bring the Europeans or even the Americans into a Pacific theater. And then what for Shanghai?

Europe slipped over the precipice, but Henchman remained focused on the races. After Hindhead's near miss in the spring, he entered the fall race meeting as a strong favorite, and most viewed his qualifying race, the Griffins Stakes, as a formality. The crowd thought him in perfect position as he broke from the gate in second place, but the race did not play out according to Henchman's script. Hindhead stayed second the whole way around the track, falling farther and farther behind and finishing six lengths back of the winner, Don Enrico. To the dismay of his owner and many supporters, Hindhead was shut out of the winner's circle altogether at the fall race meeting, failing even to qualify for Champions Day. When the main event came, Henchman's second-string, Bagshot, managed second place, but this year it was Gussie White's White Parade winning the Champions' Cup after placing three straight times. Hench would have to wait, again.

The German invasion seemed to confirm Victor Sassoon's sense that a wider war was inevitable, but not everyone shared this concern (or at least his response). Eric Moller also anticipated the expansion of Japanese influence and power in Shanghai, but rather than avoid it, he embraced it. In 1939 he made a gift of $5,000 to the Japanese Soldiers and Sailors Hospital fund, "in appreciation of the valour of army and navy officers and men."[10] Shanghailanders were accustomed to straddling all sorts of ethical fences—not least by racing ponies while Chinese refugees and news of atrocities streamed into Shanghai—but Moller's gesture was more overt than most. It was not the first time that Moller's actions elicited controversy, profitable though they were. In the 1920s, at least two Moller ships had been found to be transporting opium, illegally, among Taiwan, Japan, and the Russian Far East, their cargo falsely reported as fish.[11]

The 1940s began with the International Settlement still clinging to hope that its impossible situation might yet be sustainable. When bombs had exploded in the Settlement on Bloody Saturday, few expected the Lone Island to last the year, let alone the decade. Yet the Japanese lines around the Settlement had stabilized; the longer they stayed in place, the more permanent they seemed. Although Japan occupied eastern China north of the Yangtze and all the major coastal cities, the front was not advancing.

The outbreak of war in Europe changed little in Shanghai. Inside the Settlement, European and American consulates continued to urge their nationals to leave, but many stayed, and the foreign elites continued to focus on their distractions, the biggest of which was the races. As many as 40,000 people now packed the grandstands. Henchman greeted the new decade with high hopes. Despite the disappointment of not qualifying for the autumn 1939 Champions', Hindhead was still one of the most promising horses in the city. Henchman and Hindhead would be back, but the fall's results emphasized that success could not be taken for granted. At the end of a drab winter, Hench looked forward to the spring of 1940.

But he faced fiercer competition than before, thanks to Bob Aitkenhead's Clunie stable. Aitkenhead had been racing since his return to Shanghai from Scotland in 1933, but without much success—just some undercard victories in 1935 and 1936. After that, Aitkenhead focused all his energies elsewhere—managing an ice company and making plenty of time for tennis and lawn bowling. Not until 1939 did Aitkenhead return to the track, but this time he entered to win, acquiring at least four new China ponies and naming his stable "Clunie" after his Scottish sojourn.

Cluniecastle was a ruined rampart, sitting on a lowland hill and dating to at least the twelfth century, and Clunieburn was a trout-stocked brook winding its way through forests and meadows, but both names were now repurposed to fit ponies in Aitkenhead's stable. Cluniehill, its referent less clear, was another. But the centerpiece of the stable was Cluniehouse. In a breach of racing custom, this was the second horse Aitkenhead had given that name: the first Cluniehouse had won some minor races in 1936, but this horse—a chestnut—debuted in the spring of 1940 and promptly won the Griffins' Plate for first-year ponies.

Winning the Griffins' Plate against soft competition was one thing, but the next day Cluniehouse went on to win the Shanghai Derby as a favorite, taking the lead at the ¾-mile pole and going on to win by two full lengths. Aitkenhead announced that Cluniehouse would represent his stable in the next day's Champions' Stakes.

Aitkenhead faced a dilemma on Champions Day. The Race Club had a limited number of top jockeys. In his first two starts, Cluniehouse had been ridden by Charlie Encarnação, one of Shanghai's most successful riders. But for the Champions', Encarnação had already committed to ride the favorite, Democratic Prince, owned by stockbroker Samson Judah (Judah, one of the few Jewish members at the Race Club, raced his horses under the stable name "Jim").

With Encarnação unavailable, Aitkenhead turned to Alex Striker. Born Alexander Strijevsky, Striker had been brought to Shanghai as a boy as part of the migration of Russians prompted by the Bolshevik Revolution and the Russian Civil War. His mother, Olga Alexeevna, was from Kazan, where Alex had been born in 1909, when she was just eighteen years old. His father, Victor Mikhailovich Strijevsky, born in 1886 near the Black Sea, was a cavalry officer in the Russian Imperial Army, until forced to resign his commission because of "abnormal sexual instincts."[12] Family connections (Victor's father was governor of the province of Simbirsk, later renamed Ulyanovsk in honor of its most famous son, Vladimir Lenin) found Victor a place in the Red Cross during World War I.

After the Bolshevik Revolution, Victor, Olga, and Alex made their way, like many Russians, first to the Manchurian city of Harbin and then to Shanghai, arriving around 1924. Victor seems to have been of little use as either a husband or a father, traveling frequently among

Hong Kong, Shanghai, and Beiping, and partnering with an American, Margaret Kennedy, to operate a "high class brothel" in Shanghai. Meanwhile, Olga ran a French Concession saloon that also served as a front for gambling. Olga raised two children—Alex and a younger sister—by herself, and also operated the gambling house until she died in 1931 (suicide by poison was rumored). The two children, aged ten and fifteen at the time of her death, were all but orphaned, as Strijevsky continued to travel for new business schemes, mainly to Chinese treaty ports, but also to Europe. The Shanghai Municipal Police kept close tabs on him. Observing that he was frequently in the company of American sailors, the police expressed frustration that they could not get any charges to stick, complaining that "Strigevsky [*sic*] has no criminal record in Shanghai but has the reputation of being a sexual pervert."[13]

Alex Striker never stopped striving for the life of wealth and privilege that revolution in Russia had denied him. Not surprisingly, perhaps, he was attracted to one of Shanghai's high-profile status symbols: the automobile. Journalists celebrated Shanghai as the automobile capital of China; as early as 1916, foreign observers noted that Shanghai was "showing the rest of China the way to automobiledom."[14] Shanghai's mayor, Wu Tiecheng, was named the first president of the Automobile Club of China. By 1932, more than 10,000 private cars were registered in Shanghai's foreign concessions, a number that continued to grow.[15]

Striker's first known job as a salesman was for Dodge and Seymour, an American import-export firm that sold cars as well as other manufactures. Later he worked at Moody Motors—one of the oldest automobile garages and dealers in China—selling Packards, Plymouths, DeSotos, and Chryslers under the slogan "A Car for Every Purse"[16] on Avenue Edward VII, the wide Parisian-style boulevard that separated the French Concession from the International Settlement.

Though he made his living selling cars, Striker lived for ponies. He was a fixture at the racetrack, primarily as a jockey, but the Race Club's social scene seemed to be an end to itself for Striker. Shanghai's Municipal Police suspected him of crimes, including fraud, which internally they believed he carried out by "using his wife's attractions to make the acquaintance of people useful to him," but Striker was never charged with a crime. It may be that in hypercapitalist, and somewhat paranoid,

Shanghai, he was mistrusted as a Russian. Charges or not, the police remained suspicious of the playboy jockey on familiar terms with American naval officers and British bankers.[17] Whatever his other dealings were, Striker knew horses; only three jockeys had more victories than he did during the Lone Island period. Still, he had not ridden a Champion.

While Aitkenhead worried about putting a new jockey on Cluniehouse, Henchman trusted experience. Hindhead had qualified easily, winning the Siccawei Plate by one and a half lengths against a strong field that included White Parade and Rain, the two most recent Champions. Riding Hindhead was still Nobby Clark, who had left the Hongkong and Shanghai Bank to establish his own brokerage company but remained Henchman's leading jockey. (Clark had been compelled to leave the Bank because it was revealed that he had married, which was against company policy for many of its overseas employees.)[18]

Clark had never won the Champions' Stakes, but he had won classics for Henchman and had come up just short in the spring 1939 Champions'. This time out, at the spring race meeting of 1940, Democratic Prince was the favorite for the largest Champions' field in years— twelve horses—but both Henchman and Aitkenhead had reasons for confidence after their ponies' strong springs. When the gate opened, White Night went to the front, setting the pace for his stablemate White Parade. Along with Rain, White Parade moved past almost immediately, and the two ran neck and neck until the quarter pole, when Striker's dark-blue-and-red silks raced past on Cluniehouse.

Three different horses were within striking distance as they approached the grandstand, and Democratic Prince made a run as they headed down the stretch, but Cluniehouse pulled away and won by a length and a half, going away. Hindhead was never a factor, placing ninth out of twelve horses. Bagshot, another of Henchman's ponies, was runner-up for the second Champions' in a row, but this was cold comfort. Hindhead was his great hope, and just a few months before he had seemed poised to win the Champions'. Now, Striker, Aitkenhead, and Cluniehouse had seized not only the Shaforce Cup (since 1927, the Champions' trophy had been named in honor of "Shaforce," the British Shanghai Defence Force deployed in Shanghai), but the promise that once belonged to Hindhead and Henchman.

Hench had not risen to the top of one of the world's most important banks by accepting defeat easily, and he responded to the spring 1940 setback by overhauling Hindhead's team, starting with a new jockey. Early in its history, the Shanghai Race Club had been the domain of "gentlemen jockeys," usually people who owned and rode their own horses. They were amateurs, riding for prize money but not for pay. This, though, had changed as the stakes grew. By the 1930s, most riders were professionals, paid for their services.

Not everyone liked the change. One reader of the *Illustrated Sporting News* lamented in 1934 that "in former days, jockeys were imbued with a high sense of sportsmanship," but that this had been replaced with a cutthroat desire to win: bumping and blocking were now features of every race.[19] It's impossible to know the extent to which this situation was being described truthfully, but by the 1920s, perhaps earlier, most of the horses being raced were ridden by professional jockeys.

So, Nobby Clark had to go. Defeat in the spring of 1940—losing to a griffin—stung Henchman. Convinced that Hindhead had the stuff to be Champion, Henchman decided to change jockeys. In Clark's stead, Henchman hired Charlie Encarnação, the winningest jockey in the history of the Shanghai Race Club. Encarnação, a Portuguese trader who specialized in cotton and gold futures, had been riding winners since at least 1926 at all three Shanghai tracks. Like Hench, though, Encarnação had never won the Champions'.

Encarnação's nationality gave him a fluid and sometimes awkward status. To begin with, Encarnação, like most Shanghai "Portuguese," traced his roots not to Portugal, but to Macau, the trading outpost established three centuries before the concessions of Shanghai. Long after Macau's decline, Shanghai continued to reflect Portugal's involvement in the China trade. In the 1880s, only Britons outnumbered Portuguese—now we would term them "Macanese"—among foreigners in Shanghai. As late as the 1930s, there were more Portuguese in Shanghai than there were citizens of any European nation other than Britain, France, Russia, and perhaps Germany.

As European empires expanded in the nineteenth century, European dominance—especially the dominance of northern Europeans and Americans of northern European descent—was built in part on "racial prestige." The presence of poor whites like Russian refugees challenged the social order. So, too, could the prominence of Portuguese, deemed "less white" in the rigid hierarchy of nineteenth-century race theories. China's foreign communities used the label "Portuguese" to describe people of mixed or undetermined ancestry, illustrating their place as not Chinese, but not fully European. Henchman, though, was paying little mind to concerns or questions about Charlie Encarnação's heritage or nationality. All he cared about was finding a jockey to ride Hindhead to his full potential.

Hench changed trainers too. Nobby Clark had recommended Elise Andrews, a veteran of the club who had been racing steeplechase for several years (and also the woman Clark had secretly married, forcing his exit from the Bank). Andrews had ridden to several wins in the Shanghai Paper Hunt, where she competed regularly against Billie Liddell. Liddell and Andrews were among the only women training horses at the club, and they arrived there by very different paths. In contrast to Liddell's deep Shanghailander roots, Elise Andrews was born to English and Swedish parents in St. Petersburg, where her parents were friends of the tsar and shared his fate when revolution came in 1917. She had fled St. Petersburg after the Bolsheviks murdered her family, following thousands of others across Siberia on the railway to Harbin.

It was not coincidence that both Striker and Andrews wound up in Harbin. Founded by Russians in the 1890s, the city was a virtual Russian colony in China and a leading center of White Russian emigré culture, alongside Prague, Paris, London, and New York. Via the Trans-Siberian railway, travel was faster between Europe and Harbin than any other Chinese city, and Harbin boasted a cosmopolitanism that resembled Shanghai, with symphony orchestras, foreign consulates, churches and synagogues, and the latest European fashions. After the Russian Revolution, though, the tsar's government was gone, and the Republic of China, which had inherited the treaties laying out Harbin's legal status, refused to recognize the Bolshevik government. Russians living in Harbin were now stateless, denied meaningful legal protection and certainly without the extraterritorial privileges they had enjoyed before 1917.[20]

This uncertainty drove many Russians out of Harbin to Shanghai, where a Russian community was thriving. Many lost everything, in the revolution or during their escape, but Elise Andrews landed on her feet. Already by 1928 she was riding steeplechase at the Race Club. She was also sought after as a trainer and was known particularly for her ability to break in difficult ponies. Andrews worked all summer with Hindhead and Encarnação, preparing for the fall season. In his first race with Encarnação up, Hindhead qualified for the Champions', easily winning the Mid-Autumn Festival Stakes. A day later, Cluniehouse won the Liverpool Stakes, dispelling concerns that he was not in top shape.

On Champions Day, Cluniehouse was the overwhelming favorite to defend his crown. Both Henchman and Aitkenhead had two ponies in the fall 1940 Champions' race: Hindhead and Northwood for Henchman; Cluniehouse—the favorite—and Cluniehill for Aitkenhead. At the start, the two Clunie horses went to the front, setting a blistering pace designed to leave the other horses behind, but the strategy backfired. Cluniehill tired too quickly and fell back, leaving Striker atop Cluniehouse in the lead, all alone and running too fast. Encarnação held Hindhead back, stalking the leader from several lengths behind. As they turned to the homestretch, Hindhead, wearing Henchman's primrose-and-heliotrope silks, barreled past his exhausted rival and went on to win by three lengths.

Finally, Hench was Champion!

Cluniehouse held on for second place, narrowly beating Henchman's other entry, Northwood, with Nobby Clark up. It was customary for the owner of the Champions' winner to host the most elaborate party in Shanghai the night after the race. With not only the winning pony, but third place as well, Hench would have been keen to celebrate at his mansion on Bubbling Well Road. The team of Henchman, Andrews, Encarnação, and, of course, Hindhead was the toast of Shanghai: "Full marks should go to the veteran jockey Encarnacao who rode one of the most magnificent races of his career to combine excellent riding and good judgment . . . to defeat the raging favorite, Cluniehouse, in the most impressive style."[21] Shanghai faced another winter as a Lone Island, but for Hench, at least, it was not as dreary as usual: his horse was King of the Turf.

BY THE SPRING OF 1941, the Japanese invasion of China was nearly four years old; the war in Europe, nearly two. Britain fought Germany alone, clinging to the hope that the United States would soon enter the war. In Shanghai, the impossible was now becoming commonplace. The limb holding up the International Settlement had been sawed off long ago, but it stayed in place, defying gravity.

The longer Shanghai's strange existence went on, the more sustainable it seemed. Shanghai's tenacity certainly heartened Brits and Americans, but it frustrated many Japanese. While Japanese armies all around had not ended British power in Shanghai, Japanese residents of the Settlement—they made up about half of the voters in the Settlement by 1940—were keen to challenge the status quo from within.[22] All residents of the International Settlement, regardless of nationality, knew that the stresses of being a Lone Island had left the Settlement in financial straits, and this precarious position gave the Japanese in Shanghai an opportunity to assert themselves.

Rising inflation and diminishing revenues strained the Municipal Council's ability to pay its employees during the Lone Island period. The crisis was accentuated because the Municipal Police had to rely on a greater proportion of Chinese officers as many British men left the city to serve in the war in Europe. This was not a problem in itself, but the council paid Chinese less than British—a practice that led to rising labor tensions.

The preceding summer, voters had rejected an attempt to add five new Japanese members to the Municipal Council. The reallocation was justified as recognition of the growing Japanese population and influence in Shanghai, but it was also down to Japanese interests in the settlement dividing homes and businesses in order to lay claim to more representation. The British, who dominated the council, rejected this reallocation as violating the informal balance among the different nations of the International Settlement that had been in effect for decades. More practically, they feared that new Japanese members would facilitate the Japanese occupation of the Settlement. The five additional nominees were defeated (two Japanese were elected, as was usual).

The British responded to the Japanese attempt to fix the electorate in kind: increasing British representation on the council tenfold, while the number of Britons in the city declined over the same period.[23] Meanwhile, Chinese employees of the Shanghai Municipal Police threatened to strike in early 1941. To avoid this, the SMP agreed to raise wages for Chinese staffers, but to pay for the raise, the cash-strapped council needed more revenue, and so proposed an unprecedented tax increase, to be voted on at a special meeting of ratepayers (taxpayers).

Once again, the racecourse was at the center of it all.

Votes usually took place at City Hall, or a theater, but the expected crowd pushed the meeting to the racecourse—the largest venue in the Settlement, and perhaps the only place that could accommodate the special meeting that convened on January 23, 1941. More than two thousand voters took seats in the grandstand, overlooking the track. Danish consul Poul Scheel—by custom, the senior consul in attendance chaired the meeting—called for a vote on an amendment proposed by Hayashi Yukichi, the chairman of the Japanese Ratepayers' Association. Hayashi's amendment would block the tax increase and, presumably, destabilize British control of the Settlement.

By all accounts, after Hayashi gave a passionate and provocative speech in support of his resolution, Scheel mismanaged the vote, which broke down on racial lines that reflected the vote rigging that the British council members had engineered (underlining the peculiarity of the International Settlement, although it was Chinese sovereign territory, that no Chinese voted, because they were excluded from this general meeting). After the vote was announced, Hayashi approached Tony Keswick, the chairman of the Municipal Council who had replaced Cornell Franklin just a few months earlier. Council member Norwood Allman described what happened next:

> I was particularly unnerved by Hayashi's strange behavior, and I kept my eye on him. In a minute or two, I saw him slip out of his seat . . . and up the steps at the end opposite where I sat. . . . Before I realized what was happening, Hayashi made a boxer-like twist, and as he turned drew his revolver and fired two shots in the speaker's direction. In a split-second what had been a dignified meeting was pandemonium, hellish with indistinguishable yells.[24]

Hayashi shot Keswick twice. For a few chaotic moments, even more violence seemed likely. "No one knew definitely how badly Mr. Keswick had been hurt," reported the American consulate's observer at the meeting. "He was taken away. . . . It seemed to me extremely likely that there would be a very serious general riot," prevented only by the arrival of "Sikhs with rifles and foreign and Chinese officers with drawn revolvers" on the scene.[25] Keswick, thanks largely to his heavy overcoat, suffered only flesh wounds. While Keswick's injuries were not serious, the shooting was fatal to the Municipal Council, which responded to the crisis by suspending its elections and appointing an interim council—dominated by British interests—to govern.

The Keswick shooting illustrated the extraordinary tensions gripping Shanghai. Crime and violence rose—some of it an outgrowth of the scarcity and desperation growing in the Settlement, some of it sponsored by the Japanese in order to intimidate the Westerners who refused to acquiesce to Japanese demands. The British-run police struggled to keep up. Kidnapping, robbery, and murder surged, and political terrorism—against many different targets—became commonplace.[26] Early in 1941, the newest criminal fashion was gangs of armed men boarding public buses and robbing their passengers.[27] As the SMP struggled, the Japanese military police increased its demands that if the SMP could not maintain order in the city, the Japanese would be forced to do so.

More eager than ever for a diversion, the Settlement headed back to the races!

Crowds at the spring race meeting were large and enjoyed what observers called the best meet in years, capped, as always, by Champions Day. May 8, 1941, dawned rainy, but by midday the sun was drying the track and warming the 20,000 spectators who had gathered to watch "the now-famous feud between those two great rivals, Cluniehouse and Hindhead."[28]

Oddsmakers favored Cluniehouse to reclaim the title, making Hindhead both defending champion and underdog. Cornell Franklin had not qualified for the Champions' in several years, but in the spring of 1941 both Silver Fox and Phantom were through to the season's biggest race. Gussie White qualified White Parade and White Willie. Leslie Hutton, a British lawyer, entered Mr. Bubbins, and Vera McBain entered Magic Circle. The field was deep and fast: Cluniehouse, Hindhead, and White Parade were the three most recent Champions' winners. Magic Circle was a former Champion, as David Sassoon's Sparkling Morn. Mr. Bubbins had beaten Cluniehouse just a few weeks earlier, by a nose, in the International Recreation Club Champions'.

At the start, Phantom went to the lead as was his style. Originally christened Phantom Morn, he had been a promising horse in David

Sassoon's stables, and Franklin had snapped up the gray pony and pinned his hopes to him after the Morn stable folded. Everyone who watched the horses in Shanghai knew that Judge Franklin's horse was the swiftest in Shanghai, but could he last? Phantom had several undercard wins to his credit and a bright future, but he hadn't yet shown the ability to finish strong in big races. Most expected he was just there to push the pace.

Silver Fox and Cluniehouse followed Phantom closely around the first two turns, the lead expanding to three lengths over the tightly bunched field down the backstretch. Then, true to form, Phantom began to fall back. Cluniehouse seized the opportunity, going to the front and taking the lead into the final turn. Without Phantom out front, though, the pace slackened. Cluniehouse led, but he wasn't pulling away. Silver Fox, Magic Circle, White Parade, and Henchman's Hindhead gained with each stride until by the time they turned for home, the lead was gone.

Cluniehouse and Silver Fox, stride for stride in front as they came past the grandstand, brought the crowd to its feet. Silver Fox, though game, had never shown championship form, and even this late in the race, with just a quarter mile to go, it seemed that Cluniehouse would hold on and reclaim his title. Everyone watching knew what was next: jockey Alex Striker would let him off the bit, and Cluniehouse would run to victory.

Just the opposite happened. Instead of surging forward, Cluniehouse faltered. Chaos. It was anyone's race as White Parade, Cluniehill, Magic Circle, and most of all Hindhead closed with a rush. Down to the wire, six horses had victory within reach until, in the last yards, Charlie Encarnação coaxed Hindhead to win by a neck and defend his title! Silver Fox's second place was Judge Franklin's best Champions' finish yet, while Cluniehill edged out his stablemate to finish third. Cluniehouse, the favorite to win, finished fourth—out of the money.

Hindhead was now in elite territory: few ponies had won the Champions' back-to-back. Aitkenhead and Striker were left frustrated: twice Cluniehouse had been favored to win, and twice Hindhead had beaten him. Cluniehouse's failure to even place confounded observers; it was the first time in his career he'd finished out of the money. One writer claimed to have seen the failure coming, that the defeat seemed "to

Arriving at the Shanghai Race Club, 1928.

substantiate the earlier assertion, which I made . . . that he is not at the top of his form," even though a day earlier he had predicted victory for Aitkenhead's prize pony.[29]

As summer descended on the racecourse, Aitkenhead returned to Scotland to escape Shanghai's heat and humidity and see his youngest daughter married. Vera McBain and her husband, William, left Shanghai for the summer as well. Henchman attended to the Bank. Cornell Franklin turned back to his law practice, and the International Settlement renewed its worries about how long it could retain its bizarre neutrality surrounded by war, but its residents preferred to focus on the renewal of Hindhead versus Cluniehouse that would come in the autumn.

CHAPTER

13

. . . .

The Last Fall

Cover of the program for the
Autumn Race Meeting, 1941.

T HE UNITED STATES WAS NOT YET AT WAR IN THE SUMMER
of 1941. Millions watched Joe DiMaggio's hitting streak reach fifty-six
games while Ted Williams chased a .400 batting average, but war was
on everyone's mind. In Britain, the Blitz that had begun in the fall of

1940 had ended in the spring of 1941, but many believed it was just a pre-
lude to a German invasion. Might this be England's last free summer?
On the other side of the world, China entered another year of war with
Japan, and Shanghai approached its fourth anniversary as a Lone Island
amid the Japanese armies surrounding the International Settlement.

Their bubble of neutrality still somehow intact, Arthur Henchman,
Cornell Franklin, Robert Aitkenhead, and other Shanghailanders could
ignore the news from Europe, or from across Suzhou Creek, and look
ahead to the upcoming racing season.

At one time, the season was just one meeting, lasting only three
days. The seasonal race meetings had expanded to four days and then
five, but even that could not satisfy the public appetite for racing. Starting in 1919, the Shanghai Race Club began holding additional races
on the weekends leading up to the regular race meeting, and the number of these "Extra Race Meetings" grew steadily. There was still time
off, when the weather was either too hot or too cold for racing (or for
the spectators), and there were still two racing seasons each year, with
Champions Day the culmination of each, but by 1941 the autumn season would last more than a month, beginning in early October. There
were three Extra Race Meetings, each lasting several days of seven to
nine races each day, planned in the five weeks before the Champions'
Stakes would be run.

The longer racing season changed some features of the Champions'.
Originally, every winner in the race meeting competed in the Champions' Stakes, providing fans and bettors a chance to see the best horses
pitted against one another. Including all of the season's winners was
feasible when the entire season was just three or four days long. Now,
as many as forty ponies could qualify, far more than could reasonably
run in a single race.

Club stewards decided to limit the Champions' field to about ten
ponies. Owners who had multiple ponies qualify could choose which
ones to enter. (It's not clear how disputes—if there were any—were
resolved.) With the high stakes and prestige of being named King of
the Turf, there was no reason to worry that the top horses in Shanghai
would duck this competition. The most important aspect of the racing
season leading up to Champions Day was qualifying for the Champions' by winning at least one race.

1940–41 member's badge for the Shanghai Race Club (women's style).

The 1941 autumn season began on October 4 "on the right foot and with the proverbial bang."[1] Franklin and Aitkenhead ponies squared off in the first day's featured Perth Stakes. Franklin's Silver Fox led from the start but tired halfway through—seemingly a trademark of Franklin's horses—and gave way to Cluniehill. Cluniehill carried a three-length lead into the homestretch and held on to qualify, beating Charlie Encarnação on Bagshot by two lengths.

Two days later, Encarnação made amends, riding the twice-defending champion to victory in the Mid-Autumn Festival Stakes. Hindhead romped over a weak field that Eric Cumine dismissed as "nothing but a poor excuse for 'suckers' to lay inexplicably stupid wagers."[2] More exciting was White Night coming from behind in the final yards of the Harvest Moon Stakes to beat Vera McBain's Magic Circle and Henchman's Rye. The dramatic win established White Night as a contender for the Champions'. Cornell Franklin's Phantom hinted that he was more than just a pacesetter, winning the Virginia Stakes by two lengths and qualifying for the Champions' himself.

The racing season resumed the following weekend, and the Champions' field continued to fill. White Parade, the autumn 1939 champion, joined White Night as Gussie White's second qualifier with a one-length win over Henchman's Northwood in the Commemoration Stakes. Cluniehill's dominating six-length win—his second of the season—over a highly regarded field in the Ohio Stakes raised questions: Was he, rather than Cluniehouse, Aitkenhead's top pony?

These murmurs grew louder when Cluniehill won a third race on October 25. Aitkenhead even qualified another pony, Clunieburn, that weekend, but Cluniehouse had yet to even start. Was Cluniehouse injured? Out of shape? Had the horse—or his owner—lost confidence? Aitkenhead's champion had come up short twice since winning the spring 1940 Shaforce Cup, but he remained a favorite of the bettors.

There was confusion and consternation about Cluniehouse's failure to even race in October, when all the other contenders had been running and winning preliminary races, but most observers still thought Cluniehouse was the best pony in Shanghai. Although he had lost the Champions' as a favorite in the autumn 1940 and spring 1941 races, Cluniehouse had won the Criterion Stakes—Shanghai's oldest classic—at both meets. Oddsmakers considered his shortcomings in the previous two Champions' to be flukes. Some, furthermore, believed that Aitkenhead may have been planning a put-over (holding his best horse back to give false confidence to his rivals).

Favorite or not, Cluniehouse had to qualify, and the Extra Race Meeting on November 1 would be the last chance before the Autumn Race Meeting began on November 8. October racing had been a chance for training and gamesmanship, but when the calendar turned to November, Champions Day was around the corner, and everyone was eager to see Cluniehouse under starter's orders.

Alex Striker finally brought Cluniehouse to the line on November 1, in the Armagh Stakes, a seven-furlong race that was of interest only because Cluniehouse was running. Aitkenhead was making a safe, smart play to make sure he qualified; half of the money bet was on Cluniehouse to win. No one was concerned when Hill Song, a "second-class pony" belonging to Tony Liang, went to the front, not even when jockey Y. S. Chang held on to the lead down the backstretch, and beyond. Not until the final turn might those in the grandstands have perceived Striker's sudden urgency as he went to the whip. Finally, down the stretch, Cluniehouse streaked toward the front, closing to within a length as he passed the grandstand, but no closer. Hill Song scored the biggest upset of the season, at near-record pace.

Liang could compete in the races only thanks to a special rule, passed by the Shanghai Race Club membership that winter, permitting members at the International Recreation Club to race in SRC meets. The fact that Chinese could be members at the IRC effectively permitted Chinese members at the SRC . . . almost. "Members in good standing of the International Recreation Club are invited to participate as owners and/or riders in Race Meetings of the Shanghai Race Club," the new rule stated, "excepting always such Races as in the opinion of the Stewards should be reserved for members of the Shanghai Race Club only."[3] In other words, the Champions' would remain exclusively for the Shanghai Race Club—and only white.

Having beaten the overwhelming favorite, Hill Song brought in the biggest payday of the season to that point: a $5 bet paid more than $63.40 (more than US$1,000 in today's money). The result was a thrilling reminder that most people who came to the track came to gamble, many hoping to win big on a long shot. In 1941 Shanghai, the chance to win twelve times what you had put down might be the difference between getting a seat on a steamer out of the city and being left behind when the Japanese army crossed the Garden Bridge, as it inevitably would, and dissolved the Settlement's illusion of safety.

Hill Song represented hope. But he also represented uncertainty. It had been puzzling enough that Cluniehouse had come up short (twice!) in the Champions'. But to lose to an also-ran like Hill Song was incomprehensible. Perhaps the rust Cluniehouse had accumulated in almost six months without a race explained it, but the idea that Hill Song could defeat Aitkenhead's best horse under any circumstances shocked the crowd.

And the surprises did not end there.

Y. S. Chang barely had time to dismount and take the saddle for his next ride, the Londonderry Stakes (all the races of this day were named for sites in Northern Ireland). The grandstands were still abuzz from his upset victory aboard Hill Song when he went to the line on Slow Motion. Chang was one of the most successful Chinese jockeys at the Race Club, and he had demonstrated his skill already that fall, beating Encarnação and Jimmy Pote-Hunt just two days before in the Newmarket Stakes. He again faced Encarnação, who this time was riding the defending champion, Hindhead, looking for a last tune-up before the Autumn Race Meeting.

Chang, seeking another upset, raced stride for stride with the favorite for the entire nine furlongs. The two horses were inseparable even down to the wire, finishing in a dead heat. It was concerning enough for the punters that Hindhead could not shake Slow Motion, but far worse, it was a dead heat for second place! Northwood, another of Henchman's ponies (with Nobby Clark riding), streaked past in the stretch to win by two lengths, paying out $57 on a $5 bet, nearly as much as Hill Song had.

With the fall Extra Race Meetings drawing to a close, confusion reigned at the Shanghai Race Club. Hindhead and Cluniehouse remained the favorites of most observers, but no one could be confident. Cluniehouse had yet to even qualify for the Champions', and he would have to win in one of the Autumn Race Meeting's first days to have even a chance of regaining his title. Hindhead had won in impressive style in his first time out, but then had lost by two lengths to a lightly regarded stablemate. White Parade, White Night, Phantom, and Cluniehill all had made statements with their performances. All of them had their supporters, but success in the Extra Race Meetings was no guarantee of success in the Autumn Race Meeting that was about to begin.

BREAKING A SPELL OF fine weather—autumn is Shanghai's best season, between the oppressive humidity of summer and winter's damp cold—it rained the night before the Autumn Race Meeting was to begin. While all the trainers, owners, and jockeys had to prepare for the possibility of a muddy track, Bob Aitkenhead had a bigger problem. He still hadn't qualified his favorite.

Aitkenhead considered his options as the rain fell. After the Cham-

Horses crossing the finish line at the Shanghai Race Club, 1941.

pions', the two most important races in Shanghai were the Criterion Stakes, which had been run since 1868, and the Shanghai St. Leger, which was even older. The best horses of the season traditionally entered one of these races on the opening day of the seasonal race meeting. Cluniehouse was two-time defending champion of the Criterion, beating Henchman horses in each case. In the spring, Cluniehouse had humiliated Rye by "many lengths" (meaning more than could be reliably counted, usually about thirty). In both of these cases, the Criterion victories had made Cluniehouse the favorite for the Champions' Stakes to follow, where Cluniehouse had been upset by Henchman's Hindhead.

Cluniehouse might have been the best pony in Shanghai, but he could not enter the Champions' on reputation alone and had yet to qualify after Hill Song's upset. The Criterion Stakes attracted the strongest field of the first day, including Hindhead, Silver Fox, Magic Circle, and Cluniehill. A third straight Criterion win was itself a worthy goal, but much more important was the Champions'. Would Aitkenhead take the safer route and hold Cluniehouse out of the Criterion, looking instead for a win in a lesser race, a backdoor into the Champions'?

The next morning dawned warm and clear, the track soft from the overnight rain. Eric Cumine, reporting for the *North-China Daily News*, confirmed to a disappointed public that Cluniehouse would sit out the Criterion and instead start in the third race of the day, the Tsitsihar Stakes (named for a former Manchu border garrison that was the capital of Heilongjiang province, near the Russian border). Aitkenhead put his best horse in the race, expecting a walkover, but found himself up against an unanticipated rival, Franklin's Phantom. Phantom had finished eighth in the spring Champions' after an early lead, and started the fall season thought of as just a pacesetter, but he seemed to have found longer legs in the fall, winning twice in the Extra Race Meetings. Also entered was Libertylight, one of David Sassoon's former ponies that had contended in several Champions'. And to apply even more pressure, Hill Song was entered for a rematch of the upset just a few weeks earlier.

In Cluniehouse's previous outing, when he lost the Armagh Stakes, Striker had let Hill Song out to such a big lead that he couldn't reel him in at the finish. Determined not to make the same mistake this time, he kept Hill Song close, but Phantom went straight to the front and built an alarming lead. Aitkenhead's supposedly safe play seemed to be going wrong; instead of enjoying an easy win to qualify for the Champions', he watched from the owners' box as the field chased Phantom around the first turn, up the backstretch, and through the final turns. Just like before, Cluniehouse faced a deficit as he turned for home, needing to track down the leader in order to qualify. But just when Aitkenhead might start to panic, his horse responded. Cluniehouse surged to the lead as the field raced past the grandstand. By the time they reached the finish line, Cluniehouse was three lengths ahead of Libertylight. Phantom held on for third, while Y. S. Chang brought Hill Song home fourth. Cluniehouse wouldn't defend his Criterion title, but he was safely in the Champions' field.

With Cluniehouse now qualified, attention turned to the day's two featured races: the St. Leger and the Criterion. The St. Leger was first of the two, the sixth race. It had a long history but had declined in recent years because its length, 1¾ miles—longest of Shanghai's classics—discouraged most of the Settlement's top horses. This St. Leger was a chance, though, for C. S. Mao, one of the few Green Gang mobsters who had not fled to Hong Kong after the Japanese invasion, to win a classic: Jimmy Pote-Hunt rode Mao's Merry Sportsman to a comfortable four-length victory. It was the seventh race, the Criterion Stakes, that attracted the most attention. Ten horses entered the starting gate, half of which were serious contenders for the upcoming Champions'. Favored Hindhead was seeking his third win of the season, but Henchman could not have been overly confident, despite the bookies' support. Like Cluniehouse, Hindhead had lost his last time out to a lightly regarded rival. He was also running against Cluniehill, who was formally Aitkenhead's number two pony but had run better than Cluniehouse all season.

Aitkenhead's plan for this short, 1-mile race was to have Clunieburn set a fast pace from the start that would leave Hindhead unable to sprint to the lead at the finish as he had done twice against Cluniehouse in the Champions'. The Clunie strategy was evident right away, for Clunieburn went out more quickly even than Silver Fox, one of Cornell Franklin's reliable front-runners. With Silver Fox chasing, Clunieburn led the field for the first half mile, the two favorites—Cluniehill and Hindhead—were content to run at the back of the pack.

Clunieburn wasn't expected to keep up this pace. The plan was for him to cede the lead to his stablemate, but Cluniehill was not showing his recent top form. With three furlongs to go, Silver Fox moved to the lead, and it appeared that he might score an unexpected win for his American owner when he entered the homestretch three lengths to the good. But that lead evaporated as two other contenders—Eric Moller's Frostylight and Vera McBain's Magic Circle—moved alongside and then past Silver Fox.

In the last quarter mile, the lead changed four times. Frostylight and Magic Circle were running stride for stride toward the finish when Busted Straight took the lead on the outside, but just for a moment. Charlie Encarnação had timed the favorite's run perfectly and, with a furlong to go, took Hindhead to the lead. Even then, the race wasn't over. White Night—suddenly a fashionable choice for the Champions'—surged toward the front. Watching from his box, Henchman saw Encarnação coax a last burst from Hindhead, who crossed the line a half length ahead of White Night. Magic Circle held on for third, with the Clunie horses buried deep in the finish order.

The Autumn Race Meeting began just as Henchman had hoped: a win for Hindhead in his first race—a classic—suggesting that the horse was ready for a run at history in the Champions'. Arthur and Mary Henchman celebrated the win at their home with a large curry tiffin; what could better capture the echoes of empire that had given rise to the Shanghai races in the first place? Everyone in attendance expected more of the same from Charlie Encarnação and his mount.

The second day of the Race Meeting had been Derby Day since the 1850s, when the Shanghai Derby had first been run, a race for griffins. The roster of Derby winners was a checklist of the best ponies announcing their arrival in Shanghai, but the last Shanghai Derby had been run in the spring of 1940 because war had disrupted the annual bazaars at which ponies driven from Manchuria or Mongolia were sold. After the Japanese invasion of 1937, no more horse markets took place. Without new horses coming into Shanghai, there were no new griffins to populate the Derby field once the last new ponies were trained and entered—it could take a few seasons to train new horses to race-readiness. Rather than change the rules to run other horses in the Derby, the race was discontinued (Cluniehouse won the last one). Races for Australian horses instead dominated the meeting's second day.

So, November 10, 1941, was Derby Day with no Derby, but it was still the Race Meeting. Large crowds enjoyed the unusually warm and sunny weather as the day's races got under way with the Australian St. Leger. Mistral, the favorite, won in a canter in a race described as "a trifle dull." The Australian horses looked impressive—Mistral (14.3) stood a full hand taller than Cluniehouse (13.2), but Shanghailanders didn't care; if China ponies weren't racing, Shanghai race fans weren't that interested.

The second day's featured race was the Whangpoo Handicap, for China ponies. Its mile-and-a-quarter length matched the Champions', offering a chance to refine strategy at that distance, and several of the strongest contenders were taking advantage of the opportunity. Magic Circle, White Parade, and Mr. Bubbins were among those that odds-makers gave a chance in the Champions', now just two days away.

Mr. Bubbins puzzled oddsmakers and had cost them a lot of money. Leslie Hutton, his English owner, was, like Cornell Franklin, a lawyer, and also the only one besides Franklin never to have won the Champions'. Hutton had been arguing cases in Shanghai for more than thirty years, but this chestnut was his first real shot at the Champions'. In the spring, Mr. Bubbins had beaten Henchman's Northwood as a huge long shot: a $5 bet had returned $358 (more than US$6,000 today). This spectacular return was the equivalent of an entire year's wages for the typical unskilled laborer in Shanghai who frequented the track.[4] We don't know whether the twenty-five bettors who cashed winning tickets on Mr. Bubbins and multiplied their money seventeen times were laborers or taipans, but there were plenty of both at the races.

That had been a race run by the IRC—the club that had been founded at Jiangwan but had, since the Japanese invasion, been racing in the Settlement at the Shanghai Race Club—and the win had qualified Mr. Bubbins for the IRC Champions', where he was again lightly regarded, facing a field that included Cluniehouse, Cluniehill, and Silver Fox. But Mr. Bubbins showed his worth once more, winning in a photo finish. He had gone on to qualify for the spring Champions' at the SRC, where he finished a disappointing seventh. Many had regarded Mr. Bubbins as a horse to watch for in the fall, but so far he had disappointed. Observers kept waiting for Mr. Bubbins to regain his form, but he didn't find it in the Whangpoo Handicap, finishing fourth as Magic

Circle, White Parade, and Ashridge (another of Henchman's ponies) finished first, second, and third, all within a length of one another.

The story of the second day was Phantom. The pony had given Cluniehouse all he could handle the day before, after winning several times in the Extra Race Meetings. He was entered twice on this day—an unusual arrangement—and began by winning the 1-mile Bubbling Well Stakes going away, with a five-length advantage over one of Moller's lesser-regarded "-light" ponies. The field, though large (eighteen ponies took the start), was weak, and Phantom's win was unsurprising. What gained the attention of the racing public was Phantom's second start, this time in the Siccawei Stakes, named for the village near Shanghai that was well known to racegoers as the site of a Jesuit church, library, and orphanage.[5]

The Siccawei Stakes was not a classic, but it was one of the day's featured races, and Phantom went to the line a colossal long shot against several Champions' contenders, including Cluniehill, Silver Fox, and especially White Night. Phantom ran his typical race, running hard from the start and building a fifteen-length lead that his rivals could never overcome. White Night, who had won twice in the fall season and was being mentioned by bettors as a possible choice to upset Cluniehouse and Hindhead, finished second, two lengths behind. Cluniehill, winner of three straight races during October, was an also-ran, finishing fourth. Phantom rewarded his backers handsomely—paying $350 for a $5 bet—and established himself as not just a pacesetter, but a true contender for the Champions' race that was less than forty-eight hours away.

Day three of the Shanghai Race Meeting was traditionally an off day, with no classics scheduled. Most of the contenders were safely in the Champions' field, and there was no need for horses to tire themselves unnecessarily before the main event. For most everyone, this day was about looking forward to Champions Day.

The third day of the 1941 Autumn Race Meeting—November 11— fit this pattern. That morning, the bookmaker Dagal & Co. listed odds for the likely Champions' starters, beginning with Hindhead and Cluniehouse, each at less than 2:1. Of the fourteen ponies listed, all had qualified for the Champions' except Mr. Bubbins, whose last chance came in the Kunming Stakes. Racing against Henchman's Bagshot and

Franklin's Silver Fox, Oleg Panoff wasted no time driving Mr. Bubbins to the front. He built a ten-length lead before the rest of the field began to close, and he won by two lengths: qualified. Also qualifying was Eric Moller's gray Cherrylight, who closed with a tremendous rush to finish a short head in front of favored Columbus in the Chungking Stakes.

The field was set. Hindhead would again defend his title. Rival Cluniehouse was the favorite for the third straight Champions'. Northwood gave Henchman a second horse in the race, and Aitkenhead's second, Cluniehill, had been the best horse in Shanghai for most of the fall. Gussie White put two horses in the Champions' as well: White Night and White Parade. Cornell Franklin's Phantom, Eric Moller's Merrylight, Vera McBain's Magic Circle, and the newly qualified Mr. Bubbins rounded out the field.

These ten were expected to race for the title King of the Turf the next day: November 12, 1941. Champions Day.

PART THREE

A DAY AT THE RACES

NOVEMBER 12, 1941

Life—moving and fickle—was there.
Life as represented by 14,000 more
unpredictable than the ponies.

—*CHINA PRESS*,
NOVEMBER 14, 1941

· · ·

Champions Day

DAWN, THE RACE CLUB

B Y THE TIME ARTHUR HENCHMAN REACHED THE MOHAWK
Road stables, Elise Andrews was already there. After a decade training
horses in Shanghai, she had made it a practice to sleep in her horses' stalls
the night before a big race. If she didn't, the Chinese track stewards—
known as mafoos—would take her horses for the early morning pre-
race workouts they favored, and Andrews was not about to let anyone
tamper with her regimen. She had trained Hindhead to back-to-back
Champions' wins, and a third straight victory would put Hindhead in
rare company, achieving a feat only two ponies had accomplished in the
twentieth century. If Hindhead could join that elite club, Hench and
Andrews could set their sights on the all-time record of four straight, set
by The Dealer forty years earlier, but that would have to wait.

It was cold as Hench and Andrews looked over their champion. For
most of the Autumn Race Meeting, November had felt more like late
summer. Temperatures in the seventies prompted a string of parties
under brilliant sunshine that belied the season—music, dancing, food,
and liquor, drowning out the sounds of war, the rumors of doom, and
the warnings to evacuate. The Henchmans hosted an outdoor curry
tiffin, one of the many barbecues, picnics, and garden parties that took

advantage of the unseasonable warmth. But on the eve of Champions Day, November "stole in like a thief in the night" and brought with it the harsh winds and gray skies more typical of late autumn.[1]

Hindhead's opportunity was historic, but most of the money was on Cluniehouse, Bob Aitkenhead's spring 1940 Champion. Favored or not, Aitkenhead was taking nothing for granted as he arrived at the stable that morning. Cluniehouse had, after all, been the favorite to win the previous two Champions', but both times Hindhead had taken him down. For two years now, the rivalry between Aitkenhead and Henchman, and between these two horses, had dominated Shanghai-lander society. Today was, in the words of the local press, "yet another chapter added to the bitter and prolonged struggle for the supremacy of Shanghai's turfdom between those sworn rivals."[2]

Most observers thought the Champions' would be a two-horse race, but that didn't mean the rest of the field had given up. Cornell Franklin liked his chances too. Phantom was widely considered the speediest horse in Shanghai, but the oddsmakers didn't think he could last a mile and a quarter. After finishing second in the spring (with his horse Silver Fox), Franklin had cause to believe that the oddsmakers were underestimating his chances. An American owner had never won the Champions'; could this be the day?

The other owners with Champions' entrants were in the paddock as well. Eric Moller, Vera McBain, and Gussie White had all been Champion before, and although they weren't favored, they had spent enough time around racing to know that anything could happen. Moller had won just a few years earlier, when his son Ralph had ridden Merrylight first across the line in 1938. It had been a decade since Vera McBain (with her partner Billie Liddell) owned a Champion with Mister Cinders, and even longer—twelve years and a marriage ago—since Gussie White won with Pat in 1929. Leslie Hutton had never won the SRC Champions', but he had beaten expectations (and some of these horses) before.

Besides these seven owners with horses in the Champions' Stakes, scores of people and animals prepared for undercard events. "Eleven flat races," the ads announced (no steeplechases or other jumps). First race at 11:00 a.m., tiffin interval after the third race—so, lunch around noon. The last race would start around 4:30, in the gathering dusk. Before then, Champions Day would be a celebration of everything Shanghai.

After checking on their horses, Hench, Aitkenhead, Franklin, and the others could make their way to the clubhouse. Noisy and crowded in a few hours, it was quiet now as they climbed the stairs to the mezzanine. The bar there would be tempting later, but it was early for that, even by Shanghai's notoriously louche standards, so they would head straight to the wood-paneled coffee room. Maybe it was cold enough to start the enormous fireplace, detailed with ironwork creating an interlocking "S-R-C". There, over breakfast, they could think about what lay ahead and read the newspapers that had been delivered. Chinese, Japanese, French, German, and Russian newspapers were printed in Shanghai, but most Race Club members turned for news and opinion to the English-language newspapers—the *North-China Daily News*, *China Press*, and *Shanghai Times* among them.

Eric Cumine, writing in the *North-China Daily News* as "The Chaser," was the racing expert of choice. Cumine had been riding at the track since he was a boy, but constantly trailed behind on weak mounts. He later credited this position—chasing the field—as giving him insights into race strategy and tactics and helping him learn to gauge the strengths and weaknesses of horses and riders. He put this knowledge to use in his newspaper column, and also into the training of his own ponies. Everyone who had followed the fall racing season had opinions about how Champions Day would develop, but as club members sat down to breakfast, Hench could fold and crease the *North-China Daily News* to read Cumine's forecast, on page 6.

Cumine gave Hindhead a good chance to defend his crown and join the tiny club of small ponies that had won three straight Champions'. The weather, though, might be Hindhead's undoing, since he was, "of course, absolutely hopeless on a mud course." Under threatening skies and with rain in the forecast, Cumine reckoned that Henchman would need to rely on his second pony, Northwood, if the rains came. Even on a dry track, Cumine gave Northwood a chance to pull off the upset.[3]

Northwood had been a consistent contender for years, had won one classic, and had beaten Hindhead ten days earlier, during one of the October Extra Race Meetings. Still, Hindhead had won two straight renewals of the Champions', and until beaten, he was King of the Turf. Dagal & Co., one of the most prominent bookmakers in Shanghai, made Hindhead a narrow favorite over Cluniehouse,[4] but Cumine considered Cluniehouse the horse to beat. Despite the strength of Hench's stables, Cumine thought that Cluniehouse was too fast for the competition and would regain the title (but, Henchman would have surely pointed out, Cumine had made the same prediction before the previous two Champions', and on both occasions Hindhead had scored the upset).

Cumine gave three others a chance: McBain's Magic Circle (who had won the Champions' in 1937 as Sparkling Morn, when David Sassoon owned him), and the two White ponies, White Parade and White Night. Also expected to start was Eric Moller's Merrylight, a Champions' winner in 1938. In all, the ten-horse field contained four former Champions, plus two other horses that had finished in the top three, and every one had won a Shanghai classic (the Champions', Derby, Criterion, or St. Leger).

Father of the Nation

TEN O'CLOCK, JIANGWAN

RACING WAS YET TO GET UNDER WAY DOWNTOWN, BUT A FEW miles north of the Race Club, about three thousand people had already gathered in the plaza that Dayu Doon had designed to be the heart of a new Shanghai. This crowd was almost entirely Chinese and mostly men—some in Western-style suits, others wearing traditional Chinese gowns—brought together to observe the birthday of the Chinese Republic's founder, Sun Yat-sen.

Past celebrations had centered on a statue of the man himself, but now there stood an empty pedestal. The fighting of 1937 had destroyed Jiang Xiaojian's sculpture of Sun, but the vacant foundation may have been more appropriate to the occasion. For decades, the Republic of China had observed the anniversary of Sun Yat-sen's birth as a holiday throughout China. In years past, as many as sixty thousand people had come to the Jiangwan Civic Center to celebrate not only Sun's birthday but the renewal of Chinese sovereignty. This day's crowd, though, did not reflect most of Shanghai's Chinese population. As many as could had made their way into the International Settlement, where they were, for now, sheltered from the war. In Jiangwan, which ironically had been meant to serve as a Chinese new Shanghai, it was the Japanese now running the show—making for an uncomfortable spectacle celebrating the birthday of a Chinese patriot. The statue of Sun had been there from the start, a reminder of the government's history and identity. In 1941, though, the statue was gone, and with it, consensus about Sun's legacy.

Where the statue had once stood was now a blank space in which could be written different meanings. For many Chinese, Sun represented patriotism and resistance to Japan; this was why the Japanese had stopped celebrations of Sun's birthday after 1937. But now, for the first time since the invasion, Shanghai's city government would celebrate *guofu*—the "father of the nation"—and the Japanese would use Sun as a symbol to suggest that they were carrying on his legacy by securing China's future (under their tutelage).

More than just renewing a tradition, though, the occasion was now vastly more complex than it had been. In the 1930s, celebrants at Jiangwan had contrasted the resurgent Chinese Republic with the remnants of colonialism nearby in the International Settlement, but what could be made of a patriotic celebration in a city now under foreign occupation?

Chiang Kai-shek's Nanjing government, the successor of the Republic that Sun founded in 1912, had built the civic center and Sun's statue, but that government was now in exile. This new "Republic of China" was the Reorganized National Government formed in March 1940 by the merger of three separate Japanese-led entities under the leadership of Wang Jingwei. The new government had more autonomy

The Jiangwan Civic Center Mayor's Building, showing damage from the 1937 fighting. The plaza, where Sun's statue had been, was on the opposite side of the building.

than its predecessors, and it featured more trappings of independence, including the Nationalist flag, but it existed at Japan's pleasure. Almost everyone in Shanghai, regardless of nationality, considered Wang a Japanese puppet. Some thought he was making the best of a bad situation; others condemned him as a traitorous opportunist.

Sun's legacy presented a dilemma for Wang and his Japanese minders. Promoting Sun might emphasize that the occupying Japanese had usurped his Republic and encourage Nationalist demonstrations or violence. On the other hand, ignoring Sun could reinforce the idea that Wang's government was no heir to the Nationalists who had overthrown the Qing dynasty: Wang claimed to be leading the Republic of China; why was he not celebrating its founder? For four years, Japan had chosen the second option and there had been no official celebrations. Observances—usually small and informal—had continued throughout the Lone Island period in the Settlement, but not in Japanese-occupied parts of the city. Now, in 1941, they would try a different approach, reviving the holidays and marking the occasion with an official celebration at the civic center.

Jiang Xiaojian's sculpture of Sun was not the only thing missing from the Jiangwan Civic Center that morning. Also gone was Fu Xiaoan, the Shanghai mayor inaugurated in 1938. A target for Chinese patriots as soon as he was installed, Fu survived several assassination attempts during his brief time in office until, on October 11, 1940, one of his own bodyguards hacked him to death in his bed. Murders were common in occupied Shanghai, but this was one of the highest-profile killings, and the celebrity of the victim, as well as gruesome nature of the crime—meat cleaver wounds to the throat and forehead were the cause of death—made Fu's murder front-page news.[1]

Against the advice of the Shanghai Municipal Council, Japanese authorities insisted that Fu's funeral process through the streets of the International Settlement, taking the casket from a private home service to a public memorial at the Jiangwan Civic Center. Fearing an incident that might further provoke the Japanese, Settlement authorities cleared the streets as the motorcade drove through, the sounds of Chopin's funeral march and thirty armed policemen accompanying the procession.[2] The Japanese may have wanted a public funeral to demonstrate their presence, but it reminded onlookers that the occupiers were unable to prevent one of their collaborators from being murdered in his sleep, and the stony silence along the route only undermined their legitimacy.

Replacing Fu Xiaoan at the podium on Champions Day 1941 was Chen Gongbo, a high-ranking official in the collaborationist government who would go on to succeed Wang Jingwei as the second (and last) president of the Japanese-supported regime. (Chen would become the highest-profile collaborator to stand trial for his actions during the occupation. Found guilty of treason, he was executed by firing squad in Suzhou in 1946.)[3] A few months before the birthday celebration, Chen had announced a campaign to raise money for a new Sun statue to take the place of the old one, which he described as having "disappeared during hostilities."[4] Outside the civic center flew the new flag of the ersatz Chinese Republic, identical to the old flag, with the addition of a yellow triangle carrying the new government's slogan: "Peace, Anti-Communism, National Reconstruction." Legitimate or not in the eyes of Shanghai's population, Chen's government had the backing of the Imperial Japanese Army.

The official celebrations that Chen Gongbo presided over were small: less than one-tenth the size of the ones held in Jiangwan before the Japanese occupation. The contradictions of the celebration on November 12, 1941, were hard to ignore. In the square that was meant to be the centerpiece of Chinese nationalism, the official festivities—if that is the right word—advocated not resistance to Japan, but acquiescence. Japan's victory was inevitable, they argued, and collaborating would end the war that much sooner and stanch China's bleeding. The celebration at the Jiangwan Civic Center was presented as patriotic, but at best it celebrated the lesser of two evils, and in the eyes of many Chinese it was treason. The new government wrapped itself in the symbols of the Republic, but small differences underscored its illegitimacy: the yellow triangle, the missing statue, the murdered mayor.

Within the protective custody of the International Settlement, attitudes were different. The Chinese-language press praised Sun Yat-sen's ideals and ambitions but did not endorse the celebrations taking place in Jiangwan. *Shenbao* wrote that ceremonies commemorating Sun Yat-sen's birthday in the Settlement were "still suspended because of special circumstances," but noted that this was one of the days designated to fly the national flag and that local schools, banks, and businesses were closed to honor his memory.⁵ English-language newspapers described the unofficial birthday celebrations in Shanghai as "the most enthusiastic in years," buoyed by Chinese newspapers "that claimed China was on its way to victory in the present conflict."⁶ The city's Chinese schools held citywide tournaments—basketball and volleyball—to mark the occasion, all part of the day's "general festive atmosphere."⁷

If the day remained festive, it would defy recent history. Each November 12 since the Japanese occupation had begun, the Settlement's British-run Shanghai Municipal Police had prepared for outbursts of Chinese patriotism and Japanese reprisals (or, sometimes, the reverse). In 1938 the only incident had been the "surreptitious spreading of literature" eulogizing Dr. Sun and urging boycotts of Japanese goods.⁸ Around noon, pamphlets rained down on Nanking Road from an upper-story window, just a few blocks from the racetrack, calling on citizens (in Chinese) to support the Chiang Kai-shek government: "The Japanese hope that China will be divided, but we declare today that we are still a part of the Chinese people and are firmly united with the others. . . . We will not submit, but will fight on until our troops return to Shanghai."⁹ Police investigated the incident, questioning occupants of the office that the pamphlets had come from, but no information was forthcoming.¹⁰

In 1939 the police took more aggressive measures to prevent violence or anti-Japanese agitation. The Settlement authorities understood that they would survive only as long as the nearby Japanese armies tolerated it. Reluctant to act as agents of the Japanese, but likewise unwilling to provoke them, SMP authorities tried to tamp down nationalist activities as the holiday approached. Subinspector Roy Fernandez, a ten-year veteran of the force, led a patrol that rounded up more than fifty "undesirables" on the evening of November 11.¹¹ Another squad detained thirty more. Just before midnight, and again at dawn on the twelfth, British and Chinese detectives (many SMP officers were Chinese) searched three hotels in the blocks surrounding the racecourse on an anonymous tip, but they turned up no evidence of "arms, ammunition, or suspicious persons."¹²

While the Settlement Police worked to avoid anti-Japanese displays, it was the Japanese themselves who were often most disruptive. Also in 1939, some sixteen Japanese, Koreans, and Chinese walked along the

Bund, posting anti-Communist propaganda and also calling on people to celebrate—just like their opponents!—Sun Yat-sen's birthday.[13] The troop, now breaking curfew, plastered posters on telephone poles along the Bund and defied police attempts to disperse them, continuing along the Bund until they reached Nanking Road. They turned west, belligerently processing toward the racetrack, although the arrival of additional police forced the group off of Nanking Road and onto smaller side streets. The moving standoff continued through the streets of central Shanghai, the crowd unwilling to disperse and police unwilling to provoke them, until after 4:00 a.m. Police described the group as "high-handed and anti-Foreign: a very bad crowd of the ronin and hooligan type," adding that they were "certainly anti-Police and of the type who have no respect for law and order."[14]

The police documented dozens of posters and pamphlets from across the political spectrum. Groups with competing political agendas often took quite similar names, drawing on familiar clichés like "national salvation" and wrapping themselves in Sun Yat-sen's legacy, often through a portrait of the late leader, with the result that rivals, often calling for their mutual elimination, prefaced their pamphlets with the same picture of Sun and invoked Sun's "Three People's Principles": democracy, nationalism, and the people's welfare.

A "traitor extermination" group distributed pamphlets at the corner of Nanking and Chekiang Roads, about a quarter mile from the racetrack, calling on "all true citizens of the Republic of China" to "reject any peace movement" and instead fight for their country, rejecting the "despicable citizens turned traitors."[15]

Another group with similar aims distributed a more explicit pamphlet, claiming that the Japanese had realized that their plans to conquer China were unfeasible and were instead spreading peace propaganda through their "puppets" like Wang Jingwei, who would "deliver China into slavery." Freedom, it went on, would come through supporting the "free China" government in Chongqing. Quoting Chiang Kai-shek, they called on the youth of Shanghai to resist the Japanese and the calls for peace and surrender: "The success of the war of resistance from day-to-day does not solely depend upon force but will be due wholly to the amount of spirit in the struggle displayed by the people of the nation as a whole."[16]

Rivals distributed their own literature, supporting the Wang Jingwei government, near the same spot. These pamphlets emphasized the futility and destructiveness of the war against Japan, attributing it to a misguided grab for power by the Chinese Communists. The only hope for China's survival lay in the leadership of Wang Jingwei and an early end to the war.

The disorder of November 1939 prompted increased police vigilance, as both the Settlement police and the Japanese tried to fill cracks that might encourage dissent in the city. November 1940 had passed without incident, with just a few observances in local schools, and the calm seemed to be holding in 1941, too, at least so far. The threat of military force could pressure many in Shanghai to conform outwardly to the wishes of the Japanese, regardless of their personal sentiments. In the International Settlement, the Japanese forced the Shanghai Municipal Police to suppress expressions of anti-Japanese nationalism (it seems clear, however, that the police were inclined to maintain order without much regard for the interests of Chinese nationalism; David Bannerman Ross, who had resigned the police rather than enforce the status quo, was a rare exception). Whether because of Japanese pressure or British compliance, a strong police presence and preemptive arrests left little space for protest on November 12, 1941, and there was no violence and little disruption by Chinese nationalists in either the Settlement or the Chinese-controlled areas.

One of the only exceptions was minor vandalism of Shanghai city buses. Opponents of the Japanese-sponsored regime plastered the buses with bills calling on Chinese to stand up and resist the occupiers. A few blocks later—or perhaps it was the other way around—supporters of the regime covered the same buses with counterpropaganda, urging support for the "peace movement" (which is to say, support for the Japanese occupiers and the Chinese collaborating with them). It is likely that these pro-collaboration placards were distributed by the Wang Jingwei government itself, which had deployed propaganda units to promote its cause across the city.[17] For a few hours on the morning of November 12, buses of Shanghai General Omnibus Company's route number 10 were a mobile dialogue on China's future as they passed along the Bund, turning left near the British consulate to go up Peking Road, coming within a few blocks of the racecourse as they proceeded west.

The traveling debate continued until Japanese authorities discovered and impounded the buses when they passed the boundary of the International Settlement and entered Japanese-occupied territory. The slogans had little impact on the city; by 9:00 a.m. the buses had been taken off the road. An hour later, after the bus company had removed the offending graffiti and promised to remove any other provocative slogans that might be found,[18] the buses were returned to service.

The Hupei Stakes and the Sikong Stakes

ELEVEN O'CLOCK, THE RACE CLUB

AT 11:00 A.M., AS THE CEREMONIES AT JIANGWAN WERE concluding, the much larger crowd at the racetrack gave little thought to Sun Yat-sen, the Japanese, or anything else going on in the city, let alone the wider world. "All cares were thrown to the wind. The Far Eastern tension, the high cost of living, the rice problem, and all such worldly exigencies were forgotten. The issues at hand were of lesser gravity. Hot tips, fall frocks, surprises, dividends, pretty faces. . . . These were the features of the day,"[1] according to the *China Press*.

After weeks of Extra Race Meetings and three days of the Autumn Race Meeting, the fall 1941 Champions Day got under way with the running of the Hupei Stakes. The Race Club usually followed a daily theme in naming races—Ireland, Australia, greater Shanghai—but the Champions Day program was a hodgepodge of Chinese provinces, cities, and regions, from Manchuria to the South China Sea (few Australian place names appeared as well). Leading off, the Hupei Stakes took the name of the Chinese province now romanized as "Hubei" (even in 1941 "Hupei" was a nonstandard variant of the official postal spelling, "Hupeh"). A few hundred miles up the Yangtze River from Shanghai, Hubei is home to the lower stretches of the spectacular Three Gorges, and it was a common destination for the houseboat vacations popular among Shanghailanders before the war.

The crowd in the grandstands cared little what the race was named. People had been arriving since the gates opened, long before the first race, and now there were thousands, mainly Chinese who had walked or ridden buses from the neighborhoods surrounding the racetrack, milling around the grounds. Business was brisk at the betting windows. The owners' enclosure and members' grandstand filled more slowly. The eleven o'clock start may have felt early to those still recovering from a late night spent getting a head start on the holiday. Some owners were at the Mohawk Road stables. Others lingered over their tea or coffee in the clubhouse as the undercard races got under way. The most important races wouldn't begin for several hours yet.

Eric Moller and Cornell Franklin weren't dawdling, though; they had horses in the day's first race. Oddsmakers favored Moller's Frostylight in the Hupei Stakes, but Phantom, "Judge Franklin's wonder-pony," drew attention from bettors hoping he could reprise his performance of two days' earlier, when he had won not once, but twice. On Champions Day, Phantom would again run two races, the second one being the Champions' Stakes: if he could pull off *that* double, he would not only be Champion; he would be legendary.

The day's first contestants loaded into the starting gate.

It burst open. Champions Day was underway!

At the bell, Gabor Renner took Phantom to the lead as usual, but the experienced field did not let him get away. Mikel Hazzard, Charlie Encarnação, Alfred Noodt, and Chris Moller all knew that Phantom had upset White Parade his last time out by building a ten-length lead before the race was half over. This time Renner never got more than two lengths clear. Phantom held a slim lead around the final turn, but it was anyone's race as they turned for home. Down the stretch, the Ku stable's cherry-and-gray silks (worn by Vim), the white and red of Busted Straight, Franklin's blue and red, and Moller's chocolate and gold traded positions—a riot of color in the drizzly morning. Busted Straight, with one of Eric Moller's sons riding, burst past on the outside. The four horses crossed the line in a blanket finish, Busted Straight edging Phantom by a head, with Vim—a regular winner, though never

The Shanghai Municipal Council in its chambers, 1939 or 1940.
Chairman Cornell Franklin is seated in the center of the front row.
Tony Keswick, who was shot at the racetrack in January 1941, is
seated to Franklin's immediate right.

a contender in the classics—third. Frostylight, the favorite, failed to even place, finishing fourth and out of the money.

The day's first race had not disappointed!

The winning ponies, riders, and owners paused and posed in the winner's circle. The other winners—those holding betting tickets—headed for the windows to collect or reinvest their winnings in races to come. Lines at the betting windows ebbed and flowed as results were announced and post times approached. Each race lasted about two minutes, and just twenty-five minutes separated races, while the jockeys changed mounts and the next field was led to the start line. Members in their boxes could telephone their bets to the window, but general-admission punters had barely enough time to put down wagers in time for the next race, especially if they wanted to inspect the ponies as they walked in the parade ring.

The day's second race had an ambiguous name. "Sikong Stakes" probably referred to a mountain range in Anhui province, home to several of Buddhism's most sacred mountains and a vacation spot for Shanghailanders seeking refuge from summer's heat and humidity. Another possibility was Sikong province (officially romanized as "Sikang," though the spelling "Sikong" was common in Shanghai during the 1930s), a culturally Tibetan region in the foothills of the Himalayas, located between Sichuan province and Tibet itself. (Sikong province ceased to exist in 1955, when it was divided between Sichuan and Tibet.) Whatever its namesake, the second race of Champions Day went off around 11:30 a.m.

The Sikong Stakes presented a challenge for gamblers. The owners, trainers, and jockeys stood to win bragging rights and prize money, but most of the thousands—soon to be tens of thousands—crowding into the grandstand came to place bets. In Shanghai, as in most places, betting had initially been done as sweepstakes, or "sweeps." This arrangement was a lottery. Bettors bought tickets that were each assigned at random to a horse on the field; they had no choice about which horse they were backing. There were no odds, and there was no advantage to be gained by studying or understanding the horses. The prize money would be determined by the number of tickets bought, and the winning tickets—the tickets assigned to the winning horse—would divide the winning share, with half of the receipts going to the house. Lesser amounts would be paid out for those finishing further down in the order. There is no skill involved in sweeps, just luck. In 1941, sweeps remained a popular way to participate in the races without investing any time in choosing horses.

The luck involved in sweeps is not just about randomly getting the winning ticket. If a race were truly random, each horse in a ten-horse field would have a 10 percent chance of winning, but even casual fans know that this is not the case. Betting on racing is different from buying a lottery ticket. Some horses and some jockeys are better than others, even if the precise outcome of any race is unknowable in advance. To appeal to those who could—or believed they could—choose a winner better than a random ticket assignment could, handicapping was introduced.

Handicapping is the evaluation of horses, tracks, trainers, and jockeys with an eye to determining which horses are more, or less, likely to win certain races. At its simplest, handicapping looks at a horse's (or jockey's) win-loss record, but all sorts of other information can be analyzed too. What are the horse's training times? How about recent performances? Over certain distances? In different weather conditions? Does starting position or the size of the field have an effect? Is there an injury history? (In Thoroughbred racing, pedigree is an important part of handicapping as well, but this was all but irrelevant to racing China ponies, because horses were not bred but purchased at auction without knowledge of parentage.)

Bookmakers—associated with the track (the "house") or with private individuals or companies—make a "book" of horses' performances and accept bets. Because bettors can choose their horse, they have at least the possibility of improving their chances of winning through expertise. In these "fixed odds" arrangements, bookmakers establish odds in advance and bettors can place money at the agreed-upon price. With these "fractional" odds, the first number is the amount you can win if you put down the second number. So, 4-to-1 odds offer a chance to win $4 if putting down $1: a successful $1 bet on a horse to win at 4-to-1 odds collects $5 (the initial $1 bet, plus the $4 promised in the odds).

In this system, bookmakers establish odds by how likely they think a horse is to win, and horses given a greater chance of winning pay less to winning bettors. If odds are correctly established, a safe bet will probably win but not pay very much money. In this way, odds are a way of luring money to a horse. A high enough potential reward might entice bettors to take a chance on a long shot. By adjusting the odds, bookmakers could manipulate the wagering, encouraging bets on horses that would probably not win, and discouraging bets on likely winners that they would have to pay.

An ad for Dagal & Co. in the November 12 sports pages showed how this worked. Dagal's gave odds on each of the Champions' Stakes entrants, from Hindhead, their favorite, to the long shot Mr. Bubbins (illustrating the point that these odds were established in advance, odds were listed for horses that did not even qualify for the Champions', like Franklin's Silver Fox). Hindhead was listed at 1:1 odds ("even money"), meaning for each dollar bet, you could win, along with your original stake, a dollar, doubling your money. Dagal's priced Cluniehouse (considered the favorite by most bookmakers) similarly, at 1½:1 (today usually written as 3:2).

Both of these horses were given good chances to win, but anyone betting on them would be only modestly rewarded, especially since even the most conservative and well-informed bet will not always win. A series of even-money bets, winning some and losing some, is not likely to win, or lose, you much money, but if the odds are made correctly and you bet consistently, you have a good chance of ending your day with more money than you started. On the other hand, Dagal's was offering 40:1 odds to bet on Mr. Bubbins to win the Champions'.[2] A losing $5 bet on Mr. Bubbins meant simply losing $5, but a winning $5 bet on him would pay $200. Casual racegoers are more likely to put a small bet on long odds, hoping—against the odds—to win a lot with little investment.

By 1941, however, most of the wagering in Shanghai, as at most tracks, was not done through sweeps or fixed odds, but by the pari-mutuel, introduced to Shanghai soon after its invention in France in the 1860s. In pari-mutuel betting, gamblers are, in effect, betting against one another, not the house. All the money that is wagered, on every horse, is pooled together, and the winning bets split the receipts (after the track takes its commission). More popular bets—the favorites—have more bettors and therefore divide the pool more ways, into smaller winnings. Less popular bets might have only a few backers and so can return enormous sums in the (less likely) event they win. The bettors, rather than the oddsmakers, establish the odds (though informal or unofficial odds, or fixed odds offered by private bookies, influence how money is placed). The payout in pari-mutuel betting is constantly changing, recalculated as bets are placed, and bettors are not guaranteed the payout being offered at the time the bet is made. The final payout is not determined until post time, when the race begins and betting is closed.

Long shots are the delight of casual fans and the undoing of serious gamblers and professionals. Amateur gamblers are paying for excitement, and betting on a 100:1 shot is exciting, win or lose. Professionals rarely bet on a long shot, because it probably won't win; the reason a horse *is* a long shot to begin with is that the professionals don't like its chances.

The Sikong Stakes on Champions Day 1941 brought in the longest shot of the day—delighting a handful of fans and frustrating the oddsmakers. The favorite in this race was M. Z. Liu's Slow Motion. Liu was one of the most prominent of the Chinese owners who had moved his ponies to "town" (the Shanghai Race Club) when the encroaching war closed the Jiangwan track. Slow Motion was one of his best ponies, competing with the favorites that would run the Champions' that afternoon. The day before, Slow Motion had finished third behind Phantom and White Night, and ten days earlier, he had finished in a dead heat for second place with Hindhead, the defending King of the Turf. Emboldened by these performances, bettors picked Slow Motion to win against the lesser field of the Sikong Stakes.

Yet, keen observers would have noticed that the newspapers printed on race day had picked Tony Liang's Hill Song—the giant-killer who had beaten Cluniehouse a week earlier—to win the first race. Liang was a popular choice in the paddock and in the grandstand. Goodlooking and stylish, with an easy smile, he was one of the best athletes in the International Settlement, especially in tennis, where he competed in both the city championships (both doubles and singles) and on the interport team against Tianjin, Ningbo, and other treaty ports. Liang also owned ponies, and usually rode them himself.

Too late for the morning papers, and escaping the attention of many bettors, Liang entered Hill Song in the second race, not the first. Little noticed—just 173 bets were placed on Hill Song, as opposed to 1,663 on Slow Motion—Hill Song entered the starting gate as one of the strongest horses in the field, but a long shot to win. Three horses finished the race within a length of one another, but Liang brought Hill Song across the line first; a $5 bet returned $110.40, the richest payout of the day—enough to pay an entire year's rent for a room in one of the more desirable neighborhoods in the International Settlement.[3] Even for a professional like Nates Wong, who might have paid $30 a month to live—far more than most workers could afford—the chance to win that kind of money in a single afternoon was hard to resist.

Slow Motion failed even to place.

CHAPTER

17

· · · ·

The Wealthiest Woman in China

TWELVE NOON, AILI GARDENS

A FEW BLOCKS WEST OF THE TRACK, BUBBLING WELL
Road still echoed with the sounds of cheering race fans as two white
archways rose 30 feet into the air, framing the thoroughfare. White,
not black, is the customary color of mourning in China, and these traditional *pailou* gates announced a funeral.

Constructed in the weeks leading up to November 12 and adorned in
flowers, these archways marked the entrance to Aili Gardens, the landscape of pavilions and pagodas—also known as Hardoon Gardens—
where Liza Hardoon would finally be laid to rest, more than a month
after her death. Alongside Buddhist monks, police and private security
guards walked the grounds, some with pistols drawn, to maintain order
and to protect the Hardoon heirs.

Liza Hardoon had died at her estate on October 3, the day before
the autumn racing season began. Newspapers reported that her many
friends and associates were shocked by the news, but this was wrong
on both counts.[1] She was seventy-eight years old and increasingly frail,
so although she had been ill for only a short time, her death was hardly
unexpected. In a decade as a widow, Liza had become more and more
withdrawn. The court fight that had awarded her Silas's entire estate

had been bitter, and alienated her from some in Shanghai. Photographers who tried to verify occasional rumors of her demise were routinely ousted from the grounds, their cameras smashed.[2]

Liza had taken an active role in her late husband's businesses, primarily real estate at this point. The signature project was a new tower, well located about halfway between the Bund and the racecourse. Rising twelve stories at the corner of Nanking and Szechuan Roads, this art deco "Liza Hardoon Building" was one of the first skyscrapers in Shanghai to have central air-conditioning; its fifty apartments sold out before construction was even completed, in the spring of 1936.[3] The main tenant, Chase Bank, occupied the first two floors, starting in the spring of 1938.[4]

Aside from the business, Liza Hardoon's Buddhist faith and her children occupied her last years (the scandals surrounding son George were especially tiresome). George threatened her physically to obtain money to pay for his lifestyle as a Shanghai socialite, leading her to take out ads in the Chinese and English press claiming she had disowned him and was not responsible for his debts.[5]

Burial was scheduled for two days later, on October 6, but it didn't happen. There was an elaborate ceremony for Liza on that date, her body dressed in silks and pearls and placed in a mahogany casket befitting an empress, which her wealth certainly justified, but she was not interred. The delay—perhaps to do with finding an auspicious burial date based on geomancy or other Chinese methods—was common for a Buddhist burial, but it was certainly not in keeping with Jewish tradition, which requires the body to be buried right away. The delay raised eyebrows and fueled the controversy over the disposition of Liza's estate.[6]

November 12—Champions Day—was chosen as the new burial date.

The *China Press* called Liza Hardoon's funeral the most elaborate Shanghai had ever seen,[7] which was saying something. The city was no stranger to extravagant memorials, like Silas Hardoon's a decade earlier, which had been covered around the world, or "merchant prince" Zhu Baosan's, which had included an hours-long procession through all of Shanghai—the Chinese city, French Concession, and International Settlement. Liza's outdid all of those.

Buddhist monks, some of whom had been maintaining a vigil of

*It took several days to construct this funeral arch across Bubbling
Well Road for Liza Hardoon's funeral. On the morning of
November 12, 1941, buses like the double-decker passing beneath
the arch were vandalized with pro- and anti-Japanese propaganda.*

continuous chanting since her death on October 3, officiated against a
backdrop of Western and Chinese instruments and musicians at a ceremony blending Buddhist and Jewish rites. By some estimates, 20,000
people crowded into Aili Gardens, almost as many as at the racecourse,
and far more than were gathered in Jiangwan to honor Sun Yat-sen.
Many mourners arrived by automobile, a line of cars backing up onto
Bubbling Well Road to enter the gardens under the watchful eye of
the police. Once inside, invited guests received a badge with a photograph of the deceased before being escorted along a blue-and-white
aisle of cloth.

The vast scale of the event required a ten-minute walk to the funeral
hall, following instructions announced over loudspeakers that played
mourning music when not being used to direct the proceedings. Once
they had found their way to the funeral hall, mourners approached an
altar and bowed three times in respect for Mrs. Hardoon, then were
ushered to one of more than a hundred banquet tables to be served a
meal, with instructions to eat as quickly as possible so that all of the
5,000 official guests could join in.[8]

The attendance ought not to have been surprising. Liza Hardoon was, after all, one of the richest women in the world. When she died, her personal effects included more than eighty pieces of jewelry crafted from gold, silver, or platinum and featuring diamonds, sapphires, rubies, and emeralds, as well as dozens of pearl necklaces and bracelets, and hundreds of loose pearls.[9] Shanghai guidebooks listed her estate as a tourist attraction, with nearly a thousand servants and staff, including, it was rumored, eunuchs who had served the last emperors in Beijing before the abdication of the last Qing emperor in 1912. Dozens of Buddhist monks and nuns also lived on the estate.

Liza Hardoon's celebrity had only grown in the weeks since her death. Besides the several ceremonies and rituals that had been held to prepare for her burial, a bitter conflict over her will was ramping up in the press and in the courts. She had left virtually her entire fortune to her adopted children, and had provided for her confidant Chi Cho-mi and his family to continue living at the Hardoon estate in a will written in 1931. This will had entered probate, but a second will had been discovered in her home after her death, apparently not filed with the law firm that had kept the first. This new will, from 1937, would, if validated, supersede the earlier document. Her late husband's will had been challenged in court by Hardoon relatives in Baghdad and by the Jewish community in Shanghai. It now appeared certain that Liza Hardoon's own will would wind up in court too—unsurprisingly, given the vast fortune at stake.[10]

This second will cast Hardoon as a philanthropic and progressive figure. Her patronage of Buddhist temples and publications was important to many thousands of people in Shanghai, and her will indicated that she hoped her wealth would benefit many across the city, through property bequests to various governmental and charitable organizations: $500,000 to start a "public school for poor children in the International Settlement," $1 million to the Chinese government "for the purpose of improving the public welfare," $1 million to the Shanghai Municipal Council "for the purpose of improving public school conditions and general educational training," $1 million for a nunnery and home for the aged poor to be built in Aili Gardens, and another $500,000 to support Buddhism. She left an even larger amount of property—$6 million worth—to establish factories "to help the unemployment of workers," though without specifics that might distinguish this effort from investing in new factories generally.[11]

Liza Hardoon's 1937 will divided her fortune among her adopted children, but she left property worth many millions of dollars to different people around Shanghai. Even George Hardoon, the "millionaire playboy" who had performed alongside Ing Tang and scandalized his mother with his antics since his father's death, was conditionally included: Liza left George a sum of $140,000 (worth more than US$2 million today) to be held in trust until he was twenty-five (he was then about twenty-three), and then only released to him on the condition that Liza's appointed trustees would find him to be leading "a good and virtuous life." If not, his inheritance would be revoked. "I have made the above mentioned condition of good behavior," Hardoon wrote, "because during my life the said David George has caused me many troubles and has actually threatened me with a revolver in order to get money from me and has also attempted to defraud the public. . . . I no longer acknowledge him as my adopted son."[12]

Most controversially, Hardoon left the greatest single amount of property—$4 million—to Chi Cho-mi, who had moved in to the Hardoon estate and, along with lawyer David Abraham, was named executor. Many in Shanghai regarded Chi suspiciously, feeling that he was taking advantage of his ailing and isolated patron. One of Chi's bodyguards had even been arrested a few weeks earlier on suspicion of stealing documents related to the Hardoon estate (he was released without charge).[13] Whether his influence was inappropriate or not, Chi Cho-mi was well taken care of. In addition to the property, Hardoon gave him the right to continue living at the Hardoon estate for the rest of his life and to be buried there, near Liza and her husband.[14]

All of this was headed to court as mourners gathered on November 12. The will was being contested in numerous ways, each of which illustrated the complexities of Shanghai. Some of the drama was predictable: the Hardoon children stood to inherit substantially less under the 1937 will than under the 1931 one, so they questioned the later will's validity; George, who found his entire inheritance in jeopardy according to the new will, was particularly opposed. Other objections were more specific to Shanghai: the Chinese government challenged the will on the grounds that Liza Hardoon "had never lost her citizenship of the Republic of China," and thus she and her children were all Chinese citizens, over whom British courts had no jurisdiction.

Although the Shanghai city government protested, there was no indication that it had any power to prevent the Settlement authorities from enforcing the will. Private citizens weighed in: some Shanghailanders dismissed the Chinese government's claims as the actions of "cash-hungry politicians who would loot the properties" and instead contended that the Settlement should acquire the Hardoon estate to be a public park, partly out of the recognition that "everything that Mr. and Mrs. Hardoon possessed, and everything that their heirs now inherit, represents a debt to Shanghai."[15]

A Chinese newspaper columnist in Shanghai used a similar justification, as well as questioning the legitimacy of the adopted Hardoon children, to suggest redistributing the Hardoon fortune: "The late Mr Hardoon rose from a watchman and accumulated all his wealth in Shanghai and since he left no offspring his wealth should be returned to Shanghai."[16] He called for a public committee to determine how to spend the Hardoon estate. Arguments to determine which of the two wills would be executed were to be heard two days after the funeral, on November 14.

Legal disputes notwithstanding, a funeral procession that would lay Liza Hardoon to rest began at 1:20 on the afternoon of the twelfth, ending at a mausoleum that stonemasons had worked around the clock for days to prepare. Three bands played a mixture of Western and Chinese funeral music as part of the procession, thirty-two pallbearers carried the ornate casket draped with red silk—so heavy that even the large number of bearers had to stop frequently.

Spectators lined the entire route. Sixty photographers recorded the event for newspapers and newsreels as the Hardoons' numerous adopted children led the procession beneath a course of ceremonial gates decorated with lanterns across the gardens, each accompanied by a servant and guarded by armed police. When the procession finally reached the grave, mourners lowered the casket by ropes, while an orange-robed priest concluded the service by making sure the body was oriented on a north-south axis. Carved granite slabs, quarried in Suzhou, were placed atop the grave alongside offerings of gold and silver as the ceremony concluded. By the time the rituals, processions, offerings, feasts, and burial had all ended, there might have been barely enough time for mourners to make it to the racetrack before the big race.

CHAPTER

1 8

. . . .

The Oodnadatta Cup, Sinkiang Stakes, and Jockey Cup

TWO O'CLOCK, THE RACE CLUB

LEFT: *Original caption: "Studying the form-book: Chinese punters."*
Shanghai Race Club, 1939. RIGHT: *Original caption: "When the Chinese*
punter seeks supernatural aid in picking a winner: burning scarlet candles
and incense . . . just outside the stables." Shanghai Race Club, 1939.

THERE WAS NO WAY DAYU DOON WOULD MISS CHAMPIONS Day. The architect kept horses in his own personal stable at his French Concession home.[1] His firm on Museum Road, just behind the Bund and within sight of the Japanese lines across Suzhou Creek, was closed for the holiday like most businesses in the International Settlement. Driving to the track from the French Concession would have been harder than usual. Crowds of bettors gathered around the statues near the corner of Bubbling Well and Mohawk Roads to make offerings, whether out of force of habit or genuine belief that they would guarantee good fortune at the course. More focused on horses than on cars, luck seekers often spilled out into the roadway, snarling traffic around the racecourse. (Such concerns would lead to the statues' removal, but not until 1948.) It was not a pleasant day. The wind, now blowing at more than 20 miles per hour, made the damp November afternoon feel much colder than the 55 degrees the thermometer indicated. But however you got there and whatever the weather, the Shanghai Race Club was the place to be.

Dayu Doon came to Shanghai to make a new, Chinese city center in Jiangwan, but after narrowly escaping destruction in the 1932 war, Doon's buildings had been burned and bombed just as construction neared completion in 1937, and now they were occupied by Japanese armies and collaborating politicians. New Shanghai was in jeopardy, but this was a day to revel in Old Shanghai, if you could. And while he couldn't be a member of the Race Club, Doon had plenty of American and British friends who would bring him along for tiffin. Tiffin at the SRC was a point of pride for Shanghailanders. Fresh food could be expected; dairy, produce, chicken, beef, and pork could all be sourced from the local countryside—though availability was down, and prices up, since the Japanese had surrounded the Settlement. Nonetheless, even in 1941 a first-rate tiffin could offer as many as ten courses, including roast beef, fish, Waldorf salad, grapefruit, consommé, and even turtle soup,[2] served in the Race Club's elaborately appointed tiffin rooms. Others ate outside, despite the chilly afternoon, hosting barbecues.[3]

Of course, most racegoers weren't enjoying turtle soup or roast beef. Chinese palates in Shanghai were said to prefer "a blend of sweet, sour and salty flavors. A combination of soy sauce, vinegar, a pinch of sugar and a dash of Shaoxing rice wine . . . *xiaolongbao*, pork dumplings wrapped in translucent skin so their juicy flavors could burst in your mouth, and *shengjianbao*, made in a bread-like casing and pan-friend until brown and crispy," not to mention hundreds of varieties of tofu, that came in almost any texture, shape, and consistency.[4]

As in many major cities, a tradition of street food had grown up in Shanghai, especially in the densely populated area around the race-track. Peddlers selling all varieties of food could be found in the streets surround the Race Club; Shanghai's version of a food truck was a man carrying a portable kitchen on a bamboo pole: a "clever contraption . . . slung over the vendor's shoulders, with a coal burner for boiling or roasting; cupboards and drawers for raw ingredients; and pots, bowls and utensils."[5] Noodles, dumplings, or soup from these vendors was available on virtually every corner in the Settlement.[6]

In the Lone Island period, food in Shanghai was more varied and abundant than in most parts of China, even within reach of factory workers, clerks, and shopkeepers.[7] Restaurants all around the race-course offered hungry race fans choices befitting this city of migrants: Shaoxing pork, Sichuan *mapo* tofu, and Guangzhou oyster sauce were just some of the varieties available. On a tighter budget, rice restaurants—self-styled as "proletarian"—were plentiful in the dense urban center of Shanghai, offering rice dishes with greens and tofu for just a few cents.[8] These were the opposite of "bourgeois" restaurants, which served dishes of a greater variety (and higher cost), often with Western influences (Russian stew, for example).

Or, just a few blocks away, "Food Market Street" offered variety matched in few cities around the world. The market near the Great World Amusement Center—just across the street from the track—sold more than two thousand different types of food.[9] The Taiping Bridge food market, which had opened in 1917, was just a short walk away from the racetrack's far turn, leaving plenty of time to make it there and back in time to place a bet on the Champions'.

When racing resumed after lunch, Champions Day shifted into high gear. "Braving the first tentative feelers of winter's cold grasp, they came in their thousands," reported the *North-China Daily News*, "pouring through the enclosures, swarming round the paddock, jostling each other at the betting counters."[10] Their next opportunity to bet was the Cunnamulla Handicap, named for a small town in northeastern Australia, run in three divisions because of the large number of entries (more than ten ponies entered each one). The favorites held form, in each case by two lengths or more.

The next race was also named for a small Australian town, Oodnadatta, reputed to be the hottest and driest town on the continent. Jimmy Pote-Hunt rode Andover to win that one, finishing the mile two lengths ahead of Y. S. Chang on Golden Hen. At 3:00 p.m., the day's largest field—twenty-three starters—went off in the Sinkiang Stakes, named for the largely Muslim region of northwestern China that is today usually romanized as "Xinjiang." With so many horses running, all the major Shanghai stables were represented: Cire, Clunie, Henchman, Tony Liang, Light.

By this time of the day, most of the riders were exhausted. At most race meetings, today just as much as in 1941, riders report to the jockey room before their first race, to be weighed and checked in. Except when they are racing, they must remain in the jockeys' enclosure until their day's races are complete. At the Shanghai Race Club, the rules were more lax, particularly for the handful of owner-riders, but about a dozen jockeys rode throughout the day, some of them five or six times, meaning that they would finish one race and go immediately to their next ride, probably changing silks to represent a different stable. Finishing first and second in the Sinkiang Stakes were two of the most prominent jockeys of the time: G. P. "Sonny" Gram and Eric Cumine. Gram, the winner, was among Shanghai's winningest jockeys (1941 was not his best year; his nineteen victories that year were good for only sixth place in the jockey standings).

The last race before the Champions' Stakes was the Jockey Cup, a tradition at the club dating back to at least the 1860s. The Champions' was for winners only, but the Jockey Cup was just the opposite: a race among also-rans. Only horses and jockeys who had yet to win a race in Shanghai or Hong Kong that season were eligible. In its early years, the Jockey Cup had acted as consolation races do in many settings, a "last-chance race" that gave non-winners an opportunity to qualify for the Champions', but as the number of horses competing, the quality of the fields, and the professionalism of the entire enterprise increased, it became impossible to imagine a horse winning the Jockey Cup and then, a few minutes later, competing in the biggest race of the season.

By the twentieth century, the Jockey Cup served mainly to give those in attendance a chance to catch their breath and study the racing form one last time before placing their bets for the main event. Cornell Franklin, Robert Aitkenhead, Vera McBain, Gussie White, and the rest of the owners running in the Champions' could check on their horses before they headed to the parade ring or saddling area and then to the starting gate. Elise Andrews and the other trainers could use this moment to inspect their charges for signs of lameness or other injury. With non-winning jockeys piloting this race, Charlie Encarnação, Alex Striker, and the other riders who had been in constant motion since before could briefly rest, assessing their mount's mood and fine-tuning their race strategy. In a few minutes, their decisions and skill might well decide who was Champion and who was forgotten, but not yet. Now, they tried to calm themselves and their horses and to anticipate the moves of opponents they had raced against hundreds of times, over many years.

Standing at the rail, C. S. Mao could revel in the greatest racing day of the year and maybe reflect on the journey that had brought him here. Decades earlier, he had been destitute, fired from his job at a leather factory for stealing. Homeless and sleeping under a shed at the Shanghai docks, he was working odd jobs just to survive. He had met men there who eventually enabled him to join Du Yuesheng's Green Gang, and for years now had been one of Shanghai's most powerful men. When the Japanese invaded, Mao stayed because of the horses, racing throughout the Lone Island period.[11] He had nearly a dozen horses stabled across the street at Mohawk Road, including several winners so far this fall, but only SRC members—that is, no Chinese—could enter the Champions' Stakes. As the entrants for the big race walked in the parade ring, Mao was once against faced with the colonial restrictions that kept him an outsider.

Nates Wong, Ing Tang, and Dayu Doon didn't own or ride horses at the club, but they could bet on them. Bets would close at post time, when the race would begin—the moment to shut out war and inflation and all the worries of daily life in 1941 Shanghai. Wong had been harassed by police, disenfranchised by his employer. Tang had been disappointed by marriage and by Broadway. Doon had seen his career's greatest achievement bombed and burned. All three had spent a decade or more in Shanghai, building bridges between foreigners and Chinese so that they could translate one another's languages, play one another's games, design one another's buildings, and learn how to be what the other wanted. With war, it had all come crashing down. Their country was all but lost. The Britain they had so admired and emulated was on the verge of extinction too. America might offer opportunity, but it seemed unable to commit itself.

And of course, there were horses. Diminutive ponies dressed up and trained to go as fast as they could for a mile and a quarter. Hindhead didn't know that he had a chance to be just the sixth horse since 1869 to win three Champions' in a row. Nor did Cluniehouse realize that he had been favored twice to return to the winner's circle, only to come up short both times, disappointing thousands of backers. Phantom could help his owner get over heartbreak; White Night and Magic Circle had an opportunity to return to the glory they had once known as Champions. None of these animals knew the opportunities they faced, though surely they sensed the tension in the moment as saddles, riders, and the hopes of 20,000 people were heaped onto their broad shoulders and short legs.

It was a sideshow, but even the Jockey Cup was a contest among top stables: Arthur Henchman and Eric Moller had horses running. Hench sent out Ashridge, while Moller's Frostylight carried the chocolate and gold. In a race among perennial also-rans, the two left the gate stride for stride together, but not in the lead. A horse named Ideal King took the lead from the start, before handing it off to Bober, a horse best known for throwing its rider after being kicked in the face during one race meeting. By the time the field reached the homestretch, Ashridge and Frostylight were the only two in contention. The pair battled past the grandstand until Ashridge eked out a half-length win. Bober held on for third, three lengths behind the leaders.

Henchman had his second win of the day.

Now for the one that mattered.

Murder over New York

THREE O'CLOCK,
THE FRENCH CONCESSION

ALMOST WITHIN EARSHOT OF THE FUNERAL MUSIC FADING
as the mourners dispersed from Aili Gardens, a smaller crowd was
gathering inside the Cathay Theatre just over the border in the French
Concession—"Frenchtown," as the Brits liked to call it. The Cathay
wasn't Shanghai's first cinema, but it may have been the grandest when
it opened on New Year's Day 1932, designed in the eclectic style favored
by movie palaces of the era all over the world. Art deco geometry
defined the street front, but Ionic columns, Mediterranean arcades, and
a replica of the Venus de Milo filled the lobby. A marble staircase led to
a 1,700-seat auditorium, surrounded by archways and more columns.

As the lights went down, a soundtrack of brass and woodwinds
swelled, chromatic chords that caricatured Chinese music as the screen
showed concrete towers along a waterfront. Crowded sidewalks and
streets came into focus as ships were loaded with freight and passengers
waited at the docks. The scenes could have been mistaken for Shanghai,
but they weren't. This was Manhattan, the setting for the latest Charlie Chan movie, *Murder over New York*, which opened in Shanghai on
Champions Day—showtimes 3:00, 5:30, and 9:15 p.m..

Shanghai and cinema became global phenomena side by side in the early twentieth century. By the 1930s, more than forty cinemas were spread all across the city, showing Western—mostly Hollywood—and Chinese films. Defying predictions, the movie business thrived during the Lone Island period. The Cathay was one of a dozen first-run theaters, including the Nanking, Roxy, Grand, and Majestic, in the Settlement that showed Hollywood movies when they first arrived in China. Located on the main streets of the International Settlement and the French Concession, these enormous showplaces seated from 1,100 to 2,000 people and regularly sold out during the Lone Island period.[1]

A single management company, Asia Theaters, Inc., owned all the first-run foreign-film cinemas by 1941. Although registered in Delaware, with Cornell Franklin among its directors, most of the group's management was Chinese. Asia Theaters cinemas were expensive and served mainly the professional classes in Shanghai, with state-of-the-art sound and projection systems, plush carpets, and air-conditioning. They also pioneered secondary audio, offering headphones that plugged into individual seats (sometimes at an additional charge) to provide Chinese dubbing, underscoring the mixed nature of the audiences attending the movies.[2] There were Chinese first-run cinemas too, showing the latest productions from the Shanghai studios. Among these was the Jincheng ("Golden Palace"), another art deco gem that opened in 1933 near Nanking Road, and the Xinguang, where China's first "talkie" had premiered in 1931.

Most movie houses in the Settlement were less imposing, though the second-run theaters, which showed films at lower prices after their initial one- or two-week engagements, also evoked the "posh art deco" style of the more elite cinemas. Many more theaters showed movies on their third or fourth run for just a few cents. Most of the Settlement's population, regardless of nationality or class, had access to the same movies, though they experienced them in much different settings and not always at the same time.[3]

Even more than the races, the comfort and style of these theaters could provide a few hours' respite from the uncertainty all around, in the fantasy of Oz, the slapstick of Laurel and Hardy, or the style of screen stars at the height of Hollywood's glamor. Not everyone was a fan, and not all the movies were American. A nationalist film critic with

Scene from Murder over New York, *starring Sidney Toler as Charlie Chan (center), which opened in Shanghai on Champions Day 1941.*

the government-in-exile in Chongqing derided Shanghai as a "Solitary Island of scoundrels" interested in nothing but money, whose films "help the enemy by debilitating our fighting will."[4] Others differed, suggesting that cinema "offers the greatest source of spiritual nourishment for people in the Lone Island."[5]

The 1939 Chinese runaway hit *Mulan Joins the Army* countered suggestions that cinemas were just a place to ignore the war. Shot and produced in Shanghai by the only film company that remained in operation, the film took a familiar legend filled with nationalist messages and enhanced the commentary for Shanghai's present condition. After debuting at the Astor Theatre, the movie played to full houses in Shanghai for weeks.

For Chinese-speaking filmgoers who wanted to take advantage of the Champions Day holiday, there was plenty to see, as usual. Playing at the Jincheng was *Lonely Soul of the Dark Night (Heiye guhun)*, a love/ghost story directed by its star, Gong Jianong.[6] Li Pingqian's tragedy *The Way Out (Shenglu)* was on at the Huguang Theatre, not far from the Bund. Closer to the racetrack, the newly opened United (Guolian) Theatre was showing *In the Tiger's Lair (Longtan huxue)*, about young women breaking free of superstition. Just a few blocks away, the Xin-guang Theatre was showing Yue Feng's *A Little Lady* (*Xiaofuren*), a story of true love and rebellion against arranged marriage.[7]

Shanghailanders who wanted to see Hollywood films had even more options. The Grand, with its entrance just across Bubbling Well Road from the Race Club, was showing Edward G. Robinson and Ida Lupino in *The Sea Wolf*. At the Nanking, near the racecourse, audiences could watch Veronica Lake's "Blonde Bomber" fly Ray Milland and William Holden into the ground in *I Wanted Wings*. Vivien Leigh played oppo-site Laurence Olivier in *Lady Hamilton* at the Majestic. Olivier was also on at the Golden Gate, a second-run theater where *Pride and Preju-dice* had been held over, delaying Johnny Weissmuller's latest Tarzan installment. Buck Jones was on at the Uptown; Jimmy Stewart, Judy Garland, Hedy Lamarr, and Lana Turner, at the Roxy. Bette Davis's *The Little Foxes* was coming soon.[8]

Shanghailanders especially loved it when the movies promoted Shanghai. Though the city never appeared on-screen in *Shanghai Express*, the film, starring Marlene Dietrich and Anna May Wong, had put the city's name on marquees around the world as the highest-grossing film of 1932, but the Chinese government banned its release in China (Universal later agreed not to make any more films dealing with Chinese politics). Nonetheless, when Wong—born in America to Chi-nese parents—made a trip to the city in 1936, she came to much fanfare, headlining society events alongside visiting royalty and heads of state. When she received star billing for her 1938 film *Daughter of Shang-hai*, the local papers were disappointed that, despite the title, Shanghai played only a small role in the film. Shanghailanders were hard to sat-isfy: they objected when Shanghai was caricatured in the press or the arts, but grumbled when their metropolis did not receive its due as one of the world's great cities.

When it came to on-screen depictions of Chinese, Chinese audi-ences gravitated toward stories of national heroes or heroines challeng-ing traditional roles, like the masculine action heroes that Gong Jianong played, or the tradition-defying women of *In the Tiger's Lair* or *A Little Lady*. Not everyone in Shanghai was comfortable with these depictions. Shanghailanders found their ideal on-screen Chinese character—one not actually played by a Chinese actor—in Charlie Chan. Chan, like

Shanghai, was ambiguous: a global brand full of stereotypes and contradictions, with surprising substance and importance, but ultimately operating according to Western rules and standards. The character was always the smartest detective in the room, solving crimes that flummoxed his white counterparts. At the same time, his brilliance was two-dimensional, spoken in fortune-cookie aphorisms and trading on crude cultural stereotypes, even though his caricature was preferable to sinister depictions of Chinese men like Dr. Fu Manchu (Chinese censors routinely banned those films).

The screen version of Chan was more genial, less threatening, and more stereotyped than that found in Earl Derr Biggers's novels; some saw him as an "Uncle Tom" who had given up his dignity to serve Westerners (in one simple but telling illustration, Charlie Chan always addresses his Western colleagues by their title but is typically addressed himself as "Charlie"). White Shanghailanders found in his neat suits, refined manners, competent professionalism, and impeccable logic exactly the nonthreatening "model minority" they wanted. Charlie Chan was Chinese but wasn't a peasant, a revolutionary, or a gangster. That he was based on a real person—Detective Chang Apana of the Honolulu Police Department—seemed to make him all the more appealing.[9]

Swedish actor Warner Oland was the first to portray Chan on film—one of the most prominent examples of yellowface in cinema (Oland regularly referred to a vague Asian ancestry, but it was never documented or demonstrated). Oland's yellowface was not restricted to Charlie Chan either. He played the evil Dr. Fu Manchu—once opposite Anna May Wong—and also had a role in *Shanghai Express* as a Chinese bandit. For Shanghailanders, though, the line between Warner Oland and Charlie Chan blurred, and both became heroes.

In 1936, the Settlement had buzzed with rumors that Oland would come to Shanghai for the opening of *Charlie Chan in Shanghai*.[10] Near the start of that film, Chan says as he steams up the Huangpu River, "Most anxious to renew acquaintance with land of honorable ancestors," and Oland played nearly the same role when he arrived there, a few months before the film opened. Scheduling conflicts had made it impossible for Oland to be in Shanghai for the film's premier, but he so deeply ingratiated himself to the city during his short visit that any disappointments were forgiven.

Oland stayed in character as Charlie Chan during most of his trip, announcing in cringeworthy syntax that his reason for visiting Shanghai was to "visit graves honorable ancestor." Racist self-parody or not, his enthusiasm for the city was clear. "I got up at 5:30 this morning as I was so anxious to have a glimpse of Shanghai . . . and the first impression I got of the city was its beauty," he told reporters. Oland spent almost a week in Shanghai, touring temples, dining with the mayor, and being hosted at dinner parties, endearing himself to the city.[11] When the picture debuted in May, the reception was predictably bubbly. "Shanghai Made Glamorous Spot in Chan Film: Latest Oland Opus Is More Realistic Than Might Be Supposed," enthused the *China Press* when it opened at the Grand.[12]

It was not Warner Oland who audiences on Champions Day would see, though. After making another seven Charlie Chan movies, Oland had died suddenly two years after *Charlie Chan in Shanghai* was released. Oland's personal popularity and his perceived affection for Shanghai fueled the character's appeal, but it did not need him to succeed. A Charlie Chan comic strip began appearing in the *China Press* so that Shanghai audiences could have even more access to the "greatest detective of all time," and the films starring Oland's successor, Sidney Toler, continued to draw. The movies appeared at a breakneck pace: Toler made three Chan movies in 1939, and another four in 1940. *Murder over New York* was the last of the 1940 productions, but it did not make it to Shanghai screens until November 1941.

The opening of *Murder over New York* was more than just the latest in a highly successful franchise—more than twenty films up to that point; it was, in Shanghai, a pop culture event. Critical reviews were mixed, not that this was the point of the movie. "Quite one of the best of the series," wrote the *North-China Daily News*. "A very pleasant evening's escape from soaring prices and what-not." The *China Press* was blunter: "One cannot say that this is an excellent film, but Charlie Chan fans will not be disappointed."[13]

Party at the End of the World

FOUR O'CLOCK, THE RACE CLUB

This poster was popular in Shanghai during the 1930s, probably as part of a calendar. Visible in the background: the foreign YMCA, the China United Apartment (with the tower), and horses racing (backwards!) on the racecourse.

At the Shanghai races, 1928.

DUSK WAS GATHERING ALONG WITH ANTICIPATION AT THE racetrack. By post time, the cold had brought out overcoats and hats in the grandstand. Booze helped ward off the chill in the members' enclosure; it had been flowing since champagne corks popped at the midday tiffin—maybe earlier. On cold days such as this, the club was known to run out of brandy, leaving little doubt about the state of the members: "The enclosures and the stands were a seething mass of humanity. When the time came, they swirled round the paddock and jostled each other to get at the betting counters in an intricate weaving pattern that eventually flowed out in a disordered stream to pack the stands to capacity."[1]

Photographs of the moment illustrate the spectacle that was Champions Day. The front page of the *North-China Daily News*, under the caption "Shanghai Takes Time Out for Champions," shows the overflowing grandstand, the clubhouse rising in the background. Spectators crane to watch the horses. In the foreground, a turbaned Sikh focuses his attention on the track. Behind him, we can make out about three dozen faces. All but four or five appear to be Chinese, and only a few appear to be women, but all of them are transfixed by the action taking place on the track.

The weather also toned down the traditional fashion pageant, although it couldn't stop it altogether. "There was no suggestion of Ascot ... no broad-brimmed hats flaunted above lacy finery. A piercing wind saw to that," lamented the *North-China Daily News*.[2] Still, the fashion parade that was for some as big an attraction as the races remained a "kaleidoscopic background to the enchanting exhilarating atmosphere of the great event," even though the turn in the weather diminished the spectacle. "What's the fun," wrote Ann Sterling, society reporter for the *North-China Herald*, "of getting a snazzy new outfit for the Classic and then bundling yourself in a coat, preferably big and warm?"[3]

A brave few—or perhaps they simply didn't realize how the weather had changed from the previous day—watched the morning races in their seasonal best, but by afternoon everyone had retreated behind topcoats and furs. Fox and lynx were most popular, but otter, beaver, and monkey were there too. Inside the owners' boxes, the season's fashions grabbed attention. Mary Henchman wore a navy-blue suit, with a spray of orchids on the shoulder, to send Hindhead on his way. Dallas Franklin matched the weather in a gray dress, though her black hat drew the paparazzi's attention. Most of the other owners and their wives dressed in black, though splashes of color—chartreuse, green, red, and royal blue—added contrast.[4] The men were mostly studies in gray; gray suits, gray hats, and gray overcoats made for a drab grandstand, but not without exception: two American marines turned out as a "sturdy symphony in blue, with a powder-blue hat, blue coat and suit, and a deeper-blue sweater."[5]

Not everyone succumbed to the muted color scheme. Vera McBain, the only woman with a horse in the Champions', cheered on Magic Circle in a red felt suit, accessorized with a green-and-red checked wool cape, a red hat trimmed with green feathers, and red shoes. Betty Yanoulatte, daughter of a Greek silk merchant, wore a green-and-yellow turban. Kentucky-born Lyda Mae Francis, the personal secretary to the American consul-general and former staffer for the National Emergency Council (an oversight organization for New Deal legislation) in Washington, wore a three-piece mustard suit with a red fox muff. Louise Carriere, daughter of an American military officer, watched the races in a green checked suit, just a week before she was to leave for California to enroll at Stanford.[6]

Original caption: "The famous oriental calm gives place to animated interest: Two lovely Chinese girls wondering if their pony will win." Shanghai Race Club, 1939.

Ing Tang would have found the sudden cold snap disappointing, but not insurmountable. It was just a short distance from her home in Eric Cumine's Denis Apartments to the racetrack, right past her boutique. She would have been attired, as always for this event, in bright colors and patterns that evoked East and West. Maybe an invitation to an owner's box got her out of the wind.

Finely dressed or just trying to stay warm, bettors could visit the parade ring for a last chance to inspect the competitors before they made their way to the starting gate. All of these horses were winners, and most of them had won high-stakes classics. Rarely had Shanghai seen a field this deep. Everyone expected Mikel Hazzard to take Phantom out of the gate first, and he had been winning lately, including once over the highly rated Magic Circle. But Phantom had already run once today—finishing a close second in the day's first race. Did he look tired? Bettors could try to discern signs of fatigue as he walked in his red-and-blue silks toward the start. Most thought he would force the pace in the early going before fading midway through, but some found him an appealing risk at long odds.

There was one late change to the field. Eric Moller's stable had been expected to enter Merrylight, winner of the 1938 Fall Champions'. But at the last minute, Moller decided instead to run Cherrylight, with son Chris in the saddle. The move was puzzling. Moller's chocolate-and-

gold silks always attracted attention, and Moller was well liked personally, but few gave the gray pony a real chance. Most were surprised
that Cherrylight had even qualified, attributing his success to weak
competition, and when he did qualify, few thought that Moller would
designate him for a Champions' run. Dagal's didn't even list odds on
Cherrylight.[7]

Punters seeking a bargain might look to Leslie Hutton's enigmatic
Mr. Bubbins as Oleg Panoff rode him around the parade ring in his
stark black-and-white colors. He had shown he could do it, winning the
International Recreation Club championship in the spring over Henchman and Aitkenhead horses, but this fall he had been disappointing.
Still, 40:1 was a tempting price for bettors who believed he might recap-
ture his spring form.

Following Mr. Bubbins into the parade ring was Magic Circle, the
cerise of Vera McBain's stables easily spotted even from a distance.
McBain was a popular and successful owner, but ten years had gone
by since she and Billie Liddell had won the Champions' together. This
fall she had high hopes. Magic Circle had been Champion before, when
David Sassoon had called him Sparkling Morn, and the pedigree earned
respect. Dagal's listed Magic Circle at 10:1, and Eric Cumine labeled
him an "outsider" choice to upset the favorites. Much of that interest
was down to rider Sonny Gram. Gram was a jockey's jockey, univer-
sally praised for his hard work, persistence, and determination, not to
mention his sterling record. The *China Press* had described Gram as
"Shanghai's gift to racing," after he had ridden four winners in one 1938
afternoon.[8] Gram was among the club's all-time leaders in wins, with
several classics—but no Champions'—to his name. More than a few
bettors thought Magic Circle could challenge the leaders.

Both of Gussie White's entries were among the favorites. Dagal's
listed White Parade at 4:1, better chances than for any horse except Cluniehouse and Hindhead. White Night was 5:1, the same as Cluniehill.
Befitting one of Shanghai's oldest expatriate families, Gussie White had
two of Shanghai's most experienced jockeys wearing his gray sleeves
and orange cap. Peanut Marshall, who had ridden many a Sassoon pony
to victory, was in the saddle for White Parade, and Jimmy Pote-Hunt
rode White Night.

All of these horses were good—they had qualified by winning

Original caption: "Shanghai carries on as usual: Chinese,
Japanese and European mingle amicably at the races."
Shanghai Race Club, 1939.

races, after all—but most of the money was divided between the two favorites: Aitkenhead's Cluniehouse and Henchman's Hindhead. More than half of the nearly $36,000—perhaps half a million of today's dollars—wagered on bets to win went on one of these ponies. More than $10,000 of that was put on Cluniehouse alone, making him the clear choice of gamblers to win his second Champions'. Like White and Henchman, Aitkenhead had a second horse in the race, Cluniehill, the third-place finisher in the spring. But observers felt strongly that if Clunie's dark blue and red were going to cross the line first, they would be on Alex Striker and Cluniehouse; only $1,500 came in on Cluniehill to win.

The gray, blustery weather may have rendered the fashion parade drabber than usual, but on the track a riot of pink, red, blue, yellow, orange, and purple would soon be rushing around the course at 30 miles per hour. The ten ponies loaded into the gate.

Observers reported that the horses were "jittery" awaiting the start, perhaps sensing the gravity of the moment. Silence descended over the grandstand, punctuated occasionally by the loudspeaker as it announced results of sweeps winners who had drawn ponies in the race.[9] The crowd tensed—Henchman and Aitkenhead in the members' box, nonmembers like Nates Wong and Dayu Doon trying to get a better view in the grandstand, unless they had been lucky enough to be invited inside as guests—all of them anticipating the next chapter in the rivalry between Hindhead and Cluniehouse.

There was a moment's pause before a Chinese track attendant pulled a lever.

The bell rang. The starting gate opened.

They were off!

To 20,000 cheers, Phantom flashed to the front as expected. Spectators could see the blue and red clearly as Franklin's pony built his customary lead; Cluniehouse settled in just behind, with Hindhead about three lengths back. While the rest of the field sorted itself, Phantom led the two favorites through the first turn. In the owners' box, Hench and Aitkenhead edged forward, leaning on the marble railing overlooking the show. Heading into the first turn, Cluniehouse and Striker's darker-blue silks ate into Phantom's lead, but Franklin's horse was still in front as they emerged onto the backstretch, remaining as they had begun: Phantom, Cluniehouse, Hindhead. With the two favorites poised in second and third, the inevitable dramatic finish seemed on its way, especially since everyone—everyone except Cornell Franklin anyway—expected Phantom to tire.

Following the race's progress now through binoculars or spyglasses, spectators could see that form was holding. Phantom started to fade, and Cluniehouse pulled even with the tiring leader as they passed the half-mile post: disappointment for Franklin. Phantom had begun the fall season as an afterthought, but his record over the past month had given Franklin hope that he could finally win the coveted Champions'. It appeared, though, that his chance was slipping away.

Cluniehouse took the lead.

With a half mile to go, the field reached the Widow's Monument. This Chinese *pailou* archway had stood in the Race Club's infield since long before there was a race club. Members commonly described it as built for a virtuous widow whose name has been lost to time, but her name was Zhao, and she was the widow of a Qing dynasty merchant named Xu Yuanlai. The monument had stood since 1789, long before there were races in Shanghai and even before Shanghai was opened to European trade.[10] The Xu family had kept the monument from being torn down, as many like it had been during Shanghai's expansion, but it had fallen into disrepair until that spring, when Eric Moller sponsored its renovation.[11]

Newly restored or not, the Widow's Monument was an important marker for experienced spectators at the Shanghai Races, who knew they could ignore what happened before the Widow's Monument was reached, but from that point forward the case would be decided. With that in mind, this was where many expected Hindhead to make his move, as he had in the previous two Champions' when he had come from behind to win. Charlie Encarnação, riding Hindhead just as he had in each of those previous races, could coax the best from any horse, and he now called on the twice-defending champion.

Hindhead did not answer.

Those expecting to see Henchman's yellow-and-purple silks challenge for the lead saw them instead sliding back. Both Hindhead and Phantom, exhausted by the pace, saw the field catch and pass them.

A new vanguard had formed with three furlongs to go. Gussie White's two ponies, White Parade and White Night, caught the leader. So did Vera McBain's Magic Circle. Into the gathering dusk and the final turn, pink, orange, gray, blue, and red silks raced within one length of the lead. Twenty thousand spectators were in full throat, many of them, their hopes pinned to Hindhead, imploring the champion to find more speed.

Observant fans, though, could already tell what was going to play out down the stretch. Hindhead and Phantom were spent. Magic Circle and the two White ponies were all straining under the whip as their jockeys urged them to the front, while Alex Striker had Cluniehouse still on the bit, holding him back. After they exited the final turn, Striker let his horse run. Cruising down the homestretch, the favorite left his competition behind. Striding comfortably, Cluniehouse won going away. Alex Striker glanced over his shoulder at the finish line, and had to look five lengths back to find second-place White Parade. Magic Circle finished third, and Aitkenhead's second horse, Cluniehill, fourth. Cluniehouse's time of 2:37⅖ was unremarkable—the slowest in several years—but it didn't matter: Bob Aitkenhead was again Champion.

For Henchman, it was a different story. His twice-defending champion had faded to seventh place, out of ten, while Northwood had finished dead last.

Shoot-out at the Cathay Ballroom

EIGHT O'CLOCK,
THE INTERNATIONAL SETTLEMENT

THE CHAMPIONS' WAS DECIDED, BUT THERE WAS STILL ONE more race to be run, the Honan Stakes. Appropriately, perhaps, for a race named after one of China's most maligned provinces—today romanized as "Henan" and mocked for its pollution, poverty, and crude manners—this was a race no one cared much about. The winners were ready to celebrate, or to continue celebrations that had already begun. Losers wanted to salve their wounds, probably with friends and a bottle. Still, the race was run, in two divisions because of the large number of entries. The last race went off after sunset, and both Alex Striker and Charlie Encarnação were back in the saddle, though neither figured in the results. In the last race of the day, Eric Moller finally got his win, as his son rode Wintrylight—appropriately named in the cold and windy November evening—to a half-length victory.

With the races over for the day and the season, the people of the International Settlement turned their attention to the city's nightlife. That might mean taking in a movie; the 9:15 showing of *Murder over New York* would still leave time for dinner first. If he were in a mood to celebrate out, this was a likely option for Bob Aitkenhead. The newly crowned Champions' owner would usually host a grand party, and maybe Aitkenhead did, but by late 1941 he was not well—well enough to enjoy the races and the win, but not likely to take advantage of the many nightlife options that Shanghai offered.

Hench and Mary, stung by their defeat and coming up just short of history for Hindhead, might have wanted to avoid the revelers as well. They would have had to dodge the remnants of the Hardoon funeral—traffic diversions and temporary barriers wouldn't be completely cleared for a few days—as they made their way back to their home on Bubbling Well Road, contemplating the winter ahead. It was unfamiliar territory for Henchman; one of his horses had run first or second in six of the previous seven Champions'. He would have to talk with Elise Andrews and Charlie Encarnação to see what had gone wrong and how to get back on top.

Cornell and Dallas Franklin were younger than Hench or Aitkenhead, but they were also stung by a disappointing finish and, anyway, lived in the outskirts of the Settlement, in the grand southern-style home that Franklin had designed with Estelle Oldham (now Faulkner) in mind. If they did want company, the place to go would have been Ciro's, Victor Sassoon's nightclub that he had opened in 1937, not long before he left the city. Ciro's was an art deco showpiece and arguably Shanghai's top high-class nightspot. Unlike many of Shanghai's clubs, which were attached to, or high atop, hotels, Ciro's stood alone, on Bubbling Well Road just west of the racetrack. Ing Tang and her husband, H. L. Yung, were good bets to head to Ciro's too; they had been welcomed back to Shanghai after their marriage in Singapore in a reception at Ciro's, not long after it opened. Even farther west, the Bolero would have fit the bill, open until 4:00 a.m., with the Charles Albert Orchestra and Miss Tamara on vocals that evening.

Closer to the commercial center of Nanking Road there was no shortage of cabarets where Chinese and Western guests danced to jazz, made famous by bandleaders like Whitey Smith, whose song "Nighttime in Old Shanghai" mixed Chinese and Western styles to the taste of both audiences. The Tower Club on the ninth floor of Victor Sassoon's Cathay Hotel was still going strong at the other end of Nanking Road, overlooking the Bund. Two jazz singers, an orchestra, and a violin soloist headed the Tower's bill that evening. The Casanova Ballroom, near the Nanking Theatre and just beyond the racecourse's third turn, was open until 4:00 a.m., Filipina bandleader Gloria Andico's orchestra providing the entertainment.[1]

For more sport, or more gambling, there was a session of Jai alai beginning at 8:00 p.m. at the Parc des Sports in the French Concession, near Dayu Doon's home—a good place to keep a hot streak going or to turn one's luck around. Dog racing was also available in Frenchtown—ten races beginning at 5:30 p.m.

The Cathay Ballroom on Yu Ya Ching Road, just beyond the racecourse's second turn and near Nanking Road, was one of the most convenient places for racegoers to spend their winnings or wonder what might have been; never mind that it was a Wednesday. At about 8:30 that evening, fifteen Chinese men entered the club and ordered drinks,[2] but never drank them. Instead, they ordered other patrons out, overturned tables and chairs, and shot up the place before leaving.

The episode was the latest in a string of violent outbreaks in Shanghai nightclubs. Things would get worse just five days later, when a bomb would go off at Ciro's, killing one and seriously injuring another man. In fact, there were at least three gunfights in the Settlement on Champions Day (the two others were armed robberies earlier in the afternoon). Police had few leads to follow, based on two earlier incidents at the Cathay Ballroom, but the evidence was skimpy, and the crime, by the standards of the time, hardly merited an in-depth investigation. This was part of Shanghai, 1941.

For most race fans, the evening was not so dramatic. Most of the 20,000 who attended Champions Day made their way back to the residential neighborhoods surrounding the Race Club. Many had been off from work for the big race, but that was now over. Intellectuals like Nates Wong made their way back home, the distractions of another racing season now over. Factory workers and office clerks living in their alleyway homes would find something to eat, but it would not be a late night for most. November 12 had been Champions Day; November 13, though, was just Thursday. The anxieties that surrounded the Lone Island could be put on hold for only so long, and the city would wake up early the next day to resume wondering about what the future had in store.

PART FOUR

THE END

(1942–1945)

The Shanghai Race Club will be closed to
racing indefinitely, it was announced yesterday.

——*SHANGHAI TIMES*,
OCTOBER 16, 1942

. . .

Last Laps

L ONG-EXPECTED, THE JAPANESE INVASION OF THE INTER-
national Settlement took place on December 8, 1941, less than a month
after Champions Day. News of the Pearl Harbor attacks reached Lieu-
tenant Stephen Polkinghorn, the commander of HMS *Peterel*, moored
along the Bund, before dawn, and Japanese marines soon followed.
Outnumbered and outgunned, Polkinghorn refused to surrender, telling the Japanese commander, "Get off my bloody ship!" The firefight
that followed sent the *Peterel* to the bottom of the Huangpu River.
Docked alongside, the USS *Wake* had recently closed up the American garrison at Hankow and was soon to leave for the Philippines, but
most of her crew was still ashore this early morning, and she was seized
without a shot being fired, those on board taken prisoner. (The *Wake*
was the only US Navy vessel captured during World War II, and it
served, as the *Tatara*, in the Japanese Imperial Navy for the duration
of the war.)

The *Peterel* and the *Wake* were virtually all that remained of the
British and American military presence in Shanghai. Most of the
"Shaforce"—the British Shanghai Defence Force that sponsored
the Champions' Cup that Aitkenhead and Cluniehouse had just
reclaimed—had been withdrawn already. The American marines in
Shanghai had left the city too, boarding a troop transport on a rainy
November 28. With no other significant resistance, Japanese tanks and

trucks crossed the Garden Bridge from Hongkou to the Bund; from there, some headed west along Nanking Road, toward the Race Club, which symbolized the Anglo-American power that Japan was targeting across the Pacific, not just in Hawai'i and Shanghai, but also in Singapore, Hong Kong, Manila, and other Allied territories.[1]

The invasion did not immediately clarify Shanghai's situation. The Settlement remained in the same sort of limbo it had occupied since 1937: still run by a foreign power, but now Japanese, not British or American, although the Shanghai Municipal Council and Shanghai Municipal Police continued to enforce order in the Settlement, to the shame of some and confusion of many.[2] Daily life for many in the Settlement changed little, at least at first.

The autonomy of Allied nationals ended gradually. Little violence and few arrests followed immediately after December 8. According to the *Shanghai Evening Post and Mercury*, which reported on the events of those days sometime later, the Japanese "assured Americans and Britons that the 'international' aspects of the city would continue and that no resident had anything to fear from the Japanese who merely 'wanted to preserve peace and order.' "[3] Over time, Japanese rule became more invasive. More arrests—surprise raids in the Settlement and the French Concession carried out at all hours—began on December 20, but even then the Japanese treatment of the Settlement was inconsistent.[4] British and American consular officials were at first confined to their homes. Later in the month they were imprisoned at the Cathay Hotel, repurposed as the headquarters of the Japanese forces in the Settlement. It would take nearly a year before things looked dramatically different for most Shanghailanders.

Arthur Henchman was not among those arrested. He was on good terms with many Japanese, and friends with the manager of the Yokohama Specie Bank, who had once offered him a job advising the Japanese government on financial matters. The invasion stopped Henchman's work at the Bank, but he remained free as the occupation began, compelled like his countrymen to wear an armband identifying him as an enemy national.[5] All of the Shanghai Race Club's principal owners, including Cornell Franklin and Bob Aitkenhead, remained free, for the time being.

The Japanese left in place the Shanghai Municipal Council and

Municipal Police, to maintain order in the International Settlement, and British subjects staffed both of these institutions. The British Foreign Office replied to requests for guidance ambiguously: "We expect patriotic British subjects to refrain from assisting the enemy war effort but we should not regard as unpatriotic the participation of British subjects in the maintenance of such public services as is for the benefit of the civil population of the occupied territory."[6]

Most Chinese in the city faced a world that was fundamentally changed, yet not so very different from what it had been before. Foreign powers still controlled Shanghai, and it was still nominally Chinese territory. Nates Wong was no longer publishing anti-Japanese articles, but it was still the Shanghai Municipal Police that would enforce the rules were he to run afoul of the law. For the Chinese who worked in the city's factories and lived in the alleyway houses, the changes were, for now, mostly minor. Shortwave radios were confiscated, suspicious behavior could invite a visit from the police. The Japanese military sometimes arbitrarily commandeered civilian homes, disrupting the lives of the homeowners. These examples notwithstanding, the presence of Japanese occupiers in Shanghai was lighter than just about anywhere else in China.[7]

At times, Japanese officials vented frustration pent up for years while the British and Americans in charge of the Settlement had defied their wishes. Newspapers were shut down, especially those that had vocally criticized Japan. An exception was the *Shanghai Times*, the most American of Shanghai's newspapers (extensive coverage of every year's World Series revealed its readership). The occupiers took over and continued to print the *Times*, against the objections of its American former publishers. Beginning with a December 8 "Emergency Edition" published on the afternoon of the invasion, the paper printed news of and for the Settlement with a pro-Japanese bias that increased steadily over time.

Foreign nationals in Shanghai were encouraged—some said compelled—to carry on with their lives as usual. The racecourse was a central part of this attempt to demonstrate that Japan was a benevolent occupying force providing stability and order. This is the same message they had aimed to convey in Manchuria: that Japanese-backed authoritarian rule was preferable to the weak, chaotic Chinese government. Among other reasons, the purpose of the message was to persuade American and British audiences to give up the fight in Asia as not worth the trouble.

Amid the uncertainty of the occupation, the races symbolized the stability and status quo that Japan wanted to project. The Shanghai Race Club had hosted December races only once within anyone's memory, when the Battle of Shanghai had delayed the 1937 fall Champions' into early December. Otherwise, this month was usually dark at the City Course. On December 12, 1941, though, the *Times* looked ahead to "the very likely opening of the Race Course" and awaited confirmation that a race meeting would take place soon.[8] As promised, on Saturday, December 20—the same date as sporadic arrests began in the Settlement—"a galaxy of stars" appeared at the racecourse to entertain the Settlement. If the Japanese were hoping to give the impression that nothing had changed, these races probably satisfied them: Hindhead and Northwood—Henchman's horses—finished first and second in the day's main race, the Old Bill Handicap. Crowds were smaller than they had been, but only by a little. Familiar names from the fall Champions' filled out the field: Phantom, Magic Circle, White Night; Henchman, Aitkenhead, McBain, White, Franklin.[9]

Racing carried on during the winter of 1941–42. Henchman, Franklin, and Aitkenhead remained at the forefront when horses took to the turf for the Lunar New Year Race Meet, sanctioned by the International Recreation Club, in February. The highlight of the meet was the so-called Lunar New Year Criterion Stakes, on February 16. Evoking the Champions' duel of November 12, Alex Striker again raced against Charlie Encarnação on a Henchman mount (Northwood, not Hindhead), in a field that included Frostylight, Cluniehill, Phantom, Busted Straight, and Mr. Bubbins. A dramatic fireworks display at the racecourse concluded the race meeting on the evening of February 16, as the *Shanghai Times* put it, "where thousands near and far could see this brilliant demonstration of the dramatic capture of Singapore by the Japanese."[10]

The idea of Britons and Americans racing horses for entertainment under enemy occupation was galling to compatriots back home who thought that able-bodied men from Allied nations should be contributing to the war effort, not enjoying their hobbies under enemy protection.[11] For their part, the Shanghailanders insisted they had no choice. H. G. W. Woodhead, a columnist for the *Shanghai Evening Post and Mercury* who evaded capture by the Japanese for four months after December 8, shared the impression that the Race Club was compelled to hold its meets, observing that "much propaganda use was made of photographs of prominent 'enemy' subjects leading in winning ponies."[12] Whether or not the club was compelled, racing ponies while fireworks celebrated the fall of Singapore contrasted starkly with the experience of Allies under Japanese occupation elsewhere, and tarnished Shanghailanders' reputation.

Many of the same concerns applied to Shanghai's Chinese residents under occupation. "Few of Shanghai's urbanites," according to one study on wartime Shanghai, "earned credentials as war heroes" while they negotiated "messy compromises or protracted negotiations" that were neither resistance nor collaboration.[13] The Japanese did not, for the most part, intervene directly in the daily lives of most Chinese in the International Settlement. Though there were, of course, active collaborators and resisters—stories of espionage and heroism are part of the myth of wartime Shanghai—most Chinese in the city, regardless of their politics, lived lives under occupation that were not noticeably different from their lives before. As it had been for a century, Shanghai remained atypical: in the midst of humanity's deadliest war, Shanghai was relatively quiet. Quiet enough to watch horse races.

February 1942 was Aitkenhead's last appearance at the racetrack, perhaps because of the health concerns that would hospitalize him later that year. A dog-racing enthusiast named V. S. Chow acquired Aitkenhead's horses and renamed the Clunie stable the Old stable. Cluniehouse's name was changed to Old Victor, but he appears not to have raced again; Cluniehill became Old Timer. The only other owner who lost his horses in the first few months of the Japanese regime was Gussie White, whose best horses were taken over by a G. J. Mary, who had never owned horses before. White Parade was renamed Paladin, and White Night became Coquinet, and they continued to contend.

In the spring of 1942, the races continued. The Japanese—though not the English-language press—framed the spring race meeting as part of "allied annihilation week." Proceeds went to the Japanese military, which at one point interrupted the racing with a parade celebrating Japan's victories.[14] The Shanghai Race Club's Spring 1942 Race Meeting was held as scheduled, or as ordered by the Japanese occupiers, if sources are to be believed. Certainly, the Japanese authorities' blessing would have been needed to conduct the races. Whether Shanghailanders welcomed the glimpse of their former lives, longed for the world that no longer was, or bristled at being propaganda tools for their captors, is hard to know, but the Shanghai Champions' was run, compromised as it was, one last time, promoted as continuing the grand tradition that had emerged over nearly a century, including the fashion parade. The Settlement once again took holiday, with the paper reporting that 90 percent of shops were closed. The *Times* reported that 10,000 came to the races—a smaller crowd than at the last Champions' run under British direction, but large enough to give more than a suggestion of the old status quo.

Only five horses started, but it was a high-quality field, including Hindhead and Paladin (the old White Parade). A Chinese jockey named T. L. Wong rode Old Timer, formerly Cluniehill, to his first Champions'. Charlie Encarnação finished fourth on Northwood, out of the money. As the crowds dispersed, one story foreshadowed what was to come, by describing the end of the holiday celebrations. "Thousands of others left the Race Course with the eternal hope in their mind of winning the Autumn Champions' Sweep six months from now," the *Times* wrote optimistically. "Just like the Seven Dwarfs singing the popular ditty 'Back to work we go!' the thousands of office workers and shop assistants will troop back to their places of employment this morning."[15]

The people of Shanghai may not have appreciated the comparison, but the analogy did capture the routine that the Japanese occupiers were trying to maintain. Many Chinese in Shanghai found the differences between European and Japanese imperialism difficult to pin down, while for the British and American Shanghailanders, their almost-colony had become an almost-prison, though not a very uncomfortable one so far.

The following day, a new Japanese company was established to take control of the racecourse from the military authorities that had operated it since the invasion. This new Shanghai Heng Chan Corporation put in place a schedule and infrastructure that suggested the races were on to stay, under Japanese control.

Shanghai was no longer just surrounded by war, but rather in the thick of it, when racing resumed after the hot summer with a midautumn meeting in September and then an Extra Race Meeting in early October 1942. On the last day of that meeting, October 10—the anniversary of the Chinese revolution thirty-one years earlier—familiar ponies came again to the line: "Beneath a fine autumn sky and with winds sweeping down the stretch, more than 7,000 racing fans yesterday afternoon saw [Henchman's] Rye make a bid for the coming champion honors when in the tenth race against a field of redoubtable points, he took the lead from the start, and kept it to beat his nearest rival Mr. Bubbins by one and a half lengths."[16] Rye, Bagshot, and Roehampton each finished first or second that day; it seemed a banner day for Henchman.

Except Henchman wasn't there.

Hench had scored a much bigger prize than the Shaforce Cup in the summer of 1942: a ticket out of China. Shortly after the outbreak of war, Britain and the United States negotiated with Japan to repatriate some of their nationals. A first repatriation vessel left Shanghai in June, bringing more than 600 Americans. Several hundred Britons left the next month. News of a second vessel repatriating British citizens in China spread a frenzy to get tickets in Shanghai. Initially, most of the seats were designated for Britons living in "outports"—smaller cities without direct passage abroad—but by the time the *Kamakura Maru* sailed on August 17, nearly all the berths were filled by Shanghai residents. Arthur and Mary Henchman, and their seventeen-year-old daughter Katherine, were among them. After transferring to another vessel in (neutral) Portuguese Mozambique, the Henchmans arrived back in Liverpool in September 1942.[17] Before leaving China, Arthur had sold his horses, commenting that "the fact that I got good prices for them is merely incidental."[18]

Aitkenhead was hospitalized and Henchman gone from China, but Cornell Franklin was still there. He had stayed active in the races, running Phantom and Silver Fox until the bitter end. A chestnut named Mug's Luck, owned by a Mr. Ku, won the last race that can meaningfully be said have been run by the Shanghai Race Club. The final horse to cross the finish line was named Fine Courage. Just $28 had been placed on him to win.[19]

On October 15, 1942, the Japanese occupiers of the city announced that the racecourse was to be closed indefinitely. British, Americans, and citizens of Allied nations were no longer welcome inside the Race Club, where membership had once been their exclusive domain. New regulations barred "enemy nationals" from entering places of entertainment, including bars, clubs, cinemas, and sports venues. The announcement held open the possibility of racing in the future: "plans were rushed" to hold a race meeting as soon as possible, and the authorities made clear that ponies could be worked out by "non-enemy jockeys," but for the Shanghai Race Club of Henchman, Aitkenhead, and Franklin, this was the end.[20]

Within weeks of the Race Club's closing, the Japanese began rounding up "enemy nationals." Henchman was by this time back in England, but the other owners of the fall 1941 Champions' were targeted. On or around November 5, 1942, Japanese secret police arrested Cornell Franklin, Eric Moller, Gussie White, and Eric Cumine, who were imprisoned soon thereafter in internment camps, Franklin not far from the site of the former Jiangwan racecourse. Bob Aitkenhead and Leslie Hutton managed to avoid arrest at this time, but only because they were too ill to be imprisoned and instead were admitted to the hospital.[21]

THE RACE CLUB ILLUSTRATES the difficulties of drawing a bright line to end Old Shanghai. Franklin, Aitkenhead, and others were no longer at the racetrack, but plenty of others were willing and able to take their places. The club's secretary, Alfred Olsen, was Norwegian; his country occupied by Germany, he remained free and in place at the racecourse.[22] Charlie Encarnação, Portuguese, was neutral. Stateless Russians like Alex Striker and Oleg Panoff were likewise not interned. Eric Moller's case was even more complex. His father, Nils, had famously denied European jurisdiction over him and proclaimed himself "a citizen of Shanghai," and Eric appears also to have been fluid in his approach to nationality. He was arrested in November 1942 along with Franklin and others; however, he seems to have continued, or resumed, operating his shipping line and leased vessels to the Japanese. He might have claimed Norwegian citizenship, or perhaps he found other means to persuade the Japanese to let him continue running his business. Acquaintances of Moller who were interviewed by the FBI in 1944 raised questions about his activities during the war—questions

Longhua internment camp, where Eric Cumine, among other Shanghailanders, was held during the war.

compounded[23] by generous donations to Japanese military charities in the years leading up to 1941.[24]

To maintain the idea that little had changed, the track reopened in January 1943: "All roads lead to the Race Course and not to Rome," wrote "Ryder" in the *Shanghai Times*, "as today racing, after a lapse of more than three months, will resume with all its colour."[25] Charlie Encarnação was back, riding Hindhead. So was the Shanghai Race Club, now "administered by the Shanghai Heng Chan Corporation, Ltd.," and no longer run by its former stewards. Most of the owners and jockeys were Chinese. Many were Japanese as well, and some were of unclear European nationality, presumably Axis or neutral citizens. Hungarian Gabor Renner was riding, but so, too, was Sonny Gram, "Shanghai's gift to racing," who was apparently British yet remained in the saddle at the racecourse. A handful of Indians, like sibling jockeys Alfred and Francis Noodt, also competed. A fall racing season "under the auspices of the Shanghai Race Club" got under way in October.

Racing was a constant almost every weekend during the seasons under Japanese occupation, with many familiar names: Hindhead, Northwood, Magic Circle; Striker, Noodt, Encarnação, Renner, Gram, C. S. Mao. The Japanese even began importing new ponies from Mongolia; the first new crop of griffins to arrive in Shanghai in years came in the spring of 1943.[26] One sign of change at the track, besides the absence of the British and Americans who used to dominate the club before 1941, was inflation. In April 1943, the newly reopened track charged $10 admission for the members' and guests' enclosures; and $1.20 for the public enclosure. Just a month later, those prices had risen to $2 per day in the public enclosure and $15 in the guest enclosure, and had increased fivefold in the members' enclosure, to $50.[27] Champions Days were still run, under the authority of the International Recreation Club, but as time went on they stood out less and less from regular race days.

Even the SRC made a comeback of sorts, though it was not the Shanghai Race Club that had existed since the 1850s. A "Shanghai Recreation Club"—"formed under the direction of Sino-Japanese authorities"—was organized to replace the Shanghai Race Club in the winter of 1943–44. Y. S. Fong, the race fan and newspaper publisher, found himself club secretary after the internment of most Europeans. "All members of the Shanghai Race Club and International Race [*sic*] Club," Fong told the *Shanghai Times*, "will be accepted for membership," although most of the old club's members had been imprisoned or repatriated.[28] With this new structure in place, the racecourse was in near-constant use as the war ground on around it.

In late December 1944, the American island-hopping campaign was at full throttle. American marines had landed in the Philippines. Air raids on the Japanese home islands had begun, and Japanese kamikaze tactics had started. Planning for the invasion of Japan, and for the delivery of the atomic bomb, was underway. In Europe, Germany was fighting its last offensive, the Battle of the Bulge. Meanwhile, in Shanghai, Charlie Encarnação rode Hindhead to yet another victory, beating stablemate Rye by a length on December 30, 1944.[29]

As the war turned against the Axis, the *Shanghai Times* remained reliably propagandist, predicting Allied defeat until the last moment. News of Germany's fall followed only a few days after promises of new Nazi offensives. The races even expanded, though circumstances limited their reporting in the paper. In 1945, racing became as frequent as American naval victories. Every weekend from February to May, races were run, and they resumed again in the summer—a time when the track had always been dark. Race-day announcements appeared alongside news of Germany's surrender. The last race to be reported in the *Times* took place July 17, 1945, though there was no news about whether the favored Chefoo King lived up his potential. *Shenbao* advertised racing as late as July 29, just a week before the first atomic bomb fell on Hiroshima.[30] Japan announced it would surrender on August 15. Japanese troops stood to receive the news from their commanding officers on their parade grounds in the infield of the racecourse.[31]

A few weeks later, American and Chinese troops arrived in Shanghai to take the surrender of the Japanese there.[32] They also conveyed the news that extraterritoriality and the foreign concessions, which for a century had undergirded colonialism in Shanghai—with the Race Club as its emblem—had ended. Both Britain and the United States had signed treaties with Chiang Kai-shek's government in Chongqing surrendering extraterritorial rights in China, including the International Settlement, in February 1943, although the change was largely symbolic until after the war ended. (For their part, the Japanese had formally merged the Settlement into the Shanghai municipality in July 1943, but none of this had much practical effect until the end of the war.)

General Hayes, the British commander, met with representatives of the Shanghai British community in early September and found the Shanghailanders in denial about the changes confronting them. "I found a remarkable lack of realisation of the implications of the abolition of Extra-territoriality and of the fact that from now on Shanghai will be essentially a Chinese city," Hayes reported to his embassy. "I fear that some of my answers to their questions tended to lower rather than raise the morale of these sorely tried people. Nevertheless . . . no useful purpose would be served by allowing them to retain unjustifiable illusions."[33]

For most of the Shanghailanders at the Race Club, there was no going back. Henchman did not return to China. He continued working for the Bank, including a stint in India to assess conditions there, until resigning on December 31, 1945.[34] He retired to Sussex, where he died in 1965. Mary died there also, three years after Arthur.

Bob Aitkenhead stayed in the Shanghai Jewish hospital for two years, until all medical exemptions were revoked in June 1944. He was then interned at the Lincoln Avenue camp, in the far-western outskirts of Shanghai, designated specifically to handle sick and infirm enemy non-combatants. He remained there until the end of the war and then returned to Britain.[35] Aitkenhead lived the rest of his life in Clunie, the Scottish namesake of his Shanghai stables, passing away in January 1964.

Leslie Hutton, the lawyer and owner of Mr. Bubbins, did not survive the war. Like Aitkenhead, he had been hospitalized instead of arrested, but during the war the Red Cross informed his relatives that he had died on December 17, 1942, either in the hospital or perhaps in military custody.[36]

Vera McBain, who partnered with Billie Liddell to win the Champions' as the We Two stables and challenged for the Champions Day win with Magic Circle, illustrates how small choices can have profound consequences. She and her husband left Shanghai in June of 1941 for San Francisco, but despite the rumors of war, they returned to Shanghai in late August on the *President Garfield* in time for the fall racing season. After Champions Day in November 1941, Vera seems to have been at the racetrack in December and January, but then drops from the record until, when the war was over, she sailed—alone—from Shanghai to Honolulu,[37] presumably having spent the war in an internment camp.

Eric Moller left Shanghai after the war, making his way to Hong Kong and eventually to South Africa and Australia. He was killed in an airline crash in Singapore in 1954.[38] The racing colors that he had made famous in Shanghai and Hong Kong lived on, however: Moller stables had great success in England, including wins at Royal Ascot in the 1980s and 1990s.

Ing Tang, with her husband H. L. Yung, survived the war in Shanghai and then moved to the United States in 1947, where Yung continued his work for AIG insurance.[39] (Yung attained legendary status within AIG for burying the policy documents of his customers before the Japanese invasion, then digging them up and finding the beneficiaries after the war was over.) The couple eventually made their way to New York—Ing Tang finally did get to Broadway—where they took up residence in the apartment of AIG founder C. V. Starr. Their stay at Eighty-Seventh Street and Fifth Avenue was intended to be temporary, but the apartment remains in the family to this day.[40] H. L. Yung died in 1961, but Ing Tang went back to Shanghai—once, in the 1970s—where she was reported to be as stylish and formidable as ever, and she passed away in New York City in 1986.[41]

Nates Wong also stayed in Shanghai and survived the war. In 1945 he was working for Chinese magazines in Shanghai, translating *Look* and *Collier's* articles about the prosecution of Nazi war criminals at Nuremberg and General De Gaulle's return to France for Chinese readers. He also wrote a column for English learners that appeared as late as 1947, and in the fall of that same year, he wrote for a Buddhist periodical, *Enlightenment*, about his religious conversion.[42] After that the record falls silent.

Y. S. Fong, who ascended to become secretary of the Race Club during the Japanese occupation, stayed in Shanghai until the Communist revolution. Shortly thereafter, he fled with his family by train, crossing the border into Hong Kong in the winter of 1950. He died in Orlando, Florida, in 1987.[43]

C. S. Mao stayed in Shanghai and raced as long as he could; his horses were still running in the summer of 1945, and he stayed in the city even after the Japanese surrender and the Communist revolution. Eventually, the Communist government in Shanghai arrested him and put him on trial for collaboration with the Japanese. He was found guilty and executed in July 1951.[44]

Dayu Doon, unlike most others in this story, remained in China for the rest of his life, though he left Shanghai and the elaborate home he had built for himself on the outskirts of the French Concession (the house was converted into a factory office building after 1949, then torn down in 2002).[45] Doon continued his career in the People's Republic after 1949, designing factories and workers' dormitories in Xi'an and Hangzhou. He died in 1973.

Arguments over Liza Hardoon's will were interrupted by the Japanese invasion. A fire nearly destroyed Aili Gardens, including both Liza and Silas Hardoon's tombs, in 1943. The Communist government in Shanghai relocated the graves to the western outskirts of the city in 1953 and turned the former Hardoon estate into the Sino-Soviet Friendship Palace, which still stands as the Shanghai Exhibition Center. The disputes among the children were not settled until after 1945 (a private settlement was reached out of court).[46]

Gussie White and his family were loaded onto a steamer and sent to an internment camp at Yangzhou, about 150 miles up the Yangtze River.[47] This camp closed after a wave of repatriation in 1943, but the Whites were not so fortunate, transferred instead to an internment camp in Pudong. Gussie White stayed there for the duration of the war and then made his way to Hong Kong, which became the closest thing to Old Shanghai, and raced at Happy Valley; Billie Liddell, Elise Andrews, and Eric Cumine were all there too. White continued his career in finance and banking until he retired to Australia, where he died in 1981.

And what of Madame Helen Piper, a.k.a. Vera Hutchinson, who offered Champions Day insights into the future? Whatever gifts she may have had were not enough as the world descended around Shanghai. She lived out most of the war in internment camps but died just two months before Japan surrendered, of tuberculosis, at St. Luke's Hospital in Shanghai.[48]

EPILOGUE

· · · ·

Ghosts of Old Shanghai

*The gold statues that had stood out front of the
Shanghai Race Club for decades were torn down in 1948
because of traffic concerns.*

THERE WAS ONE SHANGHAILANDER WHO EMBODIED THE
"unjustifiable illusions" about Shanghai's future that General Hayes
spoke of in 1943: Cornell Franklin, who never seemed to admit that the
old era had ended. Arrested and interned in 1942, Franklin was, like
Arthur Henchman, repatriated as part of an exchange of nationals after

about a year in a camp. Even as his beloved races were resuming under Japanese direction, Cornell, together with his wife, Dallas, and their two daughters, left Shanghai aboard the Japanese ship *Tela Maru*. After two months at sea on board two repatriation vessels, they checked into the San Carlos Hotel in New York City on December 2, 1943.[1]

But when the war ended two years later, Franklin returned to Shanghai to pick up where he had left off. The very idea was absurd. Shanghai had suffered less during the war than most occupied places, but China was still just starting to recover after decades of fighting. The papered-over conflict between the Nationalists and Communists would soon erupt into civil war. Inflation and scarcity menaced the city's residents. All this might not have affected Franklin too much—he was, after all, a successful American lawyer—but gone were the two linchpins of his life as a Shanghailander: extraterritoriality and racing. Nonetheless, he returned, resumed his law practice, and took up the reins as secretary of the Shanghai Race Club—whatever that now meant.

Franklin negotiated with the city government to reopen the race-track, but it was never a viable option.[2] Especially with the city struggling to reestablish itself amid the remnants of war, the club was too potent an icon of imperialism to be revived. The Chinese government had worked hard to revoke the privileges of extraterritoriality, had fought alongside its former colonizers to defeat fascism, and was now a victorious ally and permanent member of the new United Nations Security Council. China was not about to tolerate the reemergence of foreign colonialism, especially for a racecourse dripping with symbolism.

There had always been some opposition to the races among Shanghai Chinese, usually focused on gambling. Yet thousands of Chinese had frequented the racetrack while it was open, and attending the races had been undeniably popular. Now, with China asserting itself, many Shanghai residents came to resent what the SRC stood for. The city land management office documented the tactics, a century earlier, by which farmers had been denied rent for land they owned, or had been forced to sell their property at low prices, and identified hundreds of families who had never received payment.[3] *Shenbao* reported extensively and not favorably on the racetrack's history: "Each British horse represents two peasant's tears," the paper wrote, expressing a common saying at the time.[4] Chiang Kai-shek, China's president, addressed 200,000 people on the racecourse in 1946 and emphasized that such a gathering was now possible because the foreign concessions had been done away with.[5]

The Shanghai city government itself considered resuming the races in order to generate desperately needed revenue. In the fall of 1946, members of the Shanghai Municipal Council debated the idea: "Shanghai cannot improve if it doesn't have any money," argued one councillor in favor of racing, while council members who opposed it focused mainly on the harmful social effects like gambling, but also on more mundane problems, like the expense of cleaning up after the horses.[6] The immense green space at the center of the city was seen as essential to making Shanghai livable, but not when it was filled with racehorses: "When the park is used for horseracing," wrote *Shenbao*, "it is like a tumor on the heart of Shanghai."[7] Instead, most councillors advocated keeping the park but transforming the buildings into a "city of culture" that would provide libraries, museums, and exhibition spaces.[8] Council member Chen Gongda summed up the feelings of many: "I lived next to the racecourse for 50 years. . . . I hate the races. It's time for the foreign horse races to take a holiday." The SMC voted 1,225 to 59 against resuming races at the Shanghai Race Club,[9] although it left open the possibility of racing at the Jiangwan course in the future (a dubious proposition at best, since war had ruined the track a decade earlier).

Like racing horses during the Japanese occupation, the debate over reopening the Race Club seemed farcical next to the larger forces shaping China's future. Even while the Municipal Council was voting on whether horse racing would be allowed, and on whether buying sweepstakes tickets for horse races constituted gambling, combat between Communist and Nationalist armies was spreading across the country. As the civil war turned against the Nationalists, city after city fell to Mao Zedong's People's Liberation Army. The Communists took Shanghai and raised the very first red flag to fly over the city directly across from the racecourse on May 25, 1949.[10] Mao stood atop Beijing's Gate of Heavenly Peace to proclaim the founding of the People's Republic of

China on October 1. Cornell Franklin was still in Shanghai five months later, when the flag of the People's Republic was raised over the former racecourse.

THE FOUNDING OF THE People's Republic did not quite end the story of the Shanghai Race Club. The clubhouse building, now nearing its centennial, still stands in the center of Shanghai, overshadowed by the skyscrapers surrounding it. Once at the center of everything Shanghai had come to be, it is now a home for ghosts and a reminder of what once was.

After 1949, the new Shanghai People's Government determined that the Race Club had illegally obtained the land on which the track had been built. Sir John Keswick, former Race Club member and officer of Jardine Matheson, negotiated the club's end, hoping to gain some goodwill rather than continue a fight he figured he would lose. In the spring of 1951, Keswick agreed—not that he had a choice—to donate the Race Club property to the government, in partial payment of its debts and taxes, requesting that it be used for public benefit. The city determined to make the enormous open space into an area for recreation, as well as for public gatherings like parades and other national celebrations.[11]

The Shanghai Bureau of Public Works undertook a survey to evaluate the destruction of imperialist monuments in the city, but decided to leave the Race Club largely in place, although its grandstands and many support buildings were razed.[12] The space was quickly converted into an art museum, and the new landlords wasted no time shoving a thumb in the eye of their predecessors, exhibiting in the former clubhouse revolutionary art depicting the evils of foreign imperialism and Chinese victory over it. Paintings of "atrocities perpetrated by the American invaders in Korea" hung in the halls where Hench and Cornell Franklin had taken tiffin a decade earlier.[13]

We don't know whether Franklin himself saw that exhibition mocking his past at the races, but he was still in Shanghai when it opened, waiting for an exit visa he had applied for in January 1951. In December of that year, the visa granted, he left China for good, the last of the Shanghailanders who had one day aspired to be Champion.[14] Cornell and Dallas Franklin retired to Virginia, where Cornell passed away in 1959, and Dallas in 1975.

Newspapers solicited suggestions from the public to rename the space that ponies had once occupied. From suggestions that included "Democracy Square," "Peace Square," "Liberation Square," and "Victory Square," city leaders chose "People's Square."[15] On National Day in 1952—the third anniversary of the PRC's founding—the Shanghai People's Government reopened what had been the racecourse as two spaces (People's Square and People's Park) separated by broad People's Avenue—no longer a playground for colonizers, but a gathering place for the ordinary residents of the city. For a time, the park even featured an artificial serpentine lake, complete with paddleboats.

The old Race Club was condemned as a lair for high rollers with loose morals, devil-may-care taipans with little regard for local law and even less for China's well-being. It was a caricature but not a lie, and it fit with the anticapitalist ideology of the Communist Party. Writing for schoolchildren during the Cultural Revolution of the 1960s and 1970s, author Lu Bo asked, "Young friends, do you know the past of People's Square and People's Park in the center of our Shanghai? Before Liberation, it was called 'the Racecourse' and it was the greatest gambling den that the imperialists built in China. . . . ."[16] [based] upon cruel and insidious exploitation and deception. . . . Their many millions are the blood and tears of the Chinese people."[17] A poem now portrayed Champions Day—the center of Arthur Henchman, Cornell Franklin, Ing Tang, and Nates Wong's old world—not as glamorous, but as parasitic:

> *Champions Day tickets, spread everywhere*
> *Sucking the blood of the Chinese people*
> *Filling the pockets of the imperialists*[18]

It never was just that. The racecourse was a social center for many thousands of Chinese, as well as for the Europeans who ran it, but there is no denying that the era of Champions Day was an era of exploitation. Shanghailanders lived well: even middle-class Europeans in Shanghai had a servant, and many had three or four. Some Chinese—like Nates Wong, Dayu Doon, Ing Tang, and others—lived very well too, but the city was a place of extremes. The Race Club (and also the Interna-

A Champions Sweepstakes ticket (front and back), of the type deplored in the poem. In addition to placing bets on individual ponies, racegoers could purchase "sweeps tickets" like these, for the Champions' Stakes, which were randomly assigned to horses and acted like a lottery.

tional Recreation Club in Jiangwan) showed off the wealth of Shanghai's upper class, but most city residents, especially Chinese, worked to generate the profits that Shanghailanders lived on.

The Communist Party—born out of those extremes in Shanghai in 1921—uses the era of the Shanghai Race Club to demonstrate that it alone has been able to restore to China the dignity and power of a great nation, and the club's usefulness as a propaganda tool does not diminish the fundamental truth of what Chinese, as early as 1915, called the "century of humiliation": from 1839 until 1945, Europeans, Americans, and Japanese kept China down at heel, and neither the Qing dynasty nor two iterations of the Republic of China were able to resist effectively. Foreigners raced horses on land extorted from Chinese farmers while China burned under Japanese occupation. Shanghai kept on racing when the Japanese attacked, while the atrocities at Nanjing were redefining cruelty, and even when Japan occupied the racetrack itself. Only when the Communist Party came to power did the races stop for good.

When Mao Zedong proclaimed the People's Republic in 1949, he called it New China. Imperialism—exemplified by the Shanghai Race Club—exploited China when it was weak. Mao declared that era to be over, with aspirations to global power. China would no longer be a place whose laws and customs could be flouted, or a victim of foreign imperialism and internal weakness.

For Shanghai, the story of China's modern history is even more complex. That century that Mao looked down on was in many ways the peak of Shanghai, and while it was an era dominated by foreigners, the people of Shanghai—even the International Settlement—were always overwhelmingly Chinese. Shanghai's restaurants and nightclubs—and the grandstands at the Race Club—were filled with both local and foreign patrons. Shanghai's golden age was framed and enabled by colonialism, but it was also a time to which many of today's Shanghai residents (no longer Shanghailanders) see their city returning. Deng Xiaoping, embarking on the reform and opening period of the 1980s, declared, "To get rich is glorious!" and Shanghai took that advice to heart.

Shanghai is mainland China's richest, most cosmopolitan city—as it was in the early twentieth century—and many Shanghai Chinese find the roots of this prosperity in the mixture of Chinese and Western culture and society that defined "Shanghai style" and persists to this day. There is nostalgia for the treaty port period, and not only among Europeans or Americans. Many Chinese residents look back through rose-colored glasses to see a model for a city that is once again one of the world's great metropolises, this time ruled and run by Chinese. At the same time, Shanghai is now one of the world's most expensive places to live, far out of reach for most people, and sharp increases in inequality, gentrification, and consumption have accompanied Shanghai's rise.

From this perspective—with the caveat that Shanghai was never technically a colony—Shanghai under the PRC can be seen as an example (maybe the best example) of decolonization. Shanghai today is a thoroughly Chinese city. The pieces of Shanghai that once symbolized Western dominance are tamed, made Chinese. Red PRC flags fly conspicuously atop every peak of every rooftop on the Bund, and all of this foreign-built cityscape is humbled by the new skyscrapers across the river in Pudong.

Recalling Chinese characters like Nates Wong, Dayu Doon, and Ing Tang, China today wants to bring in the influence (and affluence) of the West as it did in the past, but this time on its own terms. Tapping into this nostalgia, a British entrepreneur named Byron Constable purchased the rights to the name "Shanghai Race Club" in the first decade of the twenty-first century and began operating a business described as "The Shanghai Race Club est. 1862."[19] This new Shanghai Race Club "focussed on building strong global commercial demand for British racing among a new set of consumers drawn to the cultural and lifestyle aspects of the sport." Before going dark in the summer of 2019, its website featured photos and information about the Race Club going back to 1862, but the business never maintained a racecourse, conducted race meetings, or owned horses. The club took mainland Chinese interested in racing on tours of English racing landmarks like Royal Ascot, and hosted parties in Shanghai that evoked the Jazz Age heyday of the SRC.[20]

And of course, Shanghai's reemergence as a global city has seen foreigners return. From only seventy foreign residents in the early 1970s, there are now many thousands of long- and short-term expatriates living in Shanghai, some of whom revel in a romanticized version of the city's past. Lu Hanchao called this a "nostalgia for the future," an imagined future when Shanghai would build on its international and colonial roots to become truly cosmopolitan in a globalized world. "New Shanghailanders" live and work, sometimes uneasily, in many of the same spaces as earlier generations of foreigners did. They selectively remember, promote, protest, preserve, and ignore different elements of Shanghai's past, and a small industry of Shanghai nostalgia thrives.[21]

The Shanghai Race Club embodied the glamor that attracted Cornell Franklin, Arthur Henchman, Dayu Doon, and Ing Tang, as well as the exploitation that repelled authors like Lu Bo in the 1970s or Shanghai councilman Chen Gongda in the 1940s. Even though the races went on during the war, November 12, 1941, marked the end of the Shanghai Race Club as the center of a world. Never again did Western power sit unchallenged atop Shanghai.

THE RACECOURSE IT WAS built for gone, the clubhouse remains, waiting at the end of that walk up Nanjing Road from the Bund. It has stood in the same spot for nearly a century, but it seems now uncomfortable in its surroundings, a ghost of a bygone era.

After its brief stint as an art gallery in 1951, the race club was repurposed as the Shanghai Municipal Library, somehow surviving the Cultural Revolution that targeted so much of China's history. Starting in the 1990s, madcap economic growth overtook many relics of Shanghai's past, encroaching on the old clubhouse. The library moved out to its new modern home in the former French Concession in 1997, and the Shanghai Art Museum moved in, until 2012 (for much of this time, a Western-style restaurant sat on the rooftop, offering diners the view overlooking the former racecourse). For more than five years after that, the building sat mostly empty.

In the spring of 2018, the clubhouse opened as the Museum of Shanghai History, visitors entering through the same doors at the base of the tower from Bubbling Well Road—now called Nanjing West Road—that Eric Moller and Vera McBain once had. The stairs that Bob Aitkenhead and Gussie White had climbed to the mezzanine are still intact, as are the former betting halls, where Dayu Doon and Ing Tang, along with thousands of others who came to the races, could put down their wagers. The second-story coffee room, where Henchman and Franklin prepared for Champions Day, season after season, presents artifacts from Shanghai's history long before racing horses was a concern.

The museum's designers had the chance to exorcise this haunted house. Plenty of historic buildings—whether Western or Chinese in origin—are gutted or torn down in Shanghai, and all across China. Not so here, where the clubhouse retains its colonial decor, with detailed ironwork and elaborate fixtures: horseheads in the railings, the S-R-C logo in the fireplace. A new rooftop restaurant embraces the building's past with an equestrian theme, a chance to profit off of the legacy.

Within this frame, the museum tells a version of Shanghai history that clashes sharply with its setting. Foreign power, the world of the Shanghailanders, and even the Race Club itself are just a small slice; the museum gives more space to the archaeological remains of the city's prehistory. It's an odd juxtaposition: the colonial decor of the clubhouse sitting uneasily alongside an official narrative, told in the museum's exhibits, that minimizes the importance the treaty port era that defines so much of modern Shanghai. The presentation speaks to the building's new visitors, but the setting nods to its past.

Old Shanghai is today found on the third floor. There, in a room devoted to the treaty port era, is an artifact that punctuates our story of the end of Old Shanghai. To illustrate the role of the Hongkong and Shanghai Banking Corporation, the museum displays the manager's desk, preserved and moved from its original home in the corner office of the HSBC building on the Bund. This was Henchman's desk, where he negotiated the currency crises of the 1930s, wrote to his colleagues describing the destruction on Bloody Saturday in 1937, planned for dozens of Champions Days, and worried about when and how to get out of China.

Thousands of visitors now pass by the desk each day. Some may wander up another floor and enjoy a meal or a drink in the rooftop restaurant overlooking the vestiges of the racecourse surrounded by high-rises. Looking at relics of Shanghai's past, what do these visitors see? A past where powerful foreigners ignored their surroundings to focus on fancy clothes and faster horses? Or how a powerful blending of Chinese and foreign energies built a city of extraordinary openness? A cesspool of vice and poverty? Or a modern metropolis at the cutting edge of technology and fashion? All are there to be seen.

These contradictions resonate in a city that today combines unprecedented economic opportunity for many, but also increasing inequality— a city that is tightly controlled politically, yet bursting with creative energy. Shanghai is the center of a world once more, a world that is more global and cosmopolitan than the one that gave rise to Champions Day. Political, economic, social, and cultural forces fight daily to define that world. The Race Club is a cautionary tale about what happens when the powerful exploit their environment, inviting war and revolution, as well as a hopeful plea for a more open time when people and ideas and fortunes flowed into Shanghai and made it one of the world's great cities.

The morning after Champions Day 1941, Hench would have sat at the desk, looking out over the Huangpu River. Nates Wong, waking up and starting his day just a few blocks away, might have passed under Henchman's window on the Bund, or even brushed by him on the street. Perhaps Ing Tang was in that mix too, wondering if she had missed her only chance to go to Broadway. Bob Aitkenhead must have been satisfied that he had finally returned to the winner's circle. All of them, and millions more, would have wondered what was in store for Shanghai: where it had come from, and where it was going. It's unlikely that they could have guessed correctly.

The outlines of the old racetracks are easily overlooked but not invisible. The same can be said of the mixture of foreign and Chinese influences on Shanghai. This city, once run by foreigners and distinctive because it was Chinese, is now a Chinese city distinguished by its foreignness. Shanghai seeks a place in the world, and it might well wonder (as Madame Piper did decades earlier), "What of your fortune, your family, your very life? . . . If ever Humanity needed a glimpse into the future, it is now."

The former site of the Shanghai Race Club, in 1961, after the racetrack had been transformed into a lake and park.

ACKNOWLEDGMENTS

THIS BOOK STARTED AS AN IDEA MORE THAN TEN YEARS AGO. In the course of that decade many people have helped the idea develop and change and eventually become this book. My thanks to everyone listed here, and my deep apologies to anyone I have overlooked or forgotten. It goes without saying that remaining errors of fact or interpretation are mine.

I have studied and written about China for a long while, but Shanghai is a world of its own. I could never have navigated Shanghailand without help and guidance from many experts. Chief among these were Robert Bickers, Maura Elizabeth Cunningham, and Jeff Wasserstrom, all of whom are unmatched in their kindness and generosity, not to mention expertise. Without their introductions to people, sources, and scholarship, this book could not have happened. Maura has read more than one draft of this book, and commiserated over the challenges of research and writing in and about Shanghai. This book is so much better because of her contributions, and I will always be grateful for her friendship, her introduction to Shanghai, and her skill and generosity as a writer, historian, and travel guide.

At the University of Bristol, special thanks to Jamie Carstairs at Historical Photographs of China, and to the participants in the symposium "Snapshots in Time: Photography and History in Modern China."

Patrick Cranley, Tess Johnston, Tina Kanagaratnam, Greg Leck, Kent McKeever, and Bill Savadove were among other Shanghai hands who were helpful in answering questions, providing information and materials, and/or offering advice. Paul French offered advice about writing that I could not always follow, but that helped me better think about the opportunities and challenges I faced in re-creating Shanghai's past in print.

Peter Law and Sarah Mellors helped me obtain images and documents from Shanghai when I could not get there myself. Paul Pickowicz and Chen Xi at UC San Diego, and Anne Mar at Occidental College, were helpful in looking for and finding images in their library collections.

Lisa Adams, Steve Platt, and Heather Cox Richardson talked with me about the process of publishing and writing, and helped me think about both in new ways, with lasting results.

In addition to all the authors who have written about Shanghai's past and on whose work I have tried to build, I need to thank experts in several subfields, who helped me navigate some of the obstacles particular to those areas. For horse racing, Teresa Genaro and Candice Hare answered many questions, and Teresa consulted with me on my chapters that take place at the track. Thanks to Sandra Fahy for helping us get in touch. Other experts who provided invaluable assistance were, on Buddhism, Brooks Jessup and Erik Hammerstrom; on Shanghai Jews and the Hardoons, Joseph Sassoon; on architecture, Edward Denison, Seng Kuan, Cole Raskam, and Guangyu Ren; on Shanghai sports and clubs, Simon Drakeford and John Slusar; and on fashion and intellectual society in Shanghai, Andrew David Field and Paul Bevan (who also helped locate images of Ing Tang). Jonathan Howlett and Isabella Jackson offered helpful approaches to research in the UK.

Jennifer N. J. Chang of Academia Sinica hosted me for a delightful lunch in Taipei to talk about the Shanghai Races. Lydia Chen, Isabel Sun Chao, and Claire Chao shared personal and family recollections in phone, e-mail, and in-person interviews.

I was fortunate to work in many different archives and libraries, and I must thank the staffs at the Library of Congress in Washington, DC; the US National Archives in College Park, Maryland; the National Archives of the United Kingdom in Kew, London; the Royal Asiatic Society; the Shanghai Municipal Archives; and the Shanghai Library, especially the Xujiahui (Siccawei) branch. In Hong Kong, C. M. Yip helped with access and materials at the Hong Kong Jockey Club and Jockey Club Archives. Special thanks to Erin Sidwell at the Library of Congress and, above all, to Sarah Boyce and the rest of the staff at the Drexel Library at Saint Joseph's University.

Support from the Nealis Program in Asian Studies at St. Joe's helped me acquire many of the resources that made this book possible. Thanks to its benefactors, Jim and Bernadette Nealis.

The HSBC Archives in both Hong Kong and, especially, London, were invaluable. I want to thank Danielle Andrew-Lynch, Yana Fowle, and Tina Staples in London and Jenny Yu in Hong Kong. Katherine Anthony, my former student, was a diligent and thorough research assistant in London. THWND!

Sarah Dodd, Frances Weightman, and especially Peng Qipao helped me get access to unique material at the University of Leeds.

Twitter was a source of distraction, but more importantly, it helped me contact many talented scholars, authors, and even friends: Audrey Bastian, Meredith Hindley, and Bill Lascher were encouraging and enthusiastic throughout the process. Lisa Munro and Kelsey Utne helped in ways that they may not know. And Theresa Kaminski, Drew McKevitt, and Arissa Oh all very kindly read drafts of proposals and of sections of the manuscript. I look forward to returning the favor.

Katherine Flynn represented this book and helped find it a happy home at W. W. Norton. Katherine's validation of what I thought a book could be was essential. I can't thank her enough for the enthusiasm, insight, and skill she put into the proposal.

No single person has had more impact on this book than my editor at W. W. Norton, Alane Salierno Mason. Her hard work and skill as an editor, enthusiasm for the project, and patience with me have made the book immeasurably better. Thanks to Reggie Hui for important criticisms that helped a lot. "Copyediting" only begins to describe the role that Stephanie Hiebert played in finalizing the manuscript. Thanks as well to the rest of the team at Norton, including Mo Crist, but extending to many others whose work often went unseen by me.

My colleagues at Saint Joseph's University—especially Amber Abbas, Melissa Chakars, Chris Close, Emily Hage, Catherine Hughes, Susan Liebell, Elizabeth Morgan, Leslie Rogne Schumacher, Rich Warren, and Brian Yates—all read drafts of proposals, chapters, and parts of chapters, and I thank them for that. Alex Gould and Denise Thomas provided support that enabled me to do my job, and without them this book would not be done for a long while. Summer research grants from the provost's office at St. Joe's helped me conduct this research, and I thank the Board on Faculty Research and Development for approving my applications.

I could never have undertaken the research for this book over many years without the support and encouragement of Cynthia Paces.

Ingrid Creppell, Amy Fleming, Jonathan Fleming, Jeanne Malloy, Bob Mudge, and Bill Walto provided fellowship and friendship along the way—and sometimes a place to stay on research trips too! Special thanks to Jonathan for a helpful read of an early draft. Their interest in and enthusiasm for the project was reassuring at every stage. Mary Anne Cloney may not remember, but her enthusiasm about the project many years ago, when it was just an idea, helped give me the courage to push it forward. Julia and Adam were always patient when they had to hear, again, about "the horsey book"!

Special thanks to the members of the 2018 Congressional Staff Delegation to China who accompanied me on my first visit to the Shanghai Race Club building, and especially to Jess Bissett for making that trip possible. At the National Committee on US-China Relations, Jan Berris, Margot Landman, and Jon Lowet—and, of course, my many PIP friends and colleagues—helped encourage me with their interest and enthusiasm.

This book would not exist without Susan Liebell, a loving and patient partner as I have researched and written this book, always offering encouragement and enthusiasm through the many highs and lows of the process. Her sense of style and story have made this better, and her companionship brightened the often solitary practice of writing. She was also the perfect partner on "research trips" to the tracks in Saratoga and Happy Valley!

I would never have believed myself capable of writing a book like this, were it not for the support and confidence of my parents, Jim and Susan Carter. Thank you!

Above all, thanks to Charlotte and Mariel. They both heard "I need to work on my book" more than they should have, and they were constant reminders that there are more important things to do than write books.

APPENDIX

SHANGHAI RACE CLUB
CHAMPIONS' STAKES:
1869–1942

(FROM 1927 TO 1941,
THE SHAFORCE CHALLENGE CUP
AND CHAMPIONS' STAKES)

YEAR	SEASON	WIN	PLACE	SHOW
1869	AUTUMN	MORS AUX DENT	VERTUGADIN	ATABAL
1870	SPRING	CWMRW GLAN	VERTUGADIN	LAST OF THE MOHICANS
	AUTUMN	ROUGH DIAMOND	SKYTE	SKELP
1871	SPRING	SUMMER CLOUD	FIDDLE DE DEE	RATAPAN
	AUTUMN	LEECHRAFT	LAST OF THE MOHICANS	GÉNÉRAL
1872	SPRING	JULIUS CAESAR	SPONDULICK	NOUS VERRONS
	AUTUMN	SNOWDRIFT	ALMERIC	SLEEPY HOLLOW
1873	SPRING	GRASSHOPPER	KUO-PU-CHÜ	FEI YUEN
	AUTUMN	RAVENSHOE	SOUVENIR	SIR LAUNCELOT
1874	SPRING	RAVENSHOE	SOUVENIR	SINECURE
	AUTUMN	ROUBLE	TALLAPOOSA	MUDJEKEEWIS

YEAR	SEASON	WIN	PLACE	SHOW
1875	SPRING	TEEN KWANG	RAVENSHOE	ANDANTE
	AUTUMN	TEEN KWANG	WILD OATS	FURORE
1876	SPRING	BLACK SATIN	SOLDANELLA	REICHSGRAF
	AUTUMN	BLACK SATIN	WILD WHIM	WILD RUSH
1877	SPRING	SUAVITA	FIASCO	BLACK SATIN
	AUTUMN	BLACK SATIN	STRATHCLYDE	EGMONT
1878	SPRING	STRATHAVON	BLACK SATIN	EARL BRIAN
	AUTUMN	TOLERATION	BLACK SATIN	ISEGRIM
1879	SPRING	STRATHAVON	JOLLY FRIAR	WILD BOER
	AUTUMN	JOLLY FRIAR	STRATHAVON	TAJMAHAL
1880	SPRING	TAJMAHAL	RED ROBIN	STRATHAVON
	AUTUMN	PREJUDICE	BLACK SATIN	STRATHAVON
1881	SPRING	PREJUDICE	EARL HAROLD	WILD DASH
	AUTUMN	PREJUDICE	FIRST CORNET	JOLLY FRIAR
1882	SPRING	TAJMAHAL	DRIVING CLOUD	WILD DASH
	AUTUMN	FIRST CORNET	PREJUDICE	ROSE
1883	SPRING	TORPEDO	PREJUDICE	ORIOLE
	AUTUMN	SECOND VIOLIN	PICCADILLY	HERSCHEL
1884	SPRING	WILD DASH	DUNKELY	OLIAWANDA
	AUTUMN	WILD DASH	TYCOON	M.A.
1885	SPRING	PICCADILLY	BANDSMAN	HERSCHEL
	AUTUMN	COUNCILLOR	RED GAUNTLET	GAMESTER
1886	SPRING	COUNCILLOR	CUCKOO	SLIPAWAY
	AUTUMN	COUNCILLOR	MISTLETOE	DUNKELD
1887	SPRING	HARBINGER	MONT BLANC	TIOGA
	AUTUMN	SUPERSTITION	DUNKELD	TYCOON
1888	SPRING	SUSEWIND	SILKEN MEAD	CARIOLE
	AUTUMN	ORLANDO	EUREKA	BULLION
1889	SPRING	ZEPHYR	ELEGANT	SUSEWIND
	AUTUMN	ZEPHYR	HOME GUARD	ORLANDO
1890	SPRING	VATICANATOR	ZEPHYR	NOIRMONT
	AUTUMN	HERO	HOME GUARD	ZEPHYR

YEAR	SEASON	WIN	PLACE	SHOW
1891	SPRING	HERO	ZEPHYR	NOIRMONT
	AUTUMN	HERO	MERRY THOUGHT	HOME GUARD
1892	SPRING	ROYALIST	HOHENZOLLERN	LIGHTNING
	AUTUMN	HERO	MAJESTIC	BOVRIL
1893	SPRING	HERO	BLACKBERRY	TORCHLIGHT
	AUTUMN	HERO	BOVRIL	FIREFLY
1894	SPRING	SANS PAREIL	DARE DEVIL	EROS
	AUTUMN	BLACKBERRY	"ENERY" AWKINS	VAGRANT
1895	SPRING	BLACKBERRY	MISSISSIPPI	SANS DOUTE
	AUTUMN	INVADER	MENEJI	ORION
1896	SPRING	INVADER	VAQUERO	BLACK AND WHITE
	AUTUMN	BLACKBERRY	THE BROKER	HOLSTOMER
1897	SPRING	BLACKBERRY	AEOLUS	THE BROKER
	AUTUMN	CHARGER	HOLSTOMER	ORWELL
1898	SPRING	SAMMIE	BUGLER	THE BROKER
	AUTUMN	DAMASKUS	LOYALTY	SHANNON
1899	SPRING	LOYALTY	CALLISTO	BEACHNUT
	AUTUMN	DAMASKUS	LOYALTY	SHANNON
1900	SPRING	LOYALTY	RIO GRANDE	DESERT KING
	AUTUMN	THE DEALER	SET	LOYALTY
1901	SPRING	THE DEALER	SET	ICHIMURA
	AUTUMN	THE DEALER	SET	ICHIMURA
1902	SPRING	THE DEALER	HIS EXCELLENCY	RIO GRANDE
	AUTUMN	AMPHION	ALGERINE	THE DEALER
1903	SPRING	GADFLY	THE DEALER	FLOTSAM
	AUTUMN[a]	GADFLY	VANCOUVER / JETSAM	—
1904	SPRING	JETSAM	GADFLY	SPHERE
	AUTUMN	ZAMBESI	GADFLY	CORONET ROSE
1905	SPRING	ARD PATRICK	ZAMBESI	GADFLY
	AUTUMN	CELTIC	COTSWOLD	OHIO
1906	SPRING	CEDRIC	BROCKTON	ARGANTE
	AUTUMN	MORIAK	BROCKTON	ARD PATRICK

YEAR	SEASON	WIN	PLACE	SHOW
1907	SPRING	MORIAK	BROCKTON	RURIE
	AUTUMN[a]	BROCKTON	SPRING ROSE / SEA FOAM	—
1908	SPRING	MORIAK	BROCKTON	MANCHU KING
	AUTUMN	GEMINI	SAGITTARIUS	MORIAK
1909	SPRING	GEMINI	CHINA	WORCESTER
	AUTUMN	SAGITTARIUS	SPRING ROSE	LITTLE GEM
1910	SPRING[b]	SPRING ROSE	SAGITTARIUS	—
	AUTUMN	PERSIMMON TREE	SQUIRE MCGULPER	CECILE ROSE
1911	SPRING	FOREMAN	HANKOW	STADACONA
	AUTUMN	CHERRY TREE	MARENGO	ROYAL ROSE
1912	SPRING	WILLOW TREE	MARENGO	CHERRY TREE
	AUTUMN	MARENGO	BURWOOD	BATTLEFIELD
1913	SPRING	CASTLEFIELD	PRESIDENT	I'M OFF
	AUTUMN	SIR PELICAS	CASTLEFIELD	PALADIN
1914	SPRING	PALADIN	FIJIAN CHIEF	CORNFIELD
	AUTUMN	CASTLEFIELD	CONCESSION	SUFFOLK
1915	SPRING[a]	BEACONSFIELD	ROSEWOOD / SIR VICTOR	—
	AUTUMN	CASTLEFIELD	BEACONSFIELD	PERFECTION DAHLIA
1916	SPRING	BEACONSFIELD	HAZLENUT	PARAGON
	AUTUMN	BLACK DIAMOND	CASTLEFIELD	WINSOME DAHLIA
1917	SPRING	CASTLEFIELD	GLADIATOR	OSIRIS
	AUTUMN	THE ORIOLE	SILVER STREAK	GLADIATOR
1918	SPRING[c]	CASTLEWOOD	CASTLEFIELD	GLADIATOR / THE ORIOLE
	AUTUMN	CASTLEFIELD	CASTLEWOOD	SILVER STREAK
1919	SPRING	ROSEWOOD	SILVER STREAK	CASTLEFIELD
	AUTUMN	SILVER STREAK	THE ORIOLE	HALLOW E'EN
1920	SPRING	BYDAND	OLD BILL	WOODAND
	AUTUMN	THE HAWK	BYDAND	TATOUILLARD
1921	SPRING	OLD BILL	SILVER STREAK	THE HAWK
	AUTUMN	THE HAWK	MARESFIELD	OLD BILL
1922	SPRING	MARESFIELD	OLD BILL	SHENKOLAND
	AUTUMN	MARESFIELD	SALVATION	NATIONALIST

YEAR	SEASON	WIN	PLACE	SHOW
1923	SPRING	SHENKOLAND	OLD BILL	COCK O' T' NORTH
	AUTUMN	ABBEYFIELD	WHITE KNIGHT	OLD BILL
1924	SPRING	COLUMBIA	ZOUAVE	NEW ZEALAND
	AUTUMN	BONNIE SCOTLAND	BORDERLAND	ZOUAVE
1925	SPRING	WARRENFIELD	NEW ZEALAND	SAUCY
	AUTUMN	WARRENFIELD	BONNIE SCOTLAND	WHEATCROFT
1926	SPRING	BORDERLAND	OLD BILL	FIRESTONE
	AUTUMN	WHEATCROFT	MORNING FLIGHT	PICCOLO
1927	SPRING	NEW ZEALAND	MARK OVER	MORNING FLIGHT
	AUTUMN	CHARCOAL	YOUNG BILL	WHEATCROFT
1928	SPRING	WHEATCROFT	WHITE ROSEMARY	ALLIGATOR
	AUTUMN	BUSY BEE	WHEATCROFT	ALLIGATOR
1929	SPRING	PAT	WHEATCROFT	POPPYLAND
	AUTUMN	WHEATCROFT	BUSY BEE	ALLIGATOR
1930	SPRING	BUSY BEE	WHEATCROFT	ALLIGATOR
	AUTUMN	WHEATCROFT	ELECTION EVE	FIREFLASH
1931	SPRING	SAARLAND	BUSY BEE	MISTER CINDERS
	AUTUMN	SAARLAND	FIREFLASH	HAZY MORN
1932	SPRING	MISTER CINDERS	DOUR BIRD	ALLIGATOR
	AUTUMN	SLEEPY MORN	ALLIGATOR	BOOT BLACK
1933	SPRING	NATIONALIST III	BOOT BLACK	VECHEROCK
	AUTUMN	OPERA EVE	SARATOGA	TRACTION BIRD
1934	SPRING	OPERA EVE	CASTLE-RIBBON	FOUR ACES
	AUTUMN	CASTLE-RIBBON	OPERA EVE	WELCOME MORN
1935	SPRING	OPERA EVE	ROCHESTER	SILAS WEGG
	AUTUMN	RADIANT MORN	ROCHESTER	BOSTON DRILL
1936	SPRING	RADIANT MORN	STOP LOSS	ROCHESTER
	AUTUMN	RADIANT MORN	ROCHESTER	DON PEDRO
1937	SPRING	SPARKLING MORN	ROEHAMPTON	SMOKYLIGHT
	AUTUMN	RADIANT MORN	WATERLOOBEY	NAMING MORN
1938	SPRING	RADIANT MORN	ROEHAMPTON	MERRYLIGHT
	AUTUMN	MERRYLIGHT	GOLD VASE	WHITE PARADE

YEAR	SEASON	WIN	PLACE	SHOW
1939	SPRING	RAIN	HINDHEAD	WHITE WILLIE
	AUTUMN	WHITE PARADE	BAGSHOT	JOYLIGHT
1940	SPRING	CLUNIEHOUSE	BAGSHOT	DON ENRICO
	AUTUMN	HINDHEAD	CLUNIEHOUSE	NORTHWOOD
1941	SPRING	HINDHEAD	SILVER FOX	CLUNIEHILL
	AUTUMN	CLUNIEHOUSE	WHITE PARADE	MAGIC CIRCLE (LATE SPARKLING MORN)
1942	SPRING	OLD TIMER (LATE CLUNIEHILL)	COQUINET (LATE WHITE NIGHT)	PALADIN (LATE WHITE PARADE)

[a] In autumn 1903, autumn 1907, and spring 1915, there was a dead heat for second place, so no third place was awarded.

[b] In spring 1910, the winner (Marbles) was disqualified for swerving, so the horses in second and third place each moved up, and third place was not awarded.

[c] In spring 1918, there was a dead heat for third place.

NOTES

PROLOGUE: THE CENTER OF A WORLD

1. Lu Hanchao, *Beyond the Neon Lights*, 43.
2. Yang and Ye, *Jiu Shanghai fengyun renwu*, 202–9, quoted in Lu Hanchao, *Beyond the Neon Lights*, 48.

CHAPTER 1: MORNING IN SHANGHAI

1. Advertisement, *The China Press* (hereafter *TCP*), November 12, 1941, 5.
2. Advertisement, *Shanghai Times*, November 12, 1941.
3. A court case involving Vera Hutchinson—see, for example, "Madame Piper Holds Her Own in Word Battle," *North-China Daily News* (hereafter *NCDN*), October 14, 1933—revealed that Helen Piper was an alias.
4. "Shanghai," *Fortune*, 40.
5. "Liza Hardoon Dies at 78 Leaving Huge Estate," *Shanghai Times*, October 4, 1941.
6. *Racing Record*, vol. 24.
7. "Crowds Must Stay Off Roofs," *North-China Herald* (hereafter *NCH*), August 25, 1937.
8. Arthur Henchman to Vandeleur Grayburn, October 25, 1941, HQ SHGII 0124, HSBC Archives, London.
9. Shanghai Consular Correspondence, August 14, 1941, and November 8, 1941, Record Group 58 310, *Repatriation of American Citizens*, vol. 2959, National Archives (US).
10. Cover, *Pei-yang Pictorial News*, April 27, 1927.
11. Lu Hanchao, *Beyond the Neon Lights*, 146–48.
12. Ibid., 138.
13. Fang Yifeng, *Yizhongji* [A Collection], 5. Also, interview with Lydia Chen, Philadelphia, November 18, 2019.
14. Chang, *Cultural Translation*, 208.

CHAPTER 2: "THE PLEASURES OF EXILE"

1. "Ponies in Shanghai," *North-China Herald*, November 24, 1893.
2. Coates, *China Races*.
3. Platt, *Imperial Twilight*, 245.

4. Qianlong to George III, [1793], cited in Backhouse and Bland, *Annals & Memoirs*, 322–31.

5. Harrison, "Qianlong Emperor's Letter to George III."

6. Thorough recent discussion of this debate is in Platt, *Imperial Twilight*.

7. Cushing, *Opinion of the Attorney General*, 5.

8. Coates, *China Races*, 27.

9. *Shanghai Race Club Rules 1930*, 1.

10. A succinct and reliable account of the racetrack's westward movement is in Xiong, "From Racecourse to People's Park and People's Square," 477.

11. The Land Regulation of 1845 is laid out in numerous sources, including Morse, *International Relations of the Chinese Empire*, 1:350.

12. In *What Remains*, Tobie Meyer-Fong analyzes the consequences of this war.

13. Bickers, "Shanghailanders," 165–66.

14. Isabella Jackson, *Shaping Modern Shanghai*, 16–17.

15. Hawks Pott, *Short History of Shanghai*, 30.

16. Conservative estimates place this number at less than 200,000, but it is hard to know for sure. Lu Hanchao, *Beyond the Neon Lights*, 139.

17. Lu Bo, "Cong paomating dao renmin guangchang."

18. In *China Races*, Austin Coates contends that a third course was opened in 1860, between Tibet and Sinze Roads, but only four race meetings (in the spring and fall of 1860 and 1861) were held there, and that the current course is the fourth one to be built. The newspaper record, though, gives no indication of this third course. No other source supports Coates's claim.

19. "Shanghai Races," *NCH*, May 3, 1862. The *North-China Herald*, first published in 1850, was the oldest English-language newspaper in China and also the official record of the British consulate and the British Court for China and Japan. Its daily edition, the *North-China Daily News*, began in 1864.

20. Ibid.

21. D. H., "Clubland in Shanghai," *NCH*, November 24, 1893.

22. "History of the Shanghai Paper Hunt Club," quoted in Coates, *China Races*, 24.

23. Carl Sowerby, "What Is a China Pony," *NCH*, October 20, 1923.

CHAPTER 3: SHANGHAILANDERS

1. Bickers, *Scramble for China*, chapter 10.

2. Wang, *Portuguese in Shanghai*, 6–7.

3. Bickers, "Shanghailanders," 202. Historian Robert Bickers has argued persuasively that the term "Shanghailanders" meant only Britons, and specifically Britons who put down roots in Shanghai, owing loyalty to their local community even before their nation. I don't disagree, but I apply the term here in a less technical, more descriptive sense, to many Western residents of Shanghai.

4. "Law Reports," *NCH*, August 19, 1876.

5. "Mr. Nils Moller Explains," *NCH*, July 10, 1891.

6. Ibid.

7. "Public Meeting," *NCH*, August 3, 1880.

8. Various consulates, China, Registers of births, deaths, and marriages, Class FO 681, Piece 1, National Archives (UK), Kew.

9. Probate of Augustus Harold White, FO 917/1855, National Archives (UK), Kew.

10. Teng, *Eurasian: Mixed Identities*, 147.

11. D. H., "Clubland in Shanghai," *NCH*, November 24, 1893.

12. Ibid.

13. Ibid.

14. Bickers and Wasserstrom, "Shanghai's 'Dogs and Chinese Not Admitted' Sign."

15. Editorial, *NCH*, November 15, 1862. Emphasis in the original.

16. A. L. Robertson, "Ponies in Shanghai: The Pleasures of Exile," *NCH*, November 24, 1893.

17. "News of the Week," *NCH*, September 25, 1869.

18. "Autumn Race Meeting," *NCH*, November 6, 1869.

19. Stanley Jackson, *The Sassoons*.

20. "The Races," *NCH*, May 2, 1890.

21. Fairplay, "The Last Race for the Champions," *NCH*, July 7, 1893.

22. Coates, *China Races*, 126–27.

23. "Death," *NCH*, November 10, 1893, 752.

24. "Hero," *NCH*, November 16, 1893.

25. "Deaths," *NCH*, February 17, 1905.

26. "Amusements," *NCH*, November 2, 1894.

CHAPTER 4: RACE AND THE RACES

1. "Paoma leiji" [The horserace], *Shenbao*, May 5, 1875.

2. Wang Tao, *Seaside Jottings* (Shanghai, 1989), 121–22, cited in Xiong, "From Race-course to People's Park."

3. Chang, "To See and Be Seen," 96.

4. *Rules of the Shanghai Race Club 1930*, 27.

5. Nield, *China's Foreign Places*, 173–74.

6. Susan Mann Jones, "Ningpo *Pang* and Financial Power," 74–75.

7. Juliet Bredon, *Sir Robert Hart: The Romance of a Great Career*, 2nd ed. (London: Hutchinson, 1910), cited in Nield, *China's Foreign Places*, 175.

8. Goodman, *Native Place, City, and Nation*.

9. Ibid., 226.

10. "The Shanghai Race Club," *NCH*, January 29, 1897.

11. Ibid.

12. Chang, "To See and Be Seen," 100.

13. Qiong Lu, "Paoma" [Horse racing], *Shenbao*, May 7, 1914, 14, cited in Chang, "To See and Be Seen," 101.

14. Chang, "To See and Be Seen," 100.

15. "Amusements: Shanghai Autumn Race Meeting," *NCH*, November 5, 1897.

16. "International Recreation Club," *NCH*, June 3, 1910.

17. "International Recreation Club," *NCH*, April 22, 1911.

18. "International Recreation Club: Kiangwan Meeting," *NCH*, June 3, 1911.

19. "Wanguo tiyuhui chuzhi" [The International Recreation Club opening], *Shishi xinbao*, June 2, 1911.

20. Coates, *China Races*, 162.

21. "Kiangwan New Year Meeting: Opening of the New Grand Stand," *NCH*, March 3, 1923.

22. "Turned Down," *Shanghai Times*, February 14, 1919.

23. "Chinese and the Races," *Canton Times*, February 11, 1919.

24. "Shanghai News," *NCH*, May 19, 1923.

25. "Zuori fanri chubing dahui ji xiang" [Yesterday's demonstration opposing the mobilization of Japanese troops], *Shenbao*, June 13, 1927.

26. "Da lao rentou" [Assault on an old man], *Shishi xinbao*, September 1, 1925.

27. "Attack on Racing at Kiangwan: Chapei Merchants Protest to Paoshan Assembly," *NCH*, May 31, 1924.

28. "Racing at Yangtszepoo," *NCH*, November 15, 1924.

29. Chang, *Cultural Translation*, 204.

30. "Zhongguo saimahui zhi jinxing" [The opening of the Chinese Jockey Club], *Shishi xinbao*, March 8, 1926.

31. "First Official Race Meeting on Yangtsepoo Course Sunday; Program," *TCP*, March 14, 1926.

32. "Chinese Jockey Club: Inaugural Race Meeting," *NCH*, March 27, 1926, 582.

33. Ibid.

34. "The I.R.C's New Club Building," *NCH*, May 4, 1929.

35. Ibid.

36. Ibid.

37. "Large Gathering Attends Opening Ceremony," *TCP*, May 2, 1929, 5.

38. "Where Ponies Could Mean Sino-Foreign Amity," *TCP*, December 6, 1929.

CHAPTER 5: CHINESE SHANGHAILANDERS?

1. *Rules of the Shanghai Race Club 1930*, 40.

2. "Amusements: Shanghai Spring Race Meeting," *NCH*, May 2, 1890.

3. *Rules of the Shanghai Race Club 1930*, 6.

4. "Shanghai Race Meeting, Autumn 1941" [program].

5. "Obituary (1): Dr. N. A. Tang," *NCH*, August 17, 1929.

6. *Directory & Chronicle for China*, 890; *Comacrib Directory of China for 1925*, 11.

7. *Who's Who of the Chinese Students*, 67.

8. Mo, "Hong xiu," 183.

9. Chao and Chao, *Remembering Shanghai*, 153.

10. For a thorough description of the Soong sisters' remarkable lives, see Jung Chang, *Big Sister, Little Sister, Red Sister*.

11. Much of this paragraph is drawn from the cited periodicals, but also from Bevan, *Modern Miscellany*, 71–75.

12. "Shanghai Fall Fashion, Motor Car Show to Be Given for Ten Days Starting at End of October," *TCP*, September 25, 1927.

13. A Lady Correspondent, "Frocks on the Race Course," *NCH*, May 8, 1926, 283.

14. Louise B. Wilson, [First article, no title], *TCP*, November 8, 1925.

15. Phone interview, Isabel Sun Chao, October 28, 2019.

16. Data compiled by Lu Hanchao in *Beyond the Neon Lights*, 64, from Zhang Zhongli, *Jindai Shanghai chengshi yanjiu*, 724; and Zhu Bangxing et al., *Shanghai chanye yu Shanghai zhigong*, 701–2.

17. Wong's writing appeared in *Shanghai qingnian*, the journal of the YMCA—for example, Wang Naizhi, "Huayang bupingdeng lishi de yiye" [A word on the unequal history of

China and the West], *Shanghai qingnian* 45 (1930): 7–9. He wrote much later that he had been a Christian before becoming a Buddhist in the 1940s. Wang Naizhi, "Wo zhi xinyang zhuanyi zishu" [My change of faith], *Jueyouqing* [Enlightenment], date unknown.

18. Mu Shiying, "Shanghai de hu bu wu" [Shanghai foxtrot], trans. Andrew David Field, in *Mu Shiying*, ed. Field, 109.

19. Liu Na'ou, "Two People Impervious to Time," in *Dushi fengjing xian* [Urban skyline] (Shanghai: Shuimo shudian, 1930; repr., Shanghai shudian, 1988), 91–92. Translated quote from Braester, "Shanghai's Economy of the Spectacle," 43.

20. "Black Dominates the Fashions," *NCH*, November 18, 1936, 275.

21. Miriam Holloway, "Fashion Parade Gay with Color at Champions," *TCP*, May 11, 1933, 9.

22. Lady Correspondent, "Frocks on the Race Course."

23. Holloway, "Fashion Parade Gay with Color."

24. Yu Loo Tang, "Causerie Chinoise: On an Old Battlefield," *TCP*, May 9, 1926.

25. "Mr. N. A. Tang," *NCH*, August 24, 1929, 293.

26. Fitzgerald and Kuo, "Diaspora Charity."

27. William Yinson Lee, "Letter to the Editor," *NCH*, April 12, 1924, 64.

28. Ibid. For more about Lee, see Fitzgerald and Kuo, "Diaspora Charity."

29. William Yinson Lee, "Letter to the Editor," *NCH*, August 8, 1925, 137.

30. "Chinese Membership in the Foreign Clubs," *China Weekly Review* (hereafter *CWR*), August 15, 1925, 209.

31. "Shanghai Merchant Prince Mr. Chu Pao-san, Is Dead," *TCP*, September 3, 1926, 1; "Downtown Streets to Be Closed While Cortege of Mr. Chu Pao-san Is Passing," *TCP*, November 4, 1926, 1; "The Mourning Ceremonies for Mr. Chu Pao-San," *NCH*, November 6, 1926, 257.

32. Shen Zhirui, *Need for the Club*, 46.

33. Ibid.

34. Reed, *Gutenberg in Shanghai*, 186.

35. Lin Heqin, "The City and the Club," in *Need for the Club*, by Shen Zhirui, 40.

36. Liang Qichao and Yan Fu were two who thought China was doomed if it did not reform and adapt. Delury and Schell, *Wealth and Power*, 98, 101.

37. "Anglo-Chinese Garden Party," *NCH*, June 15, 1918.

38. Lin, "City and the Club."

39. Yu-loo Tang, "Causerie Chinoise," *TCP*, May 7, 1926.

40. Ibid.

41. Yu-loo Tang, "Causerie Chinoise: An Autumn Dirge," *TCP*, August 29, 1926, 12.

CHAPTER 6: CREATING A CHINESE SHANGHAI

1. Du Yangeng, "Kaipi dongfang dagang de zhongyao ji qishi shi buzhou (1)" [The importance and implementation of opening an eastern port], *Shenbao*, January 17, 1933, quoted in Roskam, *The Improvised City*, 179.

2. Isabella Jackson, *Shaping Modern Shanghai*, 73–77.

3. Coates, *China Races*, 162.

4. Roskam, *Improvised City*, 179.

5. Musgrove, *China's Contested Capital*, is the definitive account.

6. Drawn from Cody, *Building in China*.

7. Ibid., 42.

8. Ibid., 161.

9. "Henry Killam Murphy Will Draw Plans for Rebuilding of Nanking," *CWR*, December 22, 1928.

10. Denison and Ren, *Modernism in China*, 116.

11. Hibbard, *All about Shanghai and Environs*, 67.

12. Details of Doon's biography can be found in Seng, "Between Beaux-Arts and Modernism."

13. Doon, "Greater Shanghai—Greater Vision."

14. "Plans Are Outlined by Commission for Building the Future Greater Shanghai Municipal Center," *TCP*, November 10, 1929, C4.

15. Asa E. Phillips, "American Engineer Gives His Views on Plans for Local Port," *TCP*, December 3, 1929, 2.

16. "The Shanghai Dream City," *NCH*, November 16, 1929, 254.

17. "City Government Building: Foundation Stone Laying Ceremony Performed by Mayor," *NCH*, July 14, 1931, 49.

18. "Civic Center Is Reflection of New China," *TCP*, November 2, 1935.

19. "Planning Commission Awards Prizes on Civic Center Designs," *CWR*, March 22, 1930, 150.

20. "City Government Building," *NCH*.

21. "Shanghai shi zhengfu xin wudianji li ji" [Ceremony for foundation of New Shanghai government building], *Shenbao*, July 8, 1931.

22. Du Yangeng, "Kaipi dongfang dagang de zhongyao ji qishi shi buzhou" (3) [The importance and implementation of opening an eastern port], *Shenbao*, February 14, 1933. Quoted in Roskam, *Improvised City*, 194.

23. "City Government Building," *NCH*.

24. "Slain Secretary Lives to Give Graphic Story of Battle in Station," *TCP*, July 24, 1931, 1.

25. "Mr. Yu-Loo Tang Passes Away," *NCH*, July 28, 1931, 120.

26. "Scenes of Desolation," *NCH*, March 15, 1932.

27. "Work on Buildings at Civic Center to Be Resumed Soon," *TCP*, June 16, 1932, 1.

28. "Sports of All Sorts," *TCP*, February 14, 1932, B1.

29. Chang, *Cultural Translation*, 204.

CHAPTER 7: SHANGHAI RACES

1. "New Race Club Buildings," *NCH*, March 7, 1934.

2. "Burkill [*sic*] Opens New Race Club with Gold Key," *TCP*, March 1, 1934.

3. Bickers, "Settlers and Diplomats," 230.

4. Although Bickers explains how expatriates distanced themselves from Settlers, he also makes clear that the divisions between them diminished in times of crisis. For that reason, in part, I don't make great distinction between the two groups.

5. "Shanghai," *Fortune*, 40.

6. Ibid., 102.

7. "Burkhill [*sic*] Opens New Race Club," *TCP*.

8. "New Race Club Buildings," *NCH*.

9. Ibid.

10. Jerome W. Ephraim, "Expert Gives Good Advice on Hangovers: Morning after the Night Before," *TCP*, December 14, 1936.
11. "Over the Tea Cup: Looking on the Bright Side: Activities of Some of Shanghai's Bright Young Things," *NCH*, March 22, 1932.
12. Ephraim, "Expert Gives Good Advice."
13. Yu-loo Tang, "Causerie Chinoise," *TCP*, May 2, 1926.
14. "Shanghai," *Fortune*.
15. Sensibar, *Faulkner and Love*, 415.
16. "What Part Patriotism Plays in the Life of a Nation Is Told in U.S. Memorial Day Address," *TCP*, June 5, 1927.
17. Sensibar, *Faulkner and Love*, 242.
18. Based on Sensibar, *Faulkner and Love*.
19. Sensibar, *Faulkner and Love*, 395.
20. Ibid., 407.
21. Estelle Oldham (Faulkner), "Star-Spangled Banner Stuff," in Sensibar, "Introductory Note to 'Star-Spangled Banner Stuff.' "
22. Sensibar, "Introductory Note to 'Star-Spangled Banner Stuff,' " 379.
23. Sensibar, *Faulkner and Love*, 242.
24. Ibid., 469.
25. "Personal Notes," *NCH*, August 22, 1925.
26. Information on Henchman's HSBC career is drawn from King, *Hongkong Bank between the Wars*, esp. 301–2.
27. Ibid., 411.
28. "Here and There," *NCH*, December 27, 1933.
29. "Shanghai as Others See It," *NCH*, November 19, 1927.
30. "Popular Bowler's Farewell: Mr. R. C. Aitkenhead Leaving China," *NCH*, July 20, 1932, 98.
31. "Weddings," *NCH*, September 10, 1912.
32. "Passenger List," *NCH*, February 15, 1933.
33. "Shanghai," *Fortune*, 102.
34. "Flight of Fancy," English.eastday.com, October 3, 2005, http://english.eastday.com/eastday/englishedition/node20665/node20667/node22808/node45576/node45577/userobject1ai925032.html.
35. Coates, *China Races*, 251–53.
36. Jane Ram, "A Lover of Horses," Recollections (series), *South China Morning Post*, April 28, 1974, 26.
37. *Rules of the Shanghai Race Club 1930*, 42.
38. "Marriage Announcement," *NCH*, May 18, 1918, 413.
39. "Shanghai Law Reports," *NCH*, February 10, 1937, 251.
40. "Marriage Announcement," *NCH*, February 17, 1937, 308.
41. Wearing, *London Stage: 1910–1919*.
42. Coates, *China Races*.
43. M. M. P., "Lady Race Pony Owners," *NCH*, May 10, 1933, 239.
44. "Liddell-Coutts Wedding Held," *TCP*, November 22, 1927.
45. Don Warrin, "Antonio M. Jorge da Silva: An Oral History," interview conducted in 2014 (Berkeley: Oral History Center, Bancroft Library, University of California, 2015).

46. "Young Architect Welcomed," *NCH*, June 16, 1928.
47. "The Denis Apartments," *TCP*, January 30, 1930, A58.
48. Ibid.

CHAPTER 8: COSMOPOLITANS

1. *The China Directory for 1863*, 46.
2. "Optants 1872," Ancestry.com, accessed September 16, 2019.
3. Betta, "Silas Aaron Hardoon (1851–1931), 71–73.
4. Ibid., 74.
5. The story of the Sassoons and another prominent Jewish family prominent in Shanghai, the Kadoories, is told in Jonathan Kaufman, *The Last Kings of Shanghai*.
6. Chapter 3 of Betta, "Silas Aaron Hardoon," gives a thorough account of this period.
7. Betta, "Silas Aaron Hardoon," 68.
8. Ibid., 102.
9. Xu, *Hatong waizhuan*.
10. Description based on Betta, "Silas Aaron Hardoon," 77.
11. "Huge Beth Aharon Synagogue, Donated by S. A. Hardoon, Is Opened with Impressive Rites," *TCP*, July 1, 1927.
12. "A Notable Chinese Woman," *Millard's Review of the Far East*, August 9, 1919.
13. "Local and General News," *NCH*, May 25, 1912.
14. "The Garden Fete: Splendid Show for Allies' Relief Funds," *NCH*, May 29, 1915.
15. "Anglo-Chinese Garden Party," *NCH*, June 15, 1918.
16. "Charity Fete in Mr. Hardoon's Garden," *NCH*, November 10, 1917.
17. "Modern 'Women of Tang,' " *TCP*, April 8, 1928.
18. Betta, "Silas Aaron Hardoon," 110, 270.
19. The most thorough account of the complex Hardoon family is Doron, "Silas Aaron Hardoon," 76. See also Maisie J. Meyer, *From the Rivers of Babylon*, 252n100.
20. Doron, "Silas Aaron Hardoon," 79.
21. Maisie Meyer, "Sephardi Jewish Community," 32.
22. Ibid., 42.
23. The case is thoroughly discussed in Maisie J. Meyer, "Silas Aaron Hardoon Will Case," in *Shanghai's Baghdadi Jews*, 460–68.
24. "Mrs. Hardoon's Birthday," *NCH*, August 30, 1933.
25. "Hardoon's Widow Celebrates 70th Birthday Here Today," *TCP*, August 27, 1933.
26. "Here & There," *NCH*, May 8, 1935.
27. Stein, "Protected Persons?" 80.
28. Diana Yeh, *Happy Hsiungs*, 22–28.
29. Max Chaichek, "Shanghai Show World," *TCP*, April 6, 1934, 8.
30. Yeh, *Happy Hsiungs*, 39–40.
31. " 'Lady Precious Stream' Starts Vogue for Things Chinese," *TCP*, June 7, 1935, 1.
32. "Rehearsals Go Well Here on Chinese Play," *TCP*, June 5, 1935, 14.
33. "Here & There," *NCH*, May 8, 1935.
34. "Shanghai News," *NCH*, May 12, 1923.
35. "Ing Tang Lee Making Grapes When N.Y. Stage Offer Comes," *TCP*, December 15, 1935, 9.

36. " 'Lady Precious Stream': Shanghai's Presentation at Carlton Theatre," *NCH*, July 3, 1935.

37. "Re ren zhumu zhi yingwen ming ju" [Eye-catching English drama], *Shishi xinbao*, June 26, 1935.

38. "Society Turns Out for Play," *TCP*, June 26, 1935.

39. "Tang ying jiang fu mei bin Wang Baochuan" [Tang Ying will go to the United States to play Lady Precious Stream], *Tiebao*, December 15, 1935.

40. "Miss Tang Ing," *TCP*, December 20, 1935.

41. "Here and There," *NCH*, August 26, 1936.

42. Allen Wu, "Chinese Social Notes," *NCH*, November 11, 1936.

43. Bevan, *Modern Miscellany*, 70n69.

44. "Meiguo ren bu ai kan Wang Baochuan" [Americans don't like Lady Precious Stream], *Tiebao*, March 16, 1936.

45. In *Shanghai Grand*, Taras Grescoe discusses the IATS and its relation to Emily Hahn and Victor Sassoon.

46. In " 'Millionaire Playboy' Comes Home, Seeks Mother's Pardon," *TCP*, July 12, 1937, George Hardoon asserted that he was adopted at sixteen weeks old by Liza Hardoon. His age in 1937 is given, variously, as seventeen, nineteen, or twenty.

47. "Hardoon Scion Missing, May Be Disowned," *TCP*, July 10, 1937.

48. "She Loves Me Now: Prodigal Son Is Forgiven, Mrs. Hardoon Pays," *TCP*, July 13, 1937, 9.

49. "Miss Homjakoff Wins 'Miss Shanghai' Title," *TCP*, July 16, 1937.

50. Lamson, "Eurasian in Shanghai," 648.

51. Reuter, "Hybrid as a Sociological Type"; also Reuter, *Race Mixture*, 183–204.

52. Teng, *Eurasian: Mixed Identities*, 142–43.

53. Lamson, "Eurasian in Shanghai," 642.

54. Ibid., 646.

55. Hahn, *China to Me*, 70.

CHAPTER 9: NEW SHANGHAI

1. "Civic Center Is Reflection of New China," *TCP*, November 2, 1935.

2. "Shuang shi ji juxing luocheng li" [Double-ten festivals], *Shenbao*, October 7, 1933.

3. "Shifu xinsha jinri luocheng" [Completion of the new city government building], *Shenbao*, October 10, 1933.

4. "Inauguration of New Municipal Building," *TCP*, October 11, 1933.

5. "The Civic Centre," *NCH*, October 18, 1933.

6. "Zongli danchen jinian" [Premier's birthday yesterday], *Shenbao*, November 13, 1933. (*Shenbao* estimated the crowd at 60,000, though the English press placed it at half that.)

7. "Scenes of Desolation," *NCH*, March 15, 1932, 419.

8. "Towering Bronze Image Symbolises Homage to Sun Yat-Sen," *TCP*, November 13, 1933.

9. "Mingri zongli danchen jinian" [Commemoration of the birthday of the premier], *Shenbao*, November 11, 1933.

10. "Party Leader's Birthday: Fascist Leaflets at Kiangwan Meet," *NCH*, November 15, 1933, 258.

11. "Cornerstones at Civic Center Laid by Mayor," *TCP*, December 2, 1934.

12. "New Million Dollar Stadium at Civic Center Is Important Addition," *TCP*, June 16, 1935.
13. "Buildings at Kiangwan Open Mar. 1," *TCP*, December 15, 1935.
14. Seng, "Between Beaux-Arts and Modernism."
15. "Civic Centre Celebrations," *NCH*, July 14, 1937, 62.
16. "Shifu shi zhoujinian" [Tenth anniversary of city government], *Shenbao*, June 25, 1937, 16.
17. "Civic Centre Celebrations," *NCH*.
18. "Colorful Procession Last Night Preludes Show," *TCP*, July 7, 1937, 2.
19. "Civic Centre Celebrations," *NCH*.
20. Wu Tiecheng, "Shanghai shi de huigu yu zhanwang" [Looking back and forward at the city of Shanghai], *Shenbao*, July 7, 1937, 11.
21. "Shifu shi zhoujinianhui qimu" [Yesterday morning grand ceremony city hall 10th anniversary meeting], *Shenbao*, July 8, 1937.
22. "A Decade of Progress," *TCP*, July 8, 1937, 10.
23. "Civic Centre Celebrations," *NCH*.
24. Harmsen, *Shanghai 1937*, introduction.

CHAPTER 10: BEGINNING THE END

1. Harmsen, *Shanghai 1937*, 31–32.
2. "Mayor Yui Rejects Japanese Demand for Paoantui Withdrawal," *TCP*, August 12, 1937, 1.
3. Harmsen, *Shanghai 1937*, 55.
4. Hauser, *Shanghai: City for Sale*, 311. Hauser implies that Arthur Henchman was among those watching the bombs fall.
5. Henchman to Grayburn (telegram), August 14, 1937, HQ SHGII 0272, HSBC Archives, London.
6. James D. Hammond, "Ghastly Scene Witnessed in Air Bombing," *TCP*, August 15, 1937.
7. Ibid.
8. Ibid.
9. Ibid.
10. French, *Bloody Saturday*.
11. Harmsen, *Shanghai 1937*, 60. Mrs. Honigsberg is identified by name in "Deaths," *NCH*, August 18, 1937.
12. Henchman to Grayburn (telegram), August 15, 1937, HQ SHGII 0272, HSBC Archives, London.
13. Henchman to Hong Kong (telegram), August 18, 1937, HQ SHGII 0272, HSBC Archives, London.
14. Henchman to Grayburn (telegram), August 18, 1937, HQ SHGII 0272, HSBC Archives, London.
15. Henchman to Hong Kong (telegram), August 27, 1937, HQ SHGII 0272, HSBC Archives, London.
16. "Volunteers and Foreign Troops Called Out," *NCH*, August 18, 1937.
17. James A. Mills, "War Rips Finest Civic Center in Orient to Pieces," *NCH*, September 16, 1937.

18. "Damaged Civic Center to Be Rebuilt on Grandest Scale," *TCP*, September 16, 1937.
19. "Civic Centre Terribly Smashed: Main Structure Holed and Fire-Blackened," *NCH*, September 22, 1937.
20. "Liulian zhang xuezhan xunnan" [The flowing blood of martyrs], *Shishi xinbao*, October 3, 1937.
21. "Foreigners Shown Kiangwan," *NCH*, November 3, 1937.
22. "Shanghai News and Notes," *NCH*, January 12, 1938.
23. "Foreigners Shown Kiangwan," *NCH*.
24. F. Tillman Durdin, "All Captives Slain," *New York Times*, December 18, 1937.
25. Ibid.
26. "Wild Acts of Nippon Army Confirmed," *TCP*, December 25, 1937.
27. "How Lieutenants Mukai and Noda Exceeded Murder Quotas," *CWR*, January 1, 1938.
28. "Foreigners Crowd over Bridge to Have Look-See in Hongkew," *TCP*, December 28, 1937.
29. "Pork Drops in Price from 80 to 35 Cents," *TCP*, January 5, 1938.
30. "Roads Renamed in Kiangwan Area," *NCH*, February 23, 1938.
31. "Hata Reviews Nippon Troops at Kiangwan," *TCP*, March 11, 1938.
32. South Manchuria Railway Company, *Japanese Spirit in Full Bloom*, 1.
33. "The New 'Mayor,' " *TCP*, October 19, 1938.
34. Timothy Brook explains the brief and bizarre history of Su Xiwen and his "Great Way" government in "Shanghai Great Way Government."
35. "New 'Mayor,' " *TCP*.

CHAPTER 11: CROSSROADS

1. For more about *Crossroads*, see Lee, "Urban Milieu of Shanghai Cinema," 95.
2. *Shizi jietou* [Crossroads] (directed by Shen Xiling, 1937).
3. Ibid., 137.
4. Si Ying, "Tingzijian de shenghuo" [Life in the pavilion room], *Shanghai shenghuo* 1, no. 1 (March 1937): 24–25. Quoted in Lu Hanchao, *Beyond the Neon Lights*, 171.
5. Wang Naizhi, "Huayang bupingdeng lishi de yiye" [A word on the unequal history of China and the West], *Shanghai qingnian* 45 (1930): 7–9.
6. Police Report, June 20, 1938, *Files on Noulens Associates: Chinese Newspapers—Anti-Japanese Publications In*, pp. 63–67, Shanghai Municipal Police Files, 1894–1945, National Archives (US), State Papers Online, https://go.gale.com/gdsc.
7. Ibid., pp. 61–64. Emphasis in original.
8. Ibid.
9. Shanghai Municipal Police Commissioner's Files, July 9, 1940, Shanghai Municipal Archives, as acquired by Robert Bickers in the 1990s.
10. Records of US Consul Shanghai, [Telegraph from Shanghai, July 1941], RG 84, 891.1, National Archives (US).
11. "The Problem of Safety in Foreign Settlements," *China Critic*, April 6, 1939.
12. "S.M.C. Suspends Chinese Newspaper," *CWR*, May 6, 1939.
13. "S.M.C. Attitude on Flag Question," *NCH*, May 3, 1939.
14. "Reserve Unit Clears Yates Rd.," *NCH*, May 10, 1939.

CHAPTER 12: RACES RENEWED

1. In this and subsequent chapters, unless otherwise cited, descriptions of racing action are drawn from contemporary newspaper accounts in the *North-China Daily News*, *North-China Herald*, *The China Press*, *China Weekly Review*, and *Shanghai Times*.
2. "Shanghai's Wealthiest Champions Classic in Ten Years Chases Away War-Time Blues," *TCP*, May 12, 1938.
3. Ibid.
4. "David Sassoon Passes Quietly at Age of 73," *TCP*, May 23, 1938.
5. "A Leader of the House of Sassoon: Veteran Sportsman of Shanghai Buried near Scene of Victories," *TCP*, May 24, 1938.
6. "Champions Today Most Open Race in Years," *TCP*, November 9, 1938, A1.
7. David Zentner, "Sports Reflections: Biggest Champions' Crowd for Seven Years," *TCP*, November 11, 1938.
8. "Shanghai Horse Bazaar," *Shanghai Times*, May 19, 1914.
9. "From Daily News Ads," *NCH*, May 26, 1937.
10. "Mr. E. Moller Makes Gift to Japanese Forces," *NCH*, December 20, 1939.
11. Kathryn Meyer and Terry Parssinen, *Webs of Smoke*, 267.
12. "Communication Dated 25.1.27 from the Secretary of the Administrative Commission, Peiping, concerning Victor Strijevsky," February 2, 1937, p. 2, Shanghai Municipal Police Files, National Archives (US).
13. Ibid.
14. J. B. P., "The American Automobile in China," *Millard's Review of the Far East*, September 29, 1917.
15. "Cars Registered in 2 Concessions Hit 10,598 Mark," *TCP*, April 3, 1932.
16. "Mark L. Moody Co. Celebrates Fifteenth Anniversary Today," *TCP*, July 4, 1935.
17. "Alexej Viktorovich Strijevsky," August 14, 1932, Shanghai Municipal Police Files, National Archives (US).
18. King, *Hongkong Bank between the Wars*, 302.
19. "Jockey Sportsmanship," *NCH*, June 10, 1936.
20. Harbin's transition from Russian to Chinese rule is detailed in James Carter, *Creating a Chinese Harbin*.
21. "Hindhead Wins the Champions," *NCH*, November 20, 1940.
22. Isabella Jackson, *Shaping Modern Shanghai*, 89.
23. Bickers, *Out of China*, 194–95.
24. Allman and Clark, *Shanghai Lawyer*, 281.
25. American Consular Service Shanghai, Memorandum, January 23, 1941, RG59, National Archives (US).
26. Wakeman, *Shanghai Badlands*, esp. chap. 8.
27. Ibid., 99.
28. "Cluniehouse Should Win Champions Today," *NCDN*, May 7, 1941.
29. "Huge Crowd Sees Hindhead Crowned King of the Turf," *NCDN*, May 8, 1941.

CHAPTER 13: THE LAST FALL

1. "Cluniehill Runs Off with First Race of Season," *NCH*, October 8, 1941.
2. "Large Crowd Sees Hindhead Qualify for Champions," *NCH*, October 8, 1941.

3. "Shanghai Race Meeting, Autumn 1941" [program].
4. Lu Hanchao, *Beyond the Neon Lights*, 135.
5. Long ago absorbed into the city, Siccawei's library is now a branch of the Shanghai City Library, and its unequaled collection of material on Shanghai history was essential to reconstructing the story of the Shanghai races.

CHAPTER 14: CHAMPIONS DAY

1. Ann Sterling, "Romance and Reality," *NCH*, November 19, 1941, 299.
2. Ibid.
3. The Chaser, "Cluniehouse Picked to Beat Hindhead in Champions; Hindhead May Provide Upset," *NCDN*, November 12, 1941, 6.
4. "Dagal's Call Over" [advertisement], *NCDN*, November 11, 1941, 6.

CHAPTER 15: FATHER OF THE NATION

1. "Mayor Fu Siao-en Murdered," *NCH*, October 16, 1940, 90. Wakeman, *Shanghai Badlands*, is the most complete illustration of the situation in Shanghai during this time.
2. "Funeral of Mayor Fu Siao-en," *NCH*, October 30, 1940.
3. Zanasi, "Globalizing Hanjian."
4. "Men and Events," *CWR*, July 19, 1941.
5. "Qìngzhù guófù dànchén" [Celebrating the birthday of the founding father], *Shenbao*, November 12, 1941.
6. "Birthday of Dr. Sun Observed Quietly," *NCH*, November 19, 1941.
7. "Shier chan jiaofen" [Twelve battles], *Shenbao*, November 11, 1941, 7.
8. Police Reports, November 11, 1938, and November 12, 1941, *Files in Noulens Associates: Buses Operated by the China General Omnibus Company Detained by Japanese Gendarmerie*, p. 38, Shanghai Municipal Police Files, 1894–1945, National Archives (US), State Papers Online, https://go.gale.com/gdsc.
9. Morning Translation, November 12, 1938, *Files on Noulens Associates: Buses Operated by the China General Omnibus Company*, p. 31.
10. Crime Diary, Enclosure A, November 12, 1938, *Files on Noulens Associates: Buses Operated by the China General Omnibus Company*, p. 37.
11. Crime Diary, November 12, 1939, and Police Report, November 12, 1941, *Files on Noulens Associates: Buses Operated by the China General Omnibus Company*, p. 23.
12. Police Report, November 12, 1939, *Files on Noulens Associates: Buses Operated by the China General Omnibus Company*, p. 27.
13. Crime Diary, November 12, 1939, *Files on Noulens Associates: Buses Operated by the China General Omnibus Company*, pp. 24–26.
14. Ibid., p. 26.
15. Enclosure A, November 13, 1939, *Files on Noulens Associates: Buses Operated by the China General Omnibus Company*, p. 17.
16. Enclosure B, November 13, 1939, *Files on Noulens Associates: Buses Operated by the China General Omnibus Company*, p. 20.
17. Police Report, November 12, 1941, *Files on Noulens Associates: Buses Operated by the China General Omnibus Company*, p. 3.
18. Ibid. Martin Hugues has mapped out bus routes for Shanghai in the 1930s, available

at "Old Shanghai Full Bus Schedule 1931," *Shanghailander* (blog), August 20, 2017, http://shanghailander.net/2017/08/old-shanghai-full-bus-schedule-1931.

CHAPTER 16: THE HUPEI STAKES AND THE SIKONG STAKES

1. "14,000 See Cluniehouse Clinch Autumn Champions," *TCP*, November 14, 1941, 6.
2. Advertisement, *NCDN*, November 12, 1941, 6.
3. Lu Hanchao, *Beyond the Neon Lights*, 170.

CHAPTER 17: THE WEALTHIEST WOMAN IN CHINA

1. "Mrs. S. A. Hardoon Dies after a Brief Illness," *NCH*, October 8, 1941, 3.
2. "Liza Hardoon Dies at 78 Leaving Huge Estate," *Shanghai Times*, October 4, 1941.
3. "Hardoon Bldg. Space Reported as All Taken: Scaffolding on 6-Story Structure Is Now Being Removed," *TCP*, October 9, 1936.
4. "Men and Events," *CWR*, February 26, 1938.
5. " 'Millionaire Playboy' Comes Home, Seeks Mother's Pardon," *TCP*, July 12, 1937.
6. "Hardoon Burial Is Postponed," *Shanghai Times*, October 7, 1941.
7. "10,000 at Hardoon Estate to See Funeral of Late Multi-millionaire," *TCP*, November 13, 1941.
8. "Crowds See Last Rites for Mrs. L. Hardoon," *NCH*, November 19, 1941.
9. "Liza Hardoon Personal Effects," Liza Hardoon Will Case, FO 917/3970, National Archives (UK).
10. "Probate Proceedings in Matter of Will of the Late Mrs. Liza Hardoon," *NCH*, November 19, 1941.
11. "Liza Hardoon 1931 Will," Liza Hardoon Will Case, FO 917/3970, National Archives (UK).
12. "Liza Hardoon 1937 Will," Liza Hardoon Will Case, FO 917/3970, National Archives (UK).
13. "Hardoon Burial Is Postponed," *Shanghai Times*.
14. "Liza Hardoon 1937 Will," p. 9.
15. "The Hardoon Estate Should Be Donated to Shanghai," *CWR*, October 25, 1941, 217.
16. "Agitation: Use Hardoon Fortune for City," *NCH*, October 15, 1941, 92.

CHAPTER 18: THE OODNADATTA CUP, SINKIANG STAKES, AND JOCKEY CUP

1. Seng, "Between Beaux-Arts and Modernism," 181.
2. Based on menu for Park Hotel, May 17, 1941, courtesy of Bill Savadove.
3. Ann Sterling, "Romance and Reality," *NCH*, November 19, 1941, 299.
4. Chao and Chao, *Remembering Shanghai*, 110.
5. Ibid., 104.
6. Lu Hanchao, *Beyond the Neon Lights*, 200–201.
7. Ibid., 274–75.
8. Ibid., 259–60.
9. Ibid., 274–75.
10. "Huge Crowd Throngs Race Course for Champions," *NCDN*, November 13, 1941, 1.
11. Chang, *Cultural Translation*, 201.

CHAPTER 19: *MURDER OVER NEW YORK*

1. Fu, *Between Shanghai and Hong Kong*, 36.
2. Ibid., 38.
3. Ibid., 37–38.
4. Ibid.
5. Ibid., 35n89.
6. Xiao and Zhang, *Encyclopedia of Chinese Film*, 178.
7. Movie listings are from *Shenbao*, November 11, 1941, 12.
8. Advertisements, *NCDN*, November 12, 1941.
9. Yunte Huang's *Charlie Chan* is the definitive account of all aspects of Charlie Chan.
10. Paul French discusses Oland's visit to Shanghai in Chapter 4 of *Destination Shanghai*.
11. "Mr. Warner Oland in Shanghai," *NCH*, March 25, 1936.
12. "Shanghai Made Glamorous Spot in Chan Film," *TCP*, May 3, 1936.
13. "The Cinema: 'Murder Over New York,' " *NCDN*, November 13, 1941, 2; "Movie Review: 'Murder over New York,' " *TCP*, November 13, 1941, 2.

CHAPTER 20: PARTY AT THE END OF THE WORLD

1. "Huge Crowd Throngs Race Course for Champions," *NCDN*, November 13, 1941, 1.
2. Ibid.
3. Ann Sterling, "Romance and Reality," *NCH*, November 19, 1941, 299.
4. Ibid.
5. Adeline Gray, "Gorgeous Display of Fall Fashion Seen at Races," *TCP*, November 14, 1941, 7.
6. Carriere's wardrobe is described in Gray, "Gorgeous Display of Fall Fashion"; her planned enrollment at Stanford, in Sterling, "Romance and Reality."
7. The Chaser, "Cluniehouse Picked to Beat Hindhead in Champions; Hindhead May Provide Upset," *NCDN*, November 12, 1941, 6.
8. Arcana, "Gram's Four Wins Reward of Keenness," *TCP*, March 16, 1938, 6.
9. "Huge Crowd Throngs Race Course," *NCDN*.
10. "Yingren yipima-nongren liangxing lei" [One Englishman's horse—two peasant's tears], *Shenbao*, September 15, 1946.
11. "Widow's Monument Restored," *NCH*, April 9, 1941.

CHAPTER 21: SHOOT-OUT AT THE CATHAY BALLROOM

1. The definitive work on Shanghai's nightclub scene is Field, *Shanghai's Dancing World*. See also Farrer and Field, *Shanghai Nightscapes*.
2. "Chinese Dance Hall Raided by Hooligans," *NCH*, November 19, 1941.

CHAPTER 22: LAST LAPS

1. Mark Felton, "War Zone—City of Terror: The Japanese Takeover of Shanghai," *Military History Matters*, February 8, 2013, https://www.military-history.org/articles/war-zone-city-of-terror-the-japanese-takeover-of-shanghai.htm.
2. Bickers, *Out of China*, 198–99.

3. Frederick B. Opper, "Post's Editor Tells How War Came to Shanghai," *Shanghai Evening Post and Mercury*, January 1, 1943, 3.

4. Zia, *Last Boat Out of Shanghai*, 109.

5. King, *Hongkong Bank between the Wars*, 575–76.

6. Foreign Office to Washington, March 13, 1942, National Archives (US).

7. Chao and Chao, *Remembering Shanghai*, 139–45.

8. "Sports to be Resumed Here Saturday," *Shanghai Times*, December 12, 1941, 7.

9. "Results of the S.R.C. Extra Race Meeting," *Shanghai Times*, December 21, 1941, 7.

10. "Pictorial Parade: Fireworks at the Race Course," *Shanghai Times*, February 22, 1942, 7.

11. British attitudes toward Shanghailanders, both before and after Pearl Harbor, are detailed in Bickers, "Settlers and Diplomats."

12. Woodhead, *My Experiences*.

13. "Preface," in Henriot and Yeh, *In the Shadow of the Rising Sun*, xi.

14. Bickers, *Out of China*, 205–6.

15. "City Takes Holiday on Champions," *Shanghai Times*, May 7, 1942, 5.

16. "7,000 Racing Fans See Rye Triumph in Well-Earned Victory," *Shanghai Times*, October 11, 1942.

17. Leck, *Captives of Empire*, 292–94.

18. Ibid., 294.

19. "Race Results," *Shanghai Times*, October 11, 1942, 7.

20. "Race Course Is Closed to Racing Indefinitely," *Shanghai Times*, October 16, 1942, 7.

21. Greg Leck, personal communication, July 2018 and June 2019.

22. "Internment News," *Shanghai Evening Post and Mercury*, April 14, 1944, 6.

23. National Archives (US), "Record Group 65," 490/61/13/06 box 1053, National Archives (US). Courtesy Greg Leck.

24. "Mr. E. Moller Makes Gift to Japanese Forces," *NCH*, December 20, 1939.

25. Ryder, "IRC First Day Race Meeting to Start 1 p.m. Today," *Shanghai Times*, January 16, 1943, 6.

26. "New Arrivals from Mongolia Will Get Racing Test Today," *Shanghai Times*, May 15, 1943, 6.

27. Advertisement, *Shanghai Times*, April 4, 1943, and May 15, 1943.

28. "Athletic Body to Make Race Course City's Sports Center," *Shanghai Times*, January 19, 1944, 4.

29. "Hindhead Garners One Mile New Year Stakes," *Shanghai Times*, December 31, 1944, 6.

30. "Jinri Shanghai xiaji saima di er tian" [Today's Shanghai summer horse racing: day two], *Shenbao*, July 29, 1945.

31. Zia, *Last Boat Out of Shanghai*, 258.

32. *Shenbao* also reported that a horserace was planned to celebrate the Japanese surrender in late August 1945, but it seems never to have taken place. "Benshi qingzhu shengli banfa" [The city's victory celebrations], *Shenbao*, August 23, 1945.

33. [E. C. Hayes], Major General, Commanding British Troops in China, to H. M. Ambassador and Lt. Gen Sir Adrian Carton de Wiart, September 13, 1945, 3, http://news.bbc.co.uk/2/shared/bsp/hi/pdfs/02_09_15_hayes_report.pdf.

34. Henchman to [Arthur] Morse (telegram), December 16, 1945, HQ LOHII 0327, HSBC Archives, London.

35. Leck, personal communication. Also Leck, *Captives of Empire*, 456–57, 561.

36. "England, Andrews Newspaper Index Cards, 1790–1976," Ancestry.com, accessed October 4, 2019, https://www.ancestry.com/search/collections/andrewsindex.

37. US Department of Justice, List or Manifest of Alien Passengers for United States, S.S. Swede, Passengers Sailing from Shanghai, China, July 19, 1946, *Records of the Immigration and Naturalization Service, 1787–2004*, Record Group 85, National Archives (US), Ancestry.com, https://www.ancestry.com.

38. "Plane from Sydney Crashes," *[Sydney] Sun-Herald*, March 14, 1954, 1.

39. Aronson, *Ming Cho Lee*, 24.

40. Ibid., 90.

41. Ing Tang's son by her first husband, Tsufa Lee, went on to become a Tony Award–winning set designer and professor at the Yale School of Drama.

42. "Waiguo cien: Shanghai xingbutong" [Foreign mercy: doesn't work in Shanghai], *Jueyouqing* [Enlightenment], October 1, 1947.

43. Interview with Lydia Chen, Philadelphia, November 18, 2019.

44. Chang, *Cultural Translation*, 216 n220.

45. Seng Kuan, "Between Beaux-Arts and Modernism," 188.

46. Doron, "Silas Aaron Hardoon."

47. Leck, personal communication.

48. Berne to Foreign Office, July 7, 1945, RG 32: Piece 31, National Archives (UK).

EPILOGUE: GHOSTS OF OLD SHANGHAI

1. "News Chop Suey," *Shanghai Evening Post and Mercury*, December 3, 1943, 2.

2. Bickers, *Out of China*, 265.

3. "Paomating shouhui fangshi" [How to recover the racecourse], *Shenbao*, January 1, 1947.

4. "Paomating panhua zhanggu yiye yangren qinzhan shi" [History of the Shanghai Race Club and foreign invasion], *Shenbao*, September 15, 1946, 4.

5. *Shenbao*, ed., *Shanghai shi renmin shouce* [Shanghai resident handbook] (Shanghai: Shenbao chubanshe, November 1946), 4–5. Quoted in Smith and Sun, "Building 'New Shanghai,' " 61.

6. Jie Ren, "Saima haicheng wenti Zhong" [On the horseracing question], *Libao*, September 13, 1946.

7. "Jinzhi paoma keyi bubi yi wang jiaoqu zhide zantong" [Forbidden horseracing could possibly be moved to suburbs], *Shenbao*, September 21, 1946.

8. "Shouhui paomating gaijian wenhuacheng" [Convert the recovered racecourse into a Culture City], *Shenbao*, September 14, 1946.

9. "Paoma mai caipiao shifou suan dubo" [Are horseracing sweepstakes gambling?], *Shenbao*, September 25, 1946.

10. Sun and Smith, "Building 'New Shanghai,' " 62.

11. Ibid., 63.

12. Ibid.

13. John Muller, "East China Fine Arts Exhibition," *China Monthly Review*, June 1, 1951, 28.

14. Affidavit by Cornell S. Franklin to Congress, in *House Reports*, vol. 2, *Miscellaneous II*,

83rd Cong., 2nd Sess. (Washington, DC: US Government Printing Office, 1954), 101, https://hdl.handle.net/2027/mdp.39015087680800.

15. Chang, "From Racetrack to People's Square," 126.

16. Lu Bo, "Cong paomating dao renmin guangchang," 24.

17. Ibid., 30.

18. Ibid., 28.

19. Charley Lanyon, "British Entrepreneur Revives Shanghai Race Club for China's Aspiring Classes," *South China Morning Post*, October 24, 2013, https://www.scmp.com /lifestyle/article/1338860/british-entrepreneur-revives-shanghai-race-club-chinas -aspiring-classes.

20. Wayback Machine, "Shanghai Race Club," accessed September 30, 2019, https://web .archive.org/web/20190327152839/http://www.theshanghairaceclub.com.

21. James Farrer has analyzed and described the complicated nature of nostalgia among "new Shanghailanders" in " 'New Shanghailanders' or 'New Shanghainese.' "

BIBLIOGRAPHY

ARCHIVAL SOURCES

Hong Kong Jockey Club Archives
HSBC Archives, London
National Archives (UK)
National Archives (US)
Shanghai Municipal Archives

HISTORICAL NEWS SOURCES

The China Press (abbreviated *TCP* in endnotes)
The China Weekly Review (abbreviated *CWR* in endnotes)
Le journal de Shanghai. Shanghai, 1872–1949
Libao. Shanghai, 1929–1946
Liangyou huabao. Shanghai, 1926–1945
North-China Daily News (abbreviated *NCDN* in endnotes). Shanghai, 1864–1951
North-China Herald (abbreviated *NCH* in endnotes). Shanghai, 1850–1941
Shanghai Evening Post and Mercury
The Shanghai Times
Shenbao. Shanghai, 1872–1949
Shishi xinbao. Shanghai, 1911–1949
Tiebao. Shanghai, 1929–1949

SELECTED PUBLISHED SOURCES

Allman, Norwood F., and Douglas Clark. *Shanghai Lawyer: The Memoirs of America's China Spymaster*. Hong Kong: Earnshaw Books, 2017.
Aronson, Arnold. *Ming Cho Lee: A Life in Design*. New York: Theatre Communications Group, 2014.
Backhouse, E., and J. O. P. Bland. *Annals & Memoirs of the Court of Peking (From the 16th to the 20th Century)*. Boston: Houghton Mifflin, 1914.
Barr, Ruth Hill. *Ruth's Record: The Diary of an American in Japanese-Occupied Shanghai, 1941–1945*. Hong Kong: Earnshaw Books, 2016.

Barrett, David P., and Larry N. Shyu, eds. *Chinese Collaboration with Japan, 1932–1945: The Limits of Accommodation*. Stanford, CA: Stanford University Press, 2001.

Bergère, Marie-Claire. *Shanghai: China's Gateway to Modernity*. Stanford, CA: Stanford University Press, 2009.

Betta, Chiara. "From Orientals to Imagined Britons: Baghdadi Jews in Shanghai." *Modern Asian Studies* 37, no. 4 (October 2003): 999–1023.

———. "Silas Aaron Hardoon (1851–1931), Marginality and Adaptation in Shanghai." PhD diss., School of Oriental and African Studies, 1997.

Bevan, Paul. *A Modern Miscellany: Shanghai Cartoon Artists, Shao Xunmei's Circle, and the Travels of Jack Chen, 1926–1938*. Leiden, Netherlands: Brill, 2015.

Bickers, Robert. *Britain in China: Community, Culture and Colonialism, 1900–49*. Manchester, UK: Manchester University Press, 1999.

———. *Out of China: How China Ended the Era of Western Domination*. Cambridge, MA: Harvard University Press, 2017.

———. *The Scramble for China: Foreign Devils in the Qing Empire, 1832–1914*. London: Lane Allen, 2011.

———. "Settlers and Diplomats: The End of British Hegemony in the International Settlement, 1937–1945." In *In the Shadow of the Rising Sun*, edited by Christian Henriot and Wen-hsin Yeh, 229–56. Cambridge: Cambridge University Press, 2004.

———. "Shanghailanders: The Formation and Identity of the British Settler Community in Shanghai, 1843–1937." *Past and Present* 159 (May 1998): 161–211. http://www.jstor.org.ezproxy.sju.edu/stable/651233.

Bickers, Robert, and Isabella Jackson, eds. *Treaty Ports in Modern China: Law, Land & Power*. London: Routledge, 2016.

Bickers, Robert, and Jeffrey N. Wasserstrom. "Shanghai's 'Dogs and Chinese Not Admitted' Sign: Legend, History and Contemporary Symbol." *China Quarterly*, no. 142 (1995): 444–66. http://www.jstor.org/stable/655423.

Braester, Yomi. "Shanghai's Economy of the Spectacle: The Shanghai Race Club in Liu Na'ou's and Mu Shiying's Stories." *Modern Chinese Literature* 9, no. 1 (Spring 1995): 39–57.

Brook, Timothy. *Collaboration: Japanese Agents and Local Elites in Wartime China*. Cambridge, MA: Harvard University Press, 2005.

———. "The Shanghai Great Way Government." In *In the Shadow of the Rising Sun: Shanghai under Japanese Occupation*, edited by Christian Henriot and Wen-hsin Yeh, 157–86. Cambridge: Cambridge University Press, 2004.

Burt, A. R., J. B. Powell, and Carl Crow, eds. *Biographies of Prominent Chinese*. Shanghai: Biographical Publishing, n.d. [1925?].

Carter, James. *Creating a Chinese Harbin: Nationalism in an International City, 1916–1932*. Ithaca, NY: Cornell University Press, 2002.

Chang, Jung. *Big Sister, Little Sister, Red Sister: Three Women at the Heart of Twentieth-Century China*. New York: Knopf, 2019.

Chang, Ning Jennifer (as Chang Ning). *Cultural Translation: Horse Racing, Greyhound Racing, and Jai Alai in Modern Shanghai* [*Wanguo shiwu de zhuanyi: jindai Shanghai de paoma, paogou, yu huiliqiusai*]. Taipei: Institute of Modern History, Academia Sinica, 2019.

———. "From Racetrack to People's Square: The Movement to Recover the Shanghai Horseracing Track, 1946–1951." *Bulletin of the Institute of Modern History, Academia Sinica* 48 (July 2005): 97–136.

———. "Pure Sport or a Gambling Disgrace?: Dog-Racing and the Formation of Modern Shanghai." In *Creating Chinese Modernity: Knowledge and Everyday Life, 1900–1940*, edited by Peter Zarrow, 147–82. New York: Peter Lang, 2006.

———. "To See and Be Seen: Horse Racing in Shanghai, 1848–1945." In *The Habitable City in China: Urban History in the Twentieth Century*, edited by Toby Lincoln and Xu Tao, 91–111. New York: Springer, 2016.

Chao, Claire, and Isabel Sun Chao. *Remembering Shanghai: A Memoir of Socialites, Scholars and Scoundrels*. Honolulu: Plum Brook, 2018.

The China Directory for 1863. Hong Kong: A. Shortrede, 1863.

Clifford, Nicholas R. *Spoilt Children of Empire: Westerners in Shanghai and the Chinese Revolution of the 1920s*. Middlebury, VT: Middlebury College Press, 1991.

Coates, Austin. *China Races*. London: Oxford University Press, 1983.

Coble, Parks M. *Chinese Capitalists in Japan's New Order: The Occupied Lower Yangzi, 1937–1945*. Berkeley: University of California Press, 2003.

Cochran, Sherman, ed. *Inventing Nanking Road: Commercial Culture in Shanghai, 1900–1945*. Ithaca, NY: East Asia Program, Cornell University, 1999.

Cody, Jeffrey W. *Building in China: Henry K. Murphy's "Adaptive Architecture," 1914–1935*. Hong Kong: Chinese University Press, 2001.

Cody, Jeffrey W., Nancy S. Steinhardt, and Tony Atkin. *Chinese Architecture and the Beaux-Arts*. Honolulu: University of Hawaii Press, 2011.

Collis, Maurice. *Wayfoong: The Hong Kong and Shanghai Banking Corporation*. London: Faber and Faber, 1965.

The Comacrib Directory of China for 1925. Shanghai: Kelly & Walsh, 1925.

Crow, Carl. *Foreign Devils in the Flowery Kingdom*. 1940. Reprinted with a new foreword by Paul French. Hong Kong: Earnshaw Books, 2007.

Cushing, Caleb. *Opinion of the Attorney General: Concerning the Judicial Authority of the Commissioner or Minister of Consuls of the United States in China and Turkey*. Washington, DC: AOP Nicholson, 1855.

Darwent, Charles Ewart. *Shanghai: A Handbook for Travellers and Residents to the Chief Objects of Interest in and around the Foreign Settlements and Native City*. Shanghai: Kelly & Walsh, 1920.

Delury, John, and Orville Schell. *Wealth and Power: China's Long March to the Twentieth Century*. New York: Random House, 2013.

Denison, Edward, and Guang Yu Ren. *Building Shanghai: The Story of China's Gateway*. Chichester, UK: Wiley-Academy, 2006.

———. *Modernism in China: Architectural Visions and Revolutions*. London: Wiley, 2008.

Dillon, Nara, and Jean C. Oi, eds. *At the Crossroads of Empires: Middlemen, Social Networks, and State-Building in Republican Shanghai*. Stanford, CA: Stanford University Press, 2008.

The Directory & Chronicle for China, Japan, Corea, Indo-China, Straits. London: Hongkong Daily Press Office, 1912.

Dong, Stella. *Shanghai: The Rise and Fall of a Decadent City*. New York: William Morrow, 2000.

Doon, Dayoo. "Greater Shanghai—Greater Vision." *China Critic* 10, no. 5 (August 1, 1935): 103–6.

Doron, Maple Hardoon. "Silas Aaron Hardoon (1851–1931) and Family." In *Shanghai's Baghdadi Jews: A Collection of Biographical Reflections*, edited by Maisie J. Meyer, 77–87. Hong Kong: Blacksmith Books, 2015.

Eber, Irene. *Wartime Shanghai and the Jewish Refugees from Central Europe—Survival, Co-existence, and Identity in a Multi-ethnic City.* Boston: De Gruyter, 2012.

Fang Yifeng. *Yizhongji* [A Collection]. Shanghai: Shanghai Far Eastern Publishing House, 2017.

Farrer, James. " 'New Shanghailanders' or 'New Shanghainese': Western Expatriates' Narratives of Emplacement in Shanghai." *Journal of Ethnic and Migration Studies* 36, no. 8 (2010): 1211–28. https://doi.org/10.1080/13691831003687675.

Farrer, James, and Andrew David Field. *Shanghai Nightscapes: A Nocturnal Biography of a Global City.* Chicago: University of Chicago Press, 2015.

Felton, Mark. "War Zone—City of Terror: The Japanese Takeover of Shanghai," *Military History Matters,* February 8, 2013, https://www.military-history.org/articles/war-zone-city-of-terror-the-japanese-takeover-of-shanghai.htm.

Field, Andrew David. *Mu Shiying: China's Lost Modernist.* Hong Kong: Hong Kong University Press, 2014.

———. *Shanghai's Dancing World.* Hong Kong: Chinese University Press, 2011.

Finnane, Antonia. *Changing Clothes in China—Fashion, History, Nation.* New York: Columbia University Press, 2008.

Firpo, Christina Elizabeth. *The Uprooted: Race, Children, and Imperialism in French Indochina, 1890–1980.* Honolulu: University of Hawai'i Press, 2016.

Fitzgerald, John, and Mei-fen Kuo. "Diaspora Charity and Welfare Sovereignty in the Chinese Republic: Shanghai Charity Innovator William Yinson Lee (Li Yuanxin, 1884–1965)." *Twentieth-Century China* 42, no. 1 (2017): 72–96.

French, Paul. *Bloody Saturday: Shanghai's Darkest Day.* New York: Penguin Specials, 2017.

———. *City of Devils: The Two Men Who Ruled the Underworld of Old Shanghai.* New York: Picador, 2018.

———. *Destination Shanghai.* Hong Kong: Blacksmith Books, 2018.

———. *The Old Shanghai A–Z.* Hong Kong: Hong Kong University Press, 2010.

Fu, Poshek. *Between Shanghai and Hong Kong: The Politics of Chinese Cinemas.* Stanford, CA: Stanford University Press, 2003.

———. *Passivity, Resistance, and Collaboration: Intellectual Choices in Occupied Shanghai, 1937–1945.* Stanford, CA: Stanford University Press, 1993.

Gong Jin. "Jewish Past and Colonial Shanghai: Trade, Treaty-Port, and Transitive Modernity." PhD diss., University of Illinois, 2016.

Goodman, Bryna. *Native Place, City, and Nation: Regional Networks and Identities in Shanghai, 1853–1937.* Berkeley: University of California Press, 1995.

Grescoe, Taras. *Shanghai Grand: Forbidden Love and International Intrigue in a Doomed World.* New York: St. Martin's Press, 2016.

Hahn, Emily. *China to Me: A Partial Autobiography.* New York: Doubleday, 1944.

Harmsen, Peter. *Shanghai 1937: Stalingrad on the Yangtze.* Havertown, PA: Casemate, 2013.

Harrison, Henrietta, "The Qianlong Emperor's Letter to George III and the Early-Twentieth-Century Origins of Ideas about Traditional China's Foreign Relations," *American Historical Review* 122, no. 3 (June 2017): 680–701.

Hauser, Ernest O. *Shanghai: City for Sale.* New York: Harcourt Brace, 1940.

Hawks Pott, F. L. *A Short History of Shanghai: Being an Account of the Growth and Development of the International Settlement.* Shanghai: Kelly & Walsh, 1928.

Henning, Stefan. "God's Translator: Qu'ran Translation and the Struggle over a Written National Language in 1930s China." *Modern China* 41, no. 6 (November 2014): 631–55.

Henriot, Christian. *Shanghai 1927–1937: Municipal Power, Locality, and Modernization.* Berkeley: University of California Press, 1993.

Henriot, Christian, and Wen-hsin Yeh, eds. *In the Shadow of the Rising Sun: Shanghai under Japanese Occupation.* Cambridge: Cambridge University Press, 2004.

Hibbard, Peter. *All about Shanghai and Environs: The 1934–35 Standard Guide Book.* Hong Kong: Earnshaw Books, 2008.

———. *The Bund, Shanghai: China Faces West.* Hong Kong: Odyssey Books and Guides, 2008.

Huang Xuelei. *Shanghai Filmmaking: Crossing Borders, Connecting to the Globe, 1922–1938.* Leiden, Netherlands: Brill, 2014.

Huang, Yunte. *Charlie Chan: The Untold Story of the Honorable Detective and His Rendezvous with American History.* New York: W. W. Norton, 2010.

Huskey, James L. "The Cosmopolitan Connection: Americans and Chinese in Shanghai during the Interwar Years." *Diplomatic History* 11, no. 3 (Summer 1987): 227–42.

Izumi, Kuroishi, ed. *Constructing the Colonized Land: Entwined Perspectives of East Asia around WWII.* New York: Routledge, 2016.

Jackson, Isabella. *Shaping Modern Shanghai: Colonialism in China's Global City.* Cambridge: Cambridge University Press, 2018.

Jackson, Stanley. *The Sassoons: Portrait of a Dynasty.* London: Arrow Books, 1989.

Jiu Shanghai de gushi [Stories of Old Shanghai]. Shanghai: Shanghai Renmin Chubanshe, 1974.

Jones, Andrew F. *Yellow Music: Media Culture and Colonial Modernity in the Chinese Jazz Age.* Durham, NC: Duke University Press, 2001.

Jones, Susan Mann. "The Ningpo *Pang* and Financial Power at Shanghai." In *The Chinese City between Two Worlds*, edited by Mark Elvin and G. William Skinner, 73–96. Stanford, CA: Stanford University Press, 1974.

Kaufman, Jonathan. *The Last Kings of Shanghai: The Rival Jewish Dynasties That Helped Create Modern China.* New York: Viking, 2020.

King, Frank H. H. *A Concise Economic History of Modern China (1840–1961).* New York: Praeger, 1968.

———. *The Hongkong Bank between the Wars and the Bank Interned, 1919–1945: Return from Grandeur.* New York: Cambridge University Press, 1988.

Lamson, Herbert Day. "The Eurasian in Shanghai." *American Journal of Sociology* 41, no. 5 (March 1936): 642–48.

Leck, Greg. *Captives of Empire: The Japanese Internment of Allied Civilians in China (1941–1945).* Bangor, PA: Shandy Press, 2006.

Lee, Leo Ou-fan. *Shanghai Modern: The Flowering of a New Urban Culture in China, 1930–1945.* Cambridge, MA: Harvard University Press, 1999.

———. "The Urban Milieu of Shanghai Cinema, 1930–40: Some Explorations of Film Audience, Film Culture, and Narrative Conventions." In *Cinema and Urban Culture in Shanghai, 1922–1943*, edited by Zhang Yingjin, 74–96. Stanford, CA: Stanford University Press, 1999.

Li Enji. *Ai li yuan meng ying lu* [A dream record of the Aili Garden]. Beijing: Sanlian Shudian, 1984.

Li Tiangang. *Nanking Road: The Emergence of Eastern Globalism.* Shanghai: Shanghai Renmin Chubanshe, 2009.

Lu Bo. "Cong paomating dao renmin guangchang" [From racetrack to People's Square]. In *Jiu Shanghai de gushi* [Stories of Old Shanghai], 24–33. Shanghai: Shanghai Renmin Chubanshe, 1974.

Lu Hanchao. *Beyond the Neon Lights: Everyday Shanghai in the Early Twentieth Century.* Berkeley: University of California Press, 2004.

———. "Nostalgia for the Future: The Resurgence of an Alienated Culture in China." *Pacific Affairs* 75, no. 2 (2002): 169–86.

Lu Yongyi and Li Dehua. "Shanghai: Cosmopolitanism as Its Identity?" In *Architecture and Identity*, edited by Peter Herrle and Erik Weggerhoff, 335–46. Berlin: Lit, 2008.

MacKinnon, Stephen R., Diana Lary, and Ezra F. Vogel, eds. *China at War: Regions of China, 1937–1945.* Stanford, CA: Stanford University Press, 2007.

Malik, Roman, ed. *From Kaifeng . . . to Shanghai: Jews in China.* Monumenta Serica Monograph Series 46. Nettetal, Germany: Steyler, 2000.

Meyer, Kathryn, and Terry Parssinen. *Webs of Smoke: Smugglers, Warlords, Spies, and the History of the International Drug Trade.* New York: Rowman and Littlefield, 2002.

Meyer, Maisie J. *From the Rivers of Babylon to the Whangpoo: A Century of Sephardi Jewish Life in Shanghai.* Lanham, MD: University Press of America, 2003.

———. "Sephardi Jewish Community of Shanghai 1845–1939 and the Question of Identity." PhD diss., London School of Economics, 1990.

———. *Shanghai's Baghdadi Jews: A Collection of Biographical Reflections.* Hong Kong: Blacksmith Books, 2017.

Meyer-Fong, Tobie. *What Remains: Coming to Terms with Civil War in 19th-Century China.* Stanford, CA: Stanford University Press, 2013.

Mo Mo. "Hóng xiù—20 shìjì dōngfāng xiānfēng nǚxìng chuánqí" [Red beauty: Eastern women pioneers of the 20th century]. Beijing: China Democracy and Legal Publishing House, 2016.

Morse, H. B. *The International Relations of the Chinese Empire*, vol. 1. London: Longmans, Green, 1910.

Musgrove, Charles D. *China's Contested Capital: Architecture, Ritual, and Response in Nanjing.* Honolulu: University of Hawaii Press, 2013.

Nield, Robert. *China's Foreign Places: The Foreign Presence in China in the Treaty Port Era, 1940–1943.* Hong Kong: Hong Kong University Press, 2015.

Oi, Jean, and Dillon, Nara, eds. *At the Crossroads of Empires: Middlemen, Social Networks, and State-Building in Republican Shanghai.* Stanford, CA: Stanford University Press, 2007.

Pan, Lynn. *Old Shanghai: Gangsters in Paradise.* Singapore: Marshall Cavendish, 2011.

———. *Shanghai Style: Art and Design between the Wars.* San Francisco: Long River Press, 2007.

Platt, Stephen R. *Imperial Twilight: The Opium War and the End of China's Last Golden Age.* New York: Vintage, 2018.

The Racing Record, vol. 24, *A Complete Record of Racing at Shanghai for 1941.* Shanghai: Kelly & Walsh, 1942.

Reed, Christopher. *Gutenberg in Shanghai: Chinese Print Capitalism, 1876–1937.* Vancouver: University of British Columbia Press, 2004.

Reuter, Edward Byron. "The Hybrid as a Sociological Type." *Publications of the American Sociological Society* 19 (1925): 59–68.

———. *Race Mixture; Studies in Intermarriage and Miscegenation.* New York: Whittlesey House, 1931.

Ristaino, Marcia Reynders. *Ports of Last Resort: The Diaspora Communities of Shanghai*. Stanford, CA: Stanford University Press, 2001.

Rojas, Carlos, and Cheng-Yin-Chow, Eileen, eds. *The Oxford Handbook of Chinese Cinemas*. Oxford: Oxford University Press, 2013.

Roskam, Cole. *Improvised City: Architecture and Governance in Shanghai, 1843–1937*. Seattle: University of Washington Press, 2019.

———. "Recentering the City: Municipal Architecture in Shanghai, 1927–1937." In *Constructing the Colonized Land: Entwined Perspectives of East Asia around WWII*, edited by Kuroishi Izumi, 43–70. New York: Routledge, 2016. *Rules of the Shanghai Race Club 1930*. Shanghai: Kelly & Walsh, 1930.

Schoppa, R. Keith. *In a Sea of Bitterness: Refugees during the Sino-Japanese War*. Cambridge, MA: Harvard University Press, 2011.

Seng Kuan. "Between Beaux-Arts and Modernism: Dong Dayou and the Architecture of 1930s Shanghai," In *Chinese Architecture and the Beaux-Arts*, edited by Jeffrey W. Cody, Nancy S. Steinhardt, and Tony Atkin, 169–92. Honolulu: University of Hawaii Press, 2011.

Sensibar, Judith L. *Faulkner and Love: The Women Who Shaped His Art, a Biography*. New Haven, CT: Yale University Press, 2009.

———. "Introductory Note to 'Star Spangled Banner Stuff,' by Estelle Oldham (Faulkner)." *Prospects* 22 (1997): 379–417.

———. "Writing for Faulkner, Writing for Herself: Estelle Oldham's Anticolonial Fiction." *Prospects* 22 (1997): 357–78. https://doi.org/10.1017/S0361233300000168.

"Shanghai." *Fortune* 11, no. 1 (January 1935): 30–40, 99–120.

Shanghai Race Rules 1930. Shanghai: Kelly & Walsh, 1930.

Shen Ji. *Shanghai Boss: Silas Hardoon*. Shanghai: Xuelin Chubanshe, 2002.

Shen Zhirui. *The Need for the Club*, Lok. ed. Shanghai Race Club Staff Club 10 Year Anniversary Volume. Shanghai, 1937.

Shih Shu-Mei. "Gender, Race, and Semicolonialism: Liu Na'ou's Urban Shanghai Landscape." *Journal of Asian Studies* 55, no. 4 (November 1996): 934–56.

Smith, Whitey, and C. L. McDermott. *I Didn't Make a Million: How Jazz Came to China*. Hong Kong: Earnshaw Books, 2017.

South Manchuria Railway Company, *Japanese Spirit in Full Bloom: A Collection of Episodes*. Tokyo: Herald Press, 1937.

Stein, Sarah Abrevaya, "Protected Persons? The Baghdadi Jewish Diaspora, the British State, and the Persistence of Empire." *American Historical Review* 116, no. 1 (February 2011): 80–108. https://doi.org/10.1086/ahr.116.1.80.

Sun Peidong and Aminda Smith. "Building 'New Shanghai': Political Rhetoric and the Reconstruction of the Shanghai Racecourse, 1949–65." *Chinese Historical Review* 26, no. 1 (2019): 55–79. https://doi.org/10.1080/1547402X.2019.1583923.

Taylor, Jeremy E. "The Bund: Littoral Space of Empire in the Treaty Ports of East Asia." *Social History* 27, no. 2 (2002): 125–42. http://www.jstor.org/stable/4286873.

Teng, Emma Jinhua. *Eurasians: Mixed Identities in the United States, China, and Hong Kong, 1842–1943*. Berkeley: University of California Press, 2013.

Wakeman, Frederick. "Hanjian (Traitor)! Collaboration and Retribution in Wartime Shanghai." In *Becoming Chinese: Passages to Modernity and Beyond*, 323–24. Berkeley: University of California Press, 2000.

———. *Policing Shanghai, 1927–1937*. Berkeley: University of California Press, 1995.

————. *The Shanghai Badlands: Wartime Terrorism and Urban Crime, 1937–1941*. Cambridge: Cambridge University Press, 1996.

Wang Zhicheng. *Portuguese in Shanghai*. Macau: Macau Foundation, 2004.

Wasserstein, Bernard. *Secret War in Shanghai*. New York: Profile Books, 2005.

Wasserstrom, Jeffrey. *Global Shanghai, 1850–2010: A History in Fragments*. New York: Routledge, 2009.

Wearing, J. P. *The London Stage: 1910–1919: A Calendar of Productions, Performers, and Personnel*, 2nd ed. Lanham, MD: Rowman and Littlefield, 2014.

White, Cameron. "Exploring Shanghai Space: From Racecourse to People's Square and Beyond." *Princeton Journal of East Asian Studies*, special ed., *Anxious Megalopolis: Shanghai*, April 2013, 16–27.

Who's Who of the Chinese Students in America. Berkeley, CA: Lederer, Zeus, 1921.Witchard, Anne. *British Modernism and Chinoiserie*. Edinburgh: Edinburgh University Press, 2015.

Wood, Frances. *No Dogs and Not Many Chinese: Treaty Port Life in China 1843–1943*. London: John Murray, 1998.

Woodhead, H. G. W. *My Experiences in the Japanese Occupation of Shanghai*. China Society Occasional Papers 4. London: China Society, 1943.

Wu, Ellen. *The Color of Success: Asian Americans and the Origins of the Model Minority*. Princeton, NJ: Princeton University Press, 2013.

Xiao Zhiwei and Zhang Yingjin, eds. *Encyclopedia of Chinese Film*. New York: Routledge, 2002.

Xiong Yuezhi. "From Racecourse to People's Park and People's Square: Historical Transformation and Symbolic Significance." *Urban History* 38, no. 3 (2011): 475–90.

Xiong Yuezhi, Ma Xueqiang, and Yan Kejia, eds. *Shanghai de waiguoren, 1842–1949* [Foreigners in Shanghai, 1842–1949]. Shanghai: Shanghai Guji Chubanshe, 2003.

Xu Zhucheng. *Hatong woizhuan* [Unofficial biography of Hardoon]. Shanghai: Shanghai Wenhua Chubanshe, 1983.

Xue, Charlie Qiuli. *Hong Kong Architecture 1945–2015: From Colonial to Global*. Singapore: Springer, 2016.

Yang Hao and Ye Lan, eds. *Jiu Shanghai feng yun ren wu* [Men of the hour in Shanghai]. Shanghai: Shanghai renmin chubanshe, 1992.

Yeh, Diana. *The Happy Hsiungs: Performing China and the Struggle for Modernity*. Hong Kong: Hong Kong University Press, 2014.

Yeh, Wen-hsin. *Shanghai Splendor: A Cultural History, 1843–1949*. Berkeley: University of California Press, 2007.

————. *Wartime Shanghai*. New York: Routledge, 1998.

Zanasi, Margherita. "Globalizing Hanjian: The Suzhou Trials and the Post–World War II Discourse on Collaboration." *American Historical Review* 113, no. 3 (June 1, 2008): 731–51.

Zhang Yingjin, ed. *Cinema and Urban Culture in Shanghai, 1922–1943*. Stanford, CA: Stanford University Press, 1999.

Zhang Zhongli, ed. *Jindai Shanghai chengshi yanjiu* [Research on modern Shanghai city]. Shanghai: Shanghai renmin chubanshe, 1990.

Zhu Bangxing et al. *Shanghai chanye yu Shanghai zhigong* [Industries and workers in Shanghai]. Hong Kong: Yuandong chubanshe, 1939. Reprint, Shanghai: Shanghai renmin chubanshe, 1990.

Zia, Helen. *Last Boat Out of Shanghai: The Epic Story of the Chinese Who Fled Mao's Revolution*. New York: Ballantine, 2019.

ILLUSTRATION
CREDITS

165   Historical Photographs of China, University of Bristol
170   Reproduced courtesy of HSBC Archives
176   Illustrated London News/Mary Evans Picture Library
189   CriticalPast
190   Courtesy of Kent McKeever
192   Courtesy of Kent McKeever
195   Illustrated London News/Mary Evans Picture Library
203   Yad Vashem Photo Archive, Jerusalem. 4648/11
210   Image courtesy of Doreen Stoneham and Historical Photographs of China, University of Bristol
219   Historical Photographs of China, University of Bristol
226   Yad Vashem Photo Archive, Jerusalem 4648/6
231   (left and right) Illustrated London News/Mary Evans Picture Library
239   TCD/Prod.DB/Alamy
244   Illustrated London News/Mary Evans Picture Library
246   Illustrated London News/Mary Evans Picture Library
248   Illustrated London News/Mary Evans Picture Library
255   CriticalPast
265   Photograph by Oscar Seepol. Image courtesy of Susannah Stapleton and Historical Photographs of China, University of Bristol
271   Wide World Photo/AP Images
276   Courtesy of Kent McKeever
281   PA Images/Alamy Stock Photo (identifier: G7T4K6)

INDEX

Page numbers in *italics* refer to illustrations.